Guide to a
Healthy Planet

University of Essex

2006
Edited by:
Jules Pretty
Martin Sellens
Nigel South
Mike Wilson

Edited by: Jules Pretty, Martin Sellens, Nigel South and Mike Wilson

First published 2006 by
University of Essex, External Relations,
Wivenhoe Park, Colchester CO4 3SQ

ISBN 1-904059-42-2

A CIP catalogue record for this book is available from
the British Library

Co-ordinated by Lindsey Gill
Typeset and printed by University of Essex Printing Services

Authors are currently or previously accademic staff from the Departments
of Art History and Theory, Biological Sciences, Computer Science,
Government, Health and Human Sciences, Law, Mathematical Sciences,
Psychology, Sociology, the Human Rights Centre and the Institute of Social
and Economic Research

GUIDE TO A HEALTHY PLANET - AUTHORS

Naila Ahmed
Caroline Angus
Andy Ball
Graham Bailey
Neil Baker
Ralph Beneke
Joan Busfield
Vic Callaghan
Andrew Canessa
Will Cartright
Richard Cherry
Graham Clarke
Ian Colbeck
Martin Colley
Chris Cooper
Guy Coulson
Linda Crofts
Paul Dobbin
Kimmy Eldridge
Nelson Fernandez
Kimberly Fisher
Valerie Fraser
Mike Fryer
Val Gladwell
Gill Green
Murray Griffin
Hani Hagras
John Hallsworth
Richard Hammersley
Ruth Hancock
Samantha Head
Allan Hildon
Rachel Hine
Paul Hunt
Matthias Hütler
Paul Iganski
Gareth Jones
Richard Jurd
Stephanie Kirby
Elena Klenova
Renate Leithäuser
Louise Marsland
Peter Martin
Ray Meddis
Katharina Meyer

Sabine Michalowski
Dominic Micklewright
Frances Millard
Ian Morrison
Phil Mullineaux
Robin Mutter
Ceri Nicholas
Peter Nicholls
John Norton
Mark Osborn
Renos Papadopoulis
Jo Peacock
Marco Perugini
David Pevalin
Jules Pretty
George Psaroudakis
Jaynie Rance
Brandon Reeder
Marie Reid
Christopher Reynolds
Fernando Rivera-Illingworth
Karen Robson
David Rose
Terry McGenity
Gabriela Salgado
Colin Samson
Martin Sellens
Jerry Shearman
Sue Sharples
Dave Smith
Rose Smith
Nigel South
Ewen Speed
Glyn Stanway
Dima Svistunenko
Christine Temple
Paul Thornalley
Ken Timmis
Graham Upton
Vasileios Voutselas
Albert Weale
Arnold Wilkins
Mike Wilson
Anna Wittekind

CONTENTS

b. New Therapies

c. Lifestyles, Exercise and Health

d. Mental Health

e. Food and Health

f. The Environment and Health

g. Society and Health

----

h. Health Services and Policy

FOREWORD

Since the University of Essex first opened its doors to students in 1964, we have developed a worldwide reputation for academic excellence, being consistently ranked among the leading universities in the UK for research and teaching. The University also has a proud record of attracting and welcoming students from a diverse range of backgrounds nationally and internationally, with well over 100 countries now represented on campus. Its global outlook is reinforced by the international origins of its academic staff who come from 60 different countries.

Over the years, much of our research has been cross-disciplinary and comparative by nature, with staff from different departments working together on common research projects and degree schemes. It is for this reason that I particularly welcome this Guide to a Healthy Planet and its thematic focus. In recent years, research and teaching on a wide range of health-related topics have seen significant growth and development at the University. This volume contains 100 contributions from more than 80 staff in ten of our departments and centres. It is a snapshot of both the range and depth of scholarship at the University of Essex that addresses some of our most pressing health problems and issues - including understanding illness, developing new therapies, the roles of exercise and lifestyles, the importance of mental health, the roles of food, environment and society in health, and finally health services and policy.

The major health problems faced by us today cannot effectively be addressed from the viewpoint of a single discipline. The Guide to a Healthy Planet introduces readers to the contribution that researchers working together within a single university - the University of Essex - are making to understanding and resolving some of the most difficult national and global health challenges of the twenty-first century. I hope you find reading it both stimulating and enjoyable.

Professor Sir Ivor Crewe
Vice-Chancellor

THERE IS NO NEED TO SHOUT I AM NOT DEAF!

F ew people can be described as being completely deaf. Most who are 'hard of hearing' can hear something. Moreover, their world is not a silent world or even a quiet world. On the contrary, life is as noisy as ever. Their main problem is that sounds are no longer as clear as they used to be. The biggest complaint of individuals with a hearing impairment is that other people sound as if they are 'mumbling' when they speak. It is difficult to focus on what is being said especially if there are other interfering noises present. On the other hand, hearing can be almost normal if all interfering sounds are eliminated and the listener can see the speaker. This is a useful tip to bear in mind when conversing with someone with a hearing problem. Switch off the television or avoid noisy environments such as pubs and restaurants and make sure your listener can see your lips.

In addition to a lack of clarity, there is, of course, a reduction in sensitivity to sound. People with impaired hearing do have difficulty in hearing very quiet sounds. However, this does not contradict the fact that the world continues to sound as noisy as ever because most sounds (such as music or other people speaking) are well above the threshold of hearing for all but the most impaired. So where is the problem? Part of the difficulty is that the reduction in sensitivity mainly concerns sounds in the high frequency region, for the most common kind of hearing impairment. Unfortunately, high frequency speech sound components are typically very quiet. Not all speech sounds contain high frequencies but many do and a loss of sensitivity in the high frequency region can make all the difference between a meaningful word or phrase and complete nonsense.

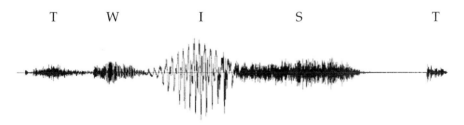

Figure 1. Sound waveform of the word 'Twist'.

Consider the waveform in Figure 1. It represents the pressure wave for the word 'Twist'. An intense component can be seen in the middle of the sound. This is the vowel sound corresponding to the '..wi..' part of the word. Listeners will rarely have difficulty hearing this component. The word begins with a low-amplitude high-frequency burst corresponding to the initial 'T..' sound. Because it is high-frequency and low-intensity, impaired listeners will often have difficulty with this section. If this intial component is not heard, the word could be received as 'whist' or 'mist'. Similarly the final section ('...st') contains high-frequency low-intensity sounds. However, these are less crucial because the final sounds can be guessed if the early sounds have been heard correctly. This is because there are not many words that begin with 'twis..'

A hard of hearing person knows that you have spoken and can sometimes guess what you have said but often the best guess is simply wrong and what you have said does not make sense. Shouting rarely helps but the situation is much improved by emphasising the high-frequency components (known as sibilants and fricatives such as 's', 't' and 'f'). The opportunity to lip read will also help with guessing accuracy. When fitting a hearing aid, an audiologist will tune the aid so that these low-intensity components are amplified. First, of course, the audiologist will make detailed measurements to see how much high-frequency emphasis is required for a particular listener.

Sadly, that is not the end of the story. Making things louder itself causes unexpected difficulties. To understand this we need to return to normal hearers. If sounds are too loud, they are experienced as painful. People with a hearing impairment are not spared this effect and, surprisingly, sounds become painful at the same levels as those for normal listeners. As a consequence, if the speaker shouts, the result can be as painful for an impaired listener as for a normal listener. This produces problems for the hearing aid designer. He may wish to use a hearing aid to amplify sounds to make them more audible but there is a limit before the sounds become painful. This limit can be surprisingly low. The range available for useful amplification can be so small as to greatly restrict the potential benefits of an aid.

Hearing aid design involves a number of other problems including the discomfort of a poorly fitting aid in the ear, painful over-amplification, whistling noise caused by electronic feedback and other irritating effects including noise caused by wind rushing past the aid microphone. Not surprisingly, hearing aids are not popular with owners who often prefer to switch them off; much to the annoyance of their friends and relatives.

But there is another problem! This one has become evident to hearing researchers only recently. It concerns auditory 'focus'. The best analogy is with vision. With normal vision we can see lines even when they are as narrow as human hairs. When vision is impaired, these lines become blurred and may not even be seen as separate if they are close together – they blur into one another. Something similar happens with hearing impairment.

Normally we can separate two simultaneous sounds that are close in frequency. We resolve these tones by 'hearing' them with different points along a membrane in the ear (called the basilar membrane). With hearing impairment, each sensitive point becomes less selective and responds to tones in a wider frequency range. As a consequence, the tones are more likely to be 'confused'. The solution to this problem in vision has been known since medieval times and involves the familiar spectacle lens. The solution for hearing impairment is not known and is the focus of an intense international research effort including scientists at the University of Essex and their collaborators in a number of laboratories in the USA and Europe.

The number of hearing impaired people in the world is enormous and the suffering caused by it is substantial. However, impaired hearing is not life-threatening and it concerns mainly old people. As a consequence, it is not a priority for medical research. Nevertheless, a method for restoring natural hearing could bring relief to many millions of people. It is also a substantial intellectual challenge to understand how normal hearing works and to know just what has gone wrong when hearing begins to fail.

One way forward is to make detailed measurements on impaired listeners and to develop computer models of normal and impaired hearing. The models should allow us to experiment 'in the computer' with new designs for hearing aids that will shape sounds so as to improve speech intelligibility and enhancement of musical appreciation. It may sound like a pipe-dream but research in this direction is already underway.

Ray Meddis

FILTERING OUT MIGRAINES

Migraine affects approximately 7% of men and 20% of women. The pain is debilitating and results in many days lost from work. The cost to US employers has been estimated at 13 billion dollars per annum. Although blurring of vision and pain in response to light are associated with most migraine attacks and are considered to be features of migraine, the role of vision in the induction of migraine attacks has received almost no study.

People with migraine are particularly susceptible to certain visual patterns, typically patterns of stripes. They find the patterns are uncomfortable to look at, inducing perceptual distortions: illusions of colour, shape and motion. The origin of the distortions is unknown but it is recognised that some individuals are far more susceptible than others, particularly individuals with frequent headaches. The susceptibility to illusions increases in the 24 hours prior to a headache. If the headaches are on one side of the head, distortions predominate to one side of vision. If the migraine attacks are accompanied by a warning (aura) the distortions tend to occur in between headaches on the side of vision affected by the aura. These links between perceptual distortions and migraine headaches may occur because the cerebral cortex is hyperexcitable in migraine.

There are several lines of evidence for the hyperexcitability. Individuals with migraine are slightly more likely than others to suffer seizures. Several anticonvulsant drugs have been shown to offer protection from migraine in randomised control trials. In people with migraine the scalp electrical activity evoked by visual stimuli does not show the usual habituation with repeated presentations of those stimuli. Magnetic pulses over the visual cortex stimulate phosphenes (flashing lights) more readily in people with migraine than in others. The brain responds to visual stimuli with an increase in blood oxygenation, and this increase is greater in migraineurs than in others, particularly for patterns that induce illusions.

It is quite possible that the aversion to strong patterns in migraine, and the increased susceptibility to the distortions they evoke is a reflection of the cortical hyperexcitability. The susceptibility to distortions occurs for precisely the same patterns as those that can induce seizures in patients with photosensitive epilepsy. The susceptibility to distortions increases after deprivation of sleep which is known to increase the likelihood of seizures.

The causes of a migraine attack are not known. Nevertheless it goes without saying that attacks can be prevented by avoiding the stimuli that trigger them, and visual stimuli may be a common trigger. When asked, about 40% of patients with migraine will report visually provoked attacks. A substantial number report that flickering light induces attacks and a smaller number are aware that patterns of stripes can also be a problem. The possibility that many headaches are visually provoked has been suggested by double-masked studies that have shown that the imperceptible high-frequency flicker from fluorescent lighting is responsible for about half the headaches experienced by office workers. Recent ophthalmic techniques for prescribing tinted lenses have also provided evidence for visually provoked headaches.

The ophthalmic tinting techniques have been developed at the University of Essex and are now in widespread use in the UK. Over 25,000 spectral filters (tints) have been prescribed in general optometric practice using the *Intuitive Colorimeter*, a coloriser that illuminates patterns with coloured light. In many individuals it is possible to find a shade of colour that reduces perceptual distortion and increases visual clarity and comfort. The appropriate colour differs from one individual to another and has to be selected with precision for optimal effect. Beneficial effects were originally demonstrated in children with reading difficulties, but have now been shown in a wide variety of other disorders, using experimental designs that control for placebo effects. The disorders include: migraine, photosensitive epilepsy, autism and head injury.

The above disorders are associated with an increased risk of seizures, consistent with cortical hyperexcitability. We hypothesize that the cortical hyperexcitability is non uniform, as is manifestly the case with epilepsy. Because of differences in the spectral sensitivity of cortical neurons and the topographic representation of colour in some cortical areas, coloured light is presumed to redistribute the cortical excitation that occurs response to a visual stimulus. We hypothesise that comfortable colours redistribute the excitation in such a way as to reduce the excitation in hyperexcitable regions. This hypothesis explains the reduction in perceptual distortion with coloured light, if these distortions are indeed due to a spread of excitation causing neurons to fire inappropriately.

In a preliminary study of migraine, using functional magnetic resonance imaging, we have demonstrated a reduction in blood oxygenation in response to patterns when tints having the appropriate colour were worn. The reduction occurred in visual area V3, an area that has been implicated with the onset of migraine. The reduction was not seen when tints having a slightly different shade of colour were used.

The Departments of Psychology and Biological Sciences at the University of Essex are now preparing to measure the change in blood oxygenation using near infra-red spectroscopy, a simpler technique that can be used on large numbers of patients. We have successfully measured the oxygenation in response to a visual stimulus and we will now try to find out whether this response is elevated in migraine, as predicted. If it is, we will try and discover whether the abnormal elevation can be reduced with the use of ophthalmic tints.

Arnold Wilkins

Figure 1.

Migraine attacks can cause a variety of visual symptoms as well as pain. 'Jesmond Barn' above is inspired by a barn seen during an attack of basilar artery migraine by the artist, Debbie Ayles, who won first prize with the painting in the Art meets Science Awards 2005. The painting was one of several used to test Arnold Wilkins' theory visual of stress.

ALL MOTHER'S FAULT? DISEASES OF THE MITOCHONDRION

About 250,000 years ago a woman – the so-called "African Eve" – was living somewhere near the Rift valley in Central Africa. She bequeathed her mitochondria to every human being alive today. Mitochondria are little organelles in all our cells important for energy transformation and hence the function of working tissues - especially important in brain, heart, and muscle.

What is special about mitochondria? They have their own chromosomes (DNA-bearing material). Though 98% of our DNA is in the cell nucleus, the remaining 2% is essential for life and located in the mitochondria. This is our legacy from African Eve. Each of us gets all our mitochondrial DNA from our mother, and hence from our maternal grandmother, and so on back in time. Think about it. If a woman has only sons and grandsons, however fertile and successful they may be, her mitochondrial DNA will be lost to later generations; in this way it is different from the other ("nuclear") DNA, which is derived from many ancestors both male and female and cycled through both. So eventually all mitochondria in a line die out except for one type. It takes that long. And the initial population was small.

The mitochondrial DNA encodes the energy transforming components of the mitochondrion – which enable us to make ATP (Adenosine Triphosphate) and other compounds that allow our brains to function, our hearts to beat, our muscles to contract, our guts to do peristalsis and digestion. Cells contain lots of mitochondria and each mitochondrion contains several (initially identical) chromosomes.

These chromosomes are simpler than those of the nucleus. They are circular DNA molecules like those of bacteria (indeed bacteria are thought to be the progenitors of mitochondria - picked up by a primordial cell billions of years ago). They reproduce like bacteria. They function like bacterial DNA. But bacteria last only a few hours or at most days before dividing and becoming new. Mitochondria also last only a few days in each type of cell but they then have to duplicate their DNA to form new chromosomes and new mitochondria. When they do this mistakes can occur. Unlike the nuclear DNA the cell cannot readily repair mitochondrial DNA. Once made it stays made. When a cell divides its nuclear DNA is carefully divided and identical sets of chromosomes assigned to each daughter cell. But the many mitochondria are assigned at random to the daughter cells. So if any are damaged some cells will get normal mitochondria but others mitochondria with the damaged DNA. As time goes by - and we nearly all live a long time - far longer than bacteria and longer than most other animals - our tissues have patches of mitochondrially good cells and patches of bad ones. Which is mainly the luck of the draw - and some kinds of damaged mitochondrial DNA (for example smaller chromosomes with bits missing) can reproduce themselves faster than the good stuff (bad DNA driving out good).

So our mitochondria, reproducing themselves and renewing themselves every few days, also age faster than the rest of us. Indeed our ageing may reflect the effects on our mitochondrial DNA.

Mitochondrial DNA has diverged immensely between different human subgroups - although in conformity with the African Eve hypothesis, most variability is still in Africa. There are numerous perfectly viable but different forms of mitochondrial DNA. But some few are damaging or even fatal. Some of these diseases are inherited. Heritable defects that affect both boys and girls but which are carried only in the maternal line suggest a problem with mitochondrial DNA. But mitochondrial defects do not always prove that it is mitochondrial DNA that is at fault. Typical mitochondrial enzymes require contributions from both nuclear and mitochondrial chromosomes.

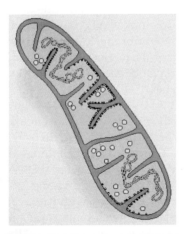

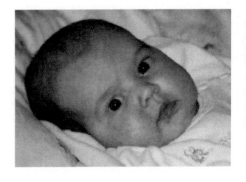

Cross-section through a mitochondrion
(from: www.kscience.co.uk/as/module1/
mitochondrion.htm)

A baby suffering from Leigh's disease -
a mitochondrial deficiency disease.

An example is cytochrome oxidase - a key enzyme of the system that reacts with oxygen in the cell. Each molecule has many subunits of which some are encoded in the nucleus and others in the mitochondria. Mutations in either group can damage mitochondrial function. Within the last few million years cytochrome oxidase has evolved in humans and their near relatives amongst the apes and monkeys quite recently. And in both the mitochondrial DNA and the associated nuclear components some deficiency diseases seem to be associated with special populations. The deficiencies also sometimes seem uniform in a tissue and sometimes heterogeneous (as might be expected for bad mitochondria). The worst deficiencies appear in infancy, with disastrous syndromes (`floppy babies' that cannot control or use their infant muscles).

But some are of late onset taking many years to develop but still proving fatal to the victims in their teens. Others are less life threatening. One case in the USA involved an American Indian girl who arrived for her bioenergetic diagnosis on a motor bike – simply complaining of feeling tired from time to time – who turned out to be defective in what until then had been thought to be an absolutely essential mitochondrial enzyme. In such cases the first symptom is commonly the accumulation of lactic acid in the blood.

Even with infants as they grow initial deficiencies may disappear (`benign' cases). Others are inevitably fatal and still effectively untreatable. Can the course of the syndrome be predicted so that parents can be given reliable advice and prognosis? This is still difficult, unless the actual genetic defect is clear and of a known kind. Similar diseases can be due either to mitochondrial DNA or to other defects. Molecular biology is rapidly clarifying the differences and soon we shall be able to identify any fault at an early stage and predict its consequences. Cures, alas, will take much longer to find. The baby shown is no longer with us.

Peter Nicholls and Mike Wilson

IF CANCER STRIKES

C ancer is a complex disease and it is not easy to understand why it strikes. There may be dietary, environmental and genetic causes, or combination of them, which can trigger cancer development and, unfortunately, this can not be narrowed down to a single process.

Cancer cells are very different from normal cells. Normally, cells grow and die in a regulated fashion; special control mechanisms also make sure that genetically damaged cells undergo a process of self-elimination. Contrary to this, cancer cells divide and grow without restrictions as they are not sensitive to inhibitory signals and can be highly responsive to growth influences. Cancer cells also develop mechanisms to resist elimination – this helps them to survive even if they are genetically damaged and dangerous for the body. As cancer cells do not adhere well to each other, they can invade other parts of the body in a process called metastasis.

There is particular concern about breast and prostate cancers, which have become two of the most common cancers of industrialised countries. Statistics tell us that prostate cancer affects one man in nine over the age of 65 and breast cancer affects one in eleven women. Considerable efforts have been directed towards understanding how to prevent breast and prostate cancer. A healthy lifestyle can certainly help to reduce the risk of cancer, but it can not guarantee that cancer does not develop. And if this happens, what can be done to find the best way to fight the disease?

The main problem in cancer treatment is that it is not very efficient when the disease is already advanced, and in many cases this happens at the time of diagnosis. However, the same treatment can be very successful if the disease is caught at the very early stage. This is why efforts of scientists and clinicians are now focused on finding the means for early cancer diagnosis and prevention. When the disease is diagnosed, it is also very important to establish how advanced it is and what would be the best way to treat it. What can modern science offer?

It has been long known that pre-cancerous and cancerous cells produce protein molecules that are not present, or present at different levels, in normal cells. The levels of proteins that help cancer cells proliferate and escape cell death are higher in cancer cells. On the other hand, levels of proteins that restrain proliferation and promote cell death, and also those mediating interactions between cells are often reduced (tables 1 and 2). Such molecules can become very useful indicators for cancer cells, or in other words, cancer biomarkers. By identifying these markers it may be possible to design a particular therapy specific to a particular cancer.

Table 1. Examples of prostate cancer biomarkers

Prostate cancer biomarker	Function	Detection in patients with prostate cancer
PSA (prostate-specific antigen)	Protease (protein that degrades other proteins)	Appears in blood stream of prostate cancer patients
G-actin	Builds the skeleton of the cell	Increased in tumours
Alpha-methylacyl coenzyme A racemase (AMACR)	Involved in bile acid synthesis and degradation of some fatty acids	Increased in tumours
pim-1	Increases cell proliferation	Increased in tumours
Hepsin	Protease (protein that degrades other proteins)	Increased in tumours
Cadherins	Mediate interactions between cells	Reduced in tumours
Tissue transglutaminase type II	Controls cell attachment and migration	Reduced in tumours

Table 2. Examples of breast cancer biomarkers

Breast cancer biomarker	Function	Detection in patients with breast tumours
Estrogen receptor (ER)	Mediate effects of female steroid hormones (estrogens) in supporting cell differentiation	Reduced/absent in some types of cancers. However, if present, ER is a favorable prognostic marker.
Progesterone receptor (PgR)	Mediate effects of a steroid progesterone in supporting cell differentiation	Similar to Estrogen Receptor
HER2	Factor that increases cell proliferation	Increased in tumours
Fibroblast growth factor-2	Factor that increases cell proliferation	Increased in tumours
Heterogeneous nuclear ribonucleoprotein A2/B1 (hnRNP-A2/B1)	Positively regulates genes that support cell proliferation	Increased in tumours
chaperone 14-3-3 sigma	Restrains cell proliferation	Reduced in tumours

Studies on breast and prostate cancer at the University of Essex

Our team at the University of Essex is currently assessing the value of two proteins, called CTCF and BORIS, in breast and prostate cancer development. We found that there is much more CTCF protein in breast tumours than in normal breast tissues; there may be correlation between the levels of CTCF and tumour progression and; BORIS has never been seen in normal tissues, but it is present in tumour tissues (see Figure).

Our data imply that:

- CTCF can play a role in protecting breast cancer cells from death.
- BORIS can be responsible for cancer development.
- Both, CTCF and BORIS, can be used as cancer biomarkers because their appearance or amount depends on the state of a tumour.
- BORIS can be used for molecular diagnostics of tumours as it can only be detected in tumours.
- N-normal breast tissue; T – breast tumour tissue.
- Tubulin is as a protein that is detected in all tissues and therefore used here as a control.

BORIS -

NTNT NTNTNTNTNTN TNTNTNT

Tubulin -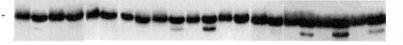

BORIS can be used for molecular diagnostics of tumours as it can only be detected in tumours.
N-normal breast tissue; T-breast tumour tissue.
Tubulin is as a protein that is detected in all tissues and therefore used here as a control.

Elena Klenova

NITRIC OXIDE – THE GOOD, THE BAD AND THE UGLY!

The good

Cells talk to each other. The language they use is called signalling. Most signalling molecules are liquids, or solids dissolved in the liquid water that makes up 80% of our bodies. However, in the 1980s one signalling molecule was discovered that is a gas. Previously thought of only as an environmental pollutant, nitric oxide (NO) gas is now known to be one of the major signalling molecules between cells. Being a small two atom gas (a nitrogen and an oxygen) no barriers to its movement exist in the body and it rapidly diffuses from source to target. Once it reaches its target NO activates an enzyme called guanylate cyclase leading to the formation of a second messenger molecule, this time a more conventional one called cyclic GMP. The cascade of subsequent events result ultimately in a variety of biochemical and physiological changes. These include controlling blood pressure and affecting memory pathways in the brain. NO-driven increases in blood flow and blood volume have highly useful effects in peripheral organs – see c13: the Viagra story.

In 1998 the Nobel Prize in Physiology and Medicine was awarded to the scientists who discovered the NO signalling pathway. The irony of this was not lost on the Nobel committee. Alfred Nobel made the money to fund his prizes by inventing ways to blow people up. Injections of one of these compounds, nitro-glycerine, were then used by doctors to treat his later heart disease. The scientists who discovered that nitro-glycerine works by releasing nitric oxide into the blood, increasing blood flow to the diseased heart, were then awarded the Nobel Prize. One assumes it is one award decision dear old Alfred would have approved of!

The bad

NO also has a role in the immune system. In this case it acts directly, rather than via the second messenger guanylate cyclase. Excess NO is toxic (remember it is an environmental pollutant) and the cell of the immune system target the toxic gas at the invading bacteria. Chemical, rather than biological warfare, being the name of the game here! However, as is often the case, sometimes the body can be its own worst enemy. The system for targeting excess NO at bacteria can break down, and instead start attacking the body's own cells. One of these NO-susceptible enzymes, mitochondrial cytochrome oxidase, is responsible for converting the oxygen we breathe into the energy our cells need. Therefore it is perhaps not a surprise that overproduction of NO is implicated in a range of diseases - septic shock, birth asphyxia, stroke, Parkinson's Disease, asthma to name but a few.

Compounds that inhibit the body's ability to make NO, or scavenge the NO once it has been made, are therefore currently being testing by drug companies as possible novel therapies for these diseases. At the same time nitro-glycerine and, indeed even NO gas, are used as treatments for diseases where not enough NO is being produced. The Greek god Janus had two heads, always arguing with each other. NO is a true Janus molecule, with a good and a bad head – the challenge for scientists and the pharmaceutical industry is how to prevent the bad effects of NO without stopping the good ones. No one wants to cure the disease, but kill the patient…

The ugly

Surprising as it seems to many people scientists are humans too, with all the frailties that attend this condition. Its chemical formula (NO), along with the fact that molecules like NO are called free radicals, has been too much to resist. Titles of talks and articles I have attended include: Just say NO! NO, a radical in control; O + NO = O NO; There's NO business like SNO business; NO chemistry is good chemistry. This only goes to prove that although scientists are very clever people, this does not necessarily translate into a heightened sense of humour.

Nitric oxide research at the University of Essex

NO research in the Department of Biological Sciences covers both "basic" and "applied" science, with the former informing the latter. The chemistry of NO inhibition of mitochondrial respiration is studied in the test tube. New physical ("spectroscopic") techniques are then designed to measure these effects and their possible development in patient diagnosis and therapy investigated. The prevention of NO overproduction in disease states is addressed by collaborations with pharmaceutical companies to design and test inhibitors of the enzyme that makes NO.

Figure 1
Nitric Oxide signalling and killing pathways

Nitric oxide (NO) can be produced by two pathways – an enzyme in the body (nitric oxide synthase) or a drug added to treat disease (nitroglycerin). The gas can then have two fates:

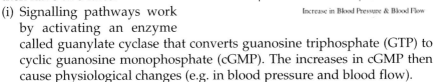

(i) Signalling pathways work by activating an enzyme called guanylate cyclase that converts guanosine triphosphate (GTP) to cyclic guanosine monophosphate (cGMP). The increases in cGMP then cause physiological changes (e.g. in blood pressure and blood flow).

(ii) Higher levels of NO are produced in response to infection and are used to kill pathogenic micro-organisms. In diseases this mechanism can misfunction causing the body to turn toxic levels of NO against itself.

Chris Cooper

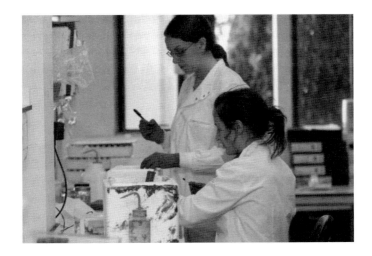

THE DARK SIDE OF HAEMOGLOBIN AND MYOGLOBIN

Haemoglobin (Hb) and its smaller relation myoglobin (Mb) are haem proteins that reversibly bind oxygen in the blood and muscle respectively. Other haem proteins have different functions, such as cytochrome *c* which transports electrons, or catalase which is an enzyme that catalyses reactions. Under certain conditions Hb and Mb can also exhibit some of the activities of other haem proteins. However, Hb and Mb cannot control these reactions safely, which can lead to tissue damage through a process termed oxidative stress. Such activities are most likely to occur if the haem protein changes from the oxygen carrying form to higher oxidation states that do not carry oxygen.

These higher oxidation sates of Mb and Hb can be highly toxic and causes damage to cells through enzymatic reactions with cell membranes and leakage of highly reactive substances called free radicals. The toxic forms of Mb and Hb can be produced by oxidants such as hydrogen peroxide, which can be formed in inflammation. These damaging reactions are normally suppressed by keeping the haem proteins in cells with high levels of antioxidants. If the haem protein is separated from its protective antioxidant environment, e.g. through trauma injuries or infection, then these 'rogue' activities of Hb and Mb can lead to serious medical complications. Research at the University of Essex looks at the mechanisms of the damaging processes that Hb and Mb can cause at a molecular level. We examine ways of how these processes could be identified in people and how these reactions could be prevented through treatment.

Myoglobin and kidney damage

Muscle damage, caused by crush injuries (or excessive exercise, alcohol or drug abuse, hyperthermia, hypothermia, seizures, deep vein thrombosis) causes Mb to be released from the muscle cells, eventually entering the kidney. A person may recover from muscle damage (known as rhabdomyolysis) only to later develop life-threatening kidney

failure. The process that causes kidney failure was largely unknown. We have developed a method for detecting and isolating altered forms of Mb using high performance liquid chromatography (HPLC, pictured). These altered forms of Mb give insights into the mechanisms of kidney damage and can be used as markers to diagnose certain types of reactions that cause oxidative stress. We have found that the Mb from kidneys of patients with rhabdomyolysis have been modified, irreversibly binding the haem to the Mb protein. This 'haem to protein cross-linked' form of Mb is far more toxic than normal Mb. Our research shows that these Mb molecules can play a major role in the mechanism of kidney damage following muscle injury. Membranes oxidised by Mb results in the formation of powerful bio-molecules called isoprostanes, which restrict blood flow to the kidney, decreasing oxygen supply (ischemia) and increasing acidity (acidosis). The increased acidity further enhances the ability of both unmodified and modified Mb to cause membrane damage and isoprostane production, hence forming a vicious cycle of tissue damage. A treatment to prevent kidney failure is to decrease the acidity of the blood/urine. Although the mechanism behind this treatment was previously unknown, we believe, based on our investigations, that this treatment decreases the ability of Mb to promote kidney damage through tissue oxidation.

Haemoglobin and brain haemorrhage

We are expanding our research to examine other situations were haem proteins are separated from their normal environment. For example, certain types of brain haemorrhage (eg subarachnoid aneurysm) releases Hb into the cerebrospinal fluid (CSF) that surrounds and protects the brain and spine. A bleed into the CSF has a high rate of mortality with a major percentage of deaths resulting from a process known as 'delayed vasospasm'. This process occurs a few days after the haemorrhage and maybe a result of isoprostane formation. We have found that haem to protein cross-linked forms of Hb are present in the CSF of patients following brain haemorrhage, showing that Hb is involved in powerful oxidation reactions in a similar way that Mb promotes kidney damage following muscle injury.

With a greater understanding of the damaging reactions caused by Mb and Hb, it is our ultimate goal to engineer Hb with a greatly decreased capacity to cause damage. We could then produce an unlimited supply of artificial blood, disease free, blood type independent and with a shelf-life of years instead of days.

Green blood

The technique we use to detect damage to the haem proteins is sensitive enough to show that small amounts of modified haem proteins are present in the blood of normal people. The structure of the haem largely determines the colour of the haem protein, which, in turn, gives blood its colour. The modified haem proteins found in blood are not red, as is normal Hb, but green.

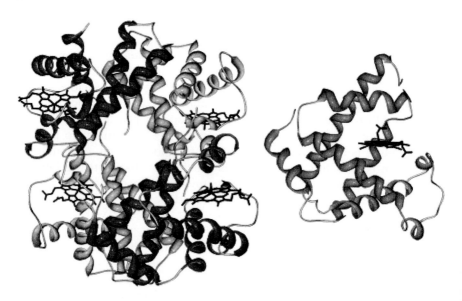

Ribbon model of Haemoglobin (left) and Myoglobin (right).
Haemoglobin contains four subunits, two a units (light ribbon) and two b units (dark ribbon). Each subunit contains a haem group (black, stick model). Myoglobin is a single polypeptide chain with one haem group.

Brandon Reeder

CYANIDE AND CARBON MONOXIDE: TWO WAYS TO STOP RESPIRATION AND PREVENT US FROM BREATHING

"a gift, a love gift, utterly unasked for by a sky ... palely and flamily igniting its carbon monoxides ... " Sylvia Plath (Poppies in October)

"The patchwork halves were cloven as they scudded the wild pigs' wood, and slime upon the trees, sucking the dark, kissed on the cyanide..." Dylan Thomas (My World Is Pyramid)

"I will fight you with a book of poetry, and a necklace of cyanide." Cyrus Mahan [Iran] (Poetry, Blood and Cyanide)

Breathe in... breathe out... breathe in again... feel better? Oxygen is essential for our life and fortunately its concentration in the air anywhere near sea level is almost constant. Unlike carbon dioxide levels, which are increasing regularly thereby contributing to global warming, the oxygen concentration has remained unchanged at least for several million years. It is produced by plant photosynthesis. So we are dependent upon plants for our lives in more ways than one. But the store of atmospheric oxygen is so great that it would take over a thousand years to see a marked change in its level, even if photosynthesis came to an end (we should starve long before we suffocated). We don't normally notice oxygen until it goes missing. It seems colourless and odourless, but at high concentrations it is actually of a bluish tinge and according to JBS Haldane tastes like dilute ink with sugar in it (how did he know? Early twentieth century professors may have had odd drinking habits).

Once in our lungs the oxygen has to travel to other parts of the body. To do this it must bind haemoglobin in the blood red cells which then carry it to the sites where it is finally taken up and reduced to water. Both the carriage and the use can be blocked by other gases in air or water. These include carbon monoxide and cyanide. Both of these are around us as pollutants. Carbon monoxide is formed when burning is incomplete, in some industrial processes, in poorly ventilated gas and oil heaters, in car engines. Stand at a busy street corner and some of your blood haemoglobin will react with the carbon monoxide from car exhausts. Smoke cigarettes regularly and the same happens. Heavy smokers have been reported to contain over

20% of their blood in this form - so they have only 80% the total oxygen carrying capacity of non-smokers. Carbon monoxide is also described as odourless; but at high concentrations - according to Professor Haldane - it smells of garlic (I'm prepared to take his word for this – though some say apples). The sensitivity of different animals towards carbon monoxide is very variable. Haldane's father experimented with canaries (subsequently used as warning devices in mines) which dropped unconscious or dead as the carbon monoxide level was raised in a closed box also containing the professor - who remained cheerfully alert writing his notes until his concerned colleagues released the door seals. We are, perhaps unfortunately, chemically much tougher than many other

JBS Haldane
(1892-1964)

animals. Haldane, arguing for the humanity of chemical weapons, describes the director of the Porton Down Research Station as casually surviving one and a half minutes in 0.05% cyanide (hydrocyanic acid gas) that swiftly killed a dog (although he claimed it left him giddy for a year).

Cyanide gas is rare in the atmosphere. Appreciable air levels would be more deadly than carbon monoxide to most of us. It can be smelled - the characteristic "almond" odour - even at low concentrations. But it is not uncommon in waters polluted by industrial chemical effluents in rivers and lakes - a danger to fish if not to non-swimming human beings. Cyanide is also naturally occurring in combined form in many plants. It can be released from several "cyanogenic" compounds as a defence mechanism against attack by insects including caterpillars. Hence is the association between cyanide and almonds. Such natural occurrence led to the use of plant concoctions as murder, suicide and execution devices.

Socrates' hemlock was probably a cyanide-releasing mixture. The Borgias were notorious for removing their enemies with cyanide-laced foods and drinks. Alan Turing, the inventor of the computer as we know it today, committed suicide with a cyanide-laced apple (cf. Snow White) after his conviction and bizarre and brutal "treatment" for homosexuality. The Czar and Czarina's advisor Rasputin was reportedly the only human being known (except perhaps the Porton Down director) with a substantial resistance to cyanide; drinking with his assassins he gaily downed a substantial amount of cyanide-treated wine and had to be dispatched by rougher methods. But sceptics suggest that his apparent cyanide resistance was due to the use of a sparkling (carbonated) wine - the carbon dioxide it contained displacing the cyanide from solution. Every spy in legend carries a cyanide capsule to ensure his departure from this world in the event of capture, without revealing secrets. The U2 pilot Gary Powers shot down in Russia in 1959 had such a capsule but failed to use it. Until the development of the "modern" lethal injection the cyanide chamber was seen by some jurisdictions in the US as a humane alternative to the electric chair. In WWI cyanide preparations were developed as part of trench insect eradication campaigns; Zyklon B was found to be highly effective in destroying lice that accumulated in soldiers' clothing. Then came the holocaust.

Carbon monoxide (CO) was also used as a death gas in early tests at the beginning of the holocaust but was later abandoned for gaseous cyanide. CO is one of the two classic components of coal gas, the other being hydrogen (obtained by passing steam over heated coal (Eq. 1) - and coal gas was until fairly recently, before natural North Sea gas came on line, the major domestic cooking fuel. The formation of coal gas from coal is very simple chemistry:

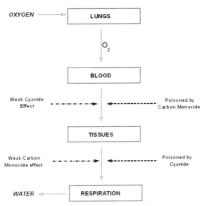

Diagram 1: Where cyanide and carbon monoxide block oxygen uptake in the body

1. C (coal) + H$_2$O (steam) —> CO (carbon monoxide) + H$_2$ (hydrogen)

"Putting one's head in the oven" became the classic euphemism for suicide and was the mechanism for several famous deaths, perhaps notably that of the poet Sylvia Plath in the bitterly cold English winter of 1963.

Carbon monoxide and cyanide can react both in the blood and in the tissues. But while the chief poisonous action of carbon monoxide is on the carriage of oxygen in the blood that of cyanide is in its action on oxygen usage by the tissues themselves (see Diagram 1). It took a long while for this to be understood. Even at the end of the nineteenth century it was still being debated.

21

Red cell haemoglobin exists in two stable forms, the reduced state that is functional, and an oxidized state (also known as methaemoglobin) that is non-functional. The latter state occurs naturally in low concentrations but is returned to the active reduced state by enzyme systems in the red cells. Only the reduced state binds oxygen; only the reduced state binds carbon monoxide. The combination with carbon monoxide is much tighter than that with oxygen. So a very small amount of carbon monoxide can compete successfully with the higher amounts of oxygen in the air and block oxygen transport by the blood. When more than 70% of the haemoglobin has bound carbon monoxide tissue respiration can no longer be maintained. The subject dies chemically asphyxiated. The oxidized form of haemoglobin can react with cyanide. But as the oxidized (met) haemoglobin is already inactive cyanide binding produces little further effect. Indeed when serious cyanide poisoning occurs, one therapy is to increase chemically and temporarily the amount of methaemoglobin in the blood so that it can bind the cyanide and prevent the latter from reaching the tissues where its action is critical.

The tissue enzyme that uses oxygen (known as cytochrome oxidase) also exists in two stable forms, reduced and oxidized. But in this case both states are functional. Tissue substrates (derived from foodstuffs) reduce the oxidized form; oxygen itself oxidizes the reduced form. Poisoning can therefore occur by a noxious substance binding either form. The oxidase is however very sensitive to cyanide, which traps the oxidized state and prevents the tissue substrates from restoring it to the reduced state. Its sensitivity to carbon monoxide is by contrast much less than that of haemoglobin and under most conditions oxygen wins the competition. Loss of oxygen supply by carbon monoxide binding the blood haemoglobin stops respiration long before the oxidase itself is affected directly. It simply runs out of its oxygen supply.

But these reactions were the original basis for the discovery of the tissue enzyme involved. Its sensitivity to cyanide determined by Otto Warburg gave the initial clues to its nature - from the similarity to haemoglobin of the blood. Warburg's work with cyanide, however, was then linked to the WWI development of the insecticide Zyklon B, which led to WWII atrocities. How sensitive do we need to be as scientists to the remoter consequences of our work? How responsible are we for these seemingly remote consequences?

The effect of carbon monoxide upon haemoglobin became a unique way of determining the chemical nature of the cellular oxidase. Haldane senior and his coworkers had made a remarkable discovery when studying the binding of carbon monoxide to haemoglobin. In winter, carbon monoxide competed well with oxygen; in summer, oxygen was more successful in binding the haemoglobin. They looked at various possibilities and eventually realised that light was the key variable (in the late 19th century laboratories were still lit by natural daylight). Light causes the release of carbon monoxide from its complex with haemoglobin. This is possible because the haemoglobin carbon monoxide compound is coloured and when a photon of light is absorbed by a molecule of the complex, the bond between the CO and the haemoglobin iron atom is broken (Eq. 2).

2. HbCO (complex) + h υ (light) —-> CO (carbon monoxide) + Hb (haemoglobin)

It is not a cure for CO poisoning because the body is not transparent enough to shine light effectively on a poisoning victim. But Otto Warburg used the phenomenon by shining light on tissue homogenates or single celled organisms such as yeasts, which are effectively transparent. He was able to reactivate CO-poisoned cells by light of specific wavelengths. Those specific wavelengths are characteristic of the enzyme involved in the cellular respiration. So he was able to "see" what it looked like indirectly even though its concentration was too low for it to be seen directly. Later isolation and characterisation of the enzyme have strikingly borne out his predictions. Photolysis of carbon monoxide complexes has become faster and faster as time has gone by.

From Haldane's months, through Warburg's minutes, we have gone to milliseconds (thousandths) with flash lamps, to microseconds (millionths) and with lasers, to nano- (billionths), pico- (trillionths), and femto-seconds (quadrillionths) with specialised optical equipment. The solution to a problem in biology has led to a better understanding of molecular chemistry and physics. And the latter disciplines have fed back explanations for the behaviour of the protein molecules. The boundaries of the sciences are continuously blurring. To understand respiration and its sicknesses we need to be biologists, biochemists, chemists and physicists. And if we fail to be polymaths we can always seek colleagues in other disciplines nearby, walk down the corridor and do science with a different perspective in another world.

Peter Nicholls

SHOULD WE FIGHT FREE RADICALS IN OUR BODY?

Our awareness of free radicals is mainly associated with the view that free radicals are wholly bad and should be fought in our body. The reason they are considered evil is because they are the key players in a number of diseases and they accelerate the process of ageing. This is, however, only half of the truth. We would not be walking around if we succeeded in eliminating all free radicals from our body.

The term "free radical" describes a special molecular state that is formed when one electron is either subtracted from a normal molecule (the process called oxidation) or added to it (reduction). Normally, molecules have an even number of electrons. Therefore, a free radical would always have an odd number of electrons. It is this unpaired number of electrons that makes a free radical a highly active chemical species. It tends either to get rid of the extra electron or to seize one from another molecule to make its own electron set even.

When we take a tablet of vitamin C, some of the molecules of the vitamin are oxidised by oxygen in our body, and a pool of free radicals is created in the stomach. These radicals of vitamin C can interact with many dangerous species (including other radicals) and terminate them. That is one of the reasons why we should take the vitamin.

Quite recently it has become known that Nature uses the high reactivity of free radicals in many enzymes. It is only about 20 years since a free radical was found in the active centre of the key enzyme of DNA synthesis, ribonucleotide reductase. This enzyme is active only if one specific amino acid, an element of the polypeptide chain of the enzyme located close to the active centre, is in a free radical state. Following that first discovery of a free radical enzyme, many other enzymes have been shown to have free radicals as key components of their catalytic mechanisms.

But it is certainly true that not all free radicals are that useful. The 'bad' free radicals are, in fact, constantly being formed in an organism. One of the most common routes of such formation is through the reaction of haem (iron) containing proteins with hydrogen peroxide, H_2O_2. There are haem enzymes are specifically designed to react with hydrogen peroxide, like those which either destroy it or use in important biosynthetic processes.

Most haem proteins, such as haemoglobin or myoglobin are not, however, designed to react safely with H_2O_2, but do nevertheless react if they happen to meet a molecule of H_2O_2 by chance. A consequence of such an interaction is the formation of a 'bad' free radical on the protein (or enzyme). Such a radical can initiate a cascade of undesirable oxidative reactions in the organism (termed "oxidative stress"). Luckily, the proteins that are not supposed to interact with H_2O_2 are isolated from it in the cells or protected by specialised systems. However, in pathological conditions things can go wrong. For example, following severe trauma, myoglobin from muscles enters the blood stream and ends up in kidneys. Having accumulated in these organs, it starts to react with H_2O_2 with catastrophic consequences: the free radicals formed in this reaction initiate the cascade of free radical reactions leading to kidney dysfunction and, ultimately, death.

Molecules with odd number of electrons can be detected by electron paramagnetic resonance (EPR) spectroscopy. An EPR spectrometer is a perfect tool for detection of free radicals and for telling the good radicals from the bad ones. Use of EPR spectroscopy can reveal many important facts about biochemical reactions happening in the organisms. An EPR spectrum of a free radical enzyme can sometimes tell us which amino acid residue of the enzymes bears the free radical. This is a key piece of information for understanding the mechanism of how the enzyme works and one that is difficult to obtain using other methods.

Both useful and 'malicious' free radicals are studied in the Biomedical EPR facility at the Department of Biological Sciences at the University of Essex. In particular interesting and, we believe, significant results have been obtained that help us to understand aspects of oxidative stress and structural biology.

Dimitri Svistunenko

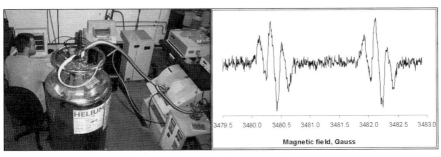

An EPR spectrometer operated at the liquid helium temperatures (-265°C)

An EPR spectrum of vitamin c radicals

DIALYSIS FLUIDS IN THE THERAPY OF KIDNEY FAILURE – A FAR FROM COMPLETE SOLUTION TO A LIFE THREATENING PROBLEM

The kidney has a vital role in human physiology. It regulates water retention in the body, acid-base balance, produces the hormone erythropoietin that controls red blood cell production, and clears waste products – renal toxins – for the body. A decline in renal function is a serious threat to health.

Severe impairment of kidney function leads to renal failure, the clinical syndrome called end-stage renal disease (ESRD). The causes of ESRD are many and varied but diabetes and inflammatory disorders are major causative factors. There are *ca.* 34,000 people with ESRD in the United Kingdom (and about 0.1% of the global population). Each year a further 5,500 people develop ESRD. This rate is set to increase in the future due to the increasing incidence and early onset of diabetes. Most diabetic patients are expected to develop ESRD after 40 years of diabetes. The current annual growth rate of patients with ESRD is 7%. Loss of kidney function is irreversible so that either the kidney must be replaced or procedures have to be undertaken to filter renal toxins from the blood. This is called renal replacement therapy (RRT).

RRT involves kidney replacement by transplantation and procedures to filter the blood to remove renal toxins – renal dialysis. Successful kidney transplantation is the only therapeutic strategy that can ensure survival for many years and a high quality of life. Unfortunately it is not always appropriate because of other health problems and a suitable donor organ may be unavailable. There is also the risk that the causative factor that damaged the original kidney will, in time, also impair the function of the donated kidney. Approximately half of ESRD patients in the UK are unsuitable for kidney transplantation. There is also a shortage of suitable donors, significant transplantation failure (25% after 5 years) and associated costs. About 47% of patients with ESRD eventually receive a kidney transplant, there are about 2000 kidney transplantations performed per year in the U.K. For all other ESRD patients, and for ESRD patients waiting for a suitable donor organ, renal dialysis therapy procedures are implemented.

Dialysis therapy is a poor substitute for a normal kidney. ESRD patient survival on dialysis is poor – with the best medical care available, the median life expectancy is about 8 years from the diagnosis of renal failure. In the UK, after 4 years of dialysis therapy, 48% of ESRD patients are dead. The major problem with dialysis therapy is that renal toxins are not eliminated effectively and increased heart disease leads to premature death. Dialysis procedures used clinically are haemodialysis (HD) and peritoneal dialysis (PD). Considerable research effort is required to improve the performance of dialysis procedures to enhance ESRD patient survival.

In HD, venous blood is circulated out of the body over a semi-permeable membrane. This allows renal toxins to diffuse through the membrane into a second circulating dialysis fluid. HD patients visit a dialysis centre 3 times per week and remain attached to the mechanical dialysis machine for 4 h. Interaction of white blood cells in the circulating blood with the dialysis membrane causes inflammation in the blood vessels that increases the risk of heart disease and, paradoxically, may increase the production of some renal toxins. HD is inconvenient and expensive – the average cost is £29,000 per patient year. An improvement in patient survival on HD is achievable by daily dialysis sessions but there would be an associated 2-3 fold increase in cost of patient care.

In PD therapy, a special dialysis fluid (typically 2 litres) is infused into the peritoneal cavity – the space within the abdomen around the intestines, the stomach, and the liver, left to dwell there for 4 h or overnight, and is then drained out. Renal toxins flow across the surrounding peritoneal membrane and are thereby removed. PD is done daily with typically 4 changes of PD fluid per day. PD is less expensive than HD – ca. £20,000 per patient year. It is associated with a lower inflammatory response since white blood cells that trigger inflammatory responses do not come into contact with synthetic membranes used in HD. Since inflammatory responses initiate and sustain damage to arteries associated with heart disease in dialysis therapy, it is surprising that PD does not have a significantly better clinical outcome than HD.

Currently, worldwide the use of HD and PD is split 85% to 15%. PD is patient preferred and it is thought that global PD will increase to 30-40% of dialysis therapy. In the UK, 55% of ESRD patients receive HD and 45% PD therapy; recently 50% of all new ESRD subjects have received PD therapy. In continental Europe and the USA, most ESRD patients (90%) are on HD; in some developing countries (eg Mexico) 90% of patients receive PD therapy.

There is an emerging consensus that HD and PD therapies in ESRD are complementary. Ideally, PD is a particularly suitable technique to start renal replacement therapy until the ultrafiltration properties of the peritoneal membrane are impaired when a timely switch to HD therapy is required. The reason why filtration by the peritoneal membrane fails is damaging effects of the PD fluids in the peritoneal cavity. High concentrations of glucose (1 - 4%, 76 – 214 mM) are included in PD fluids to create an osmotic flow across the peritoneal membrane, driving the filtration of renal toxins into the peritoneal cavity. Heat sterilisation of the glucose-containing PD fluids leads to loss of biocompatibility by formation of toxic dicarbonyls compounds. Sterilisation of PD fluids by filtration is not a viable alternative because of high cost. The major dialysis companies worldwide have research programmes to improve the biocompatibility of PD fluids and research at the University of Essex is contributing to this effort.

Paul Thornalley

CANCER MARKERS FOR DISEASE DIAGNOSIS AND DRUG DEVELOPMENT

The rather sobering statistics predict that one person in three will be afflicted with cancer at sometime in their life. As a disease affecting ageing populations, cancer is on the rise, and if current trends continue, the number of cases is expected to double by 2050. Thankfully, many types of cancer are often curable, although the outlook for some of the commonest cancers such as lung and colorectal cancer is less optimistic. Surgery, often in combination with radiotherapy and chemotherapy provide the usual treatment options. Until recently, the arsenal of front-line anti-cancer drugs on offer (eg 5-fluorouracil, cytosine arabinoside, methotrexate) has remained remarkably unchanged for several decades. In the absence of anything better, these drugs have stood the test of time and have proven their worth in helping to eliminate tumour cells in some patients and in prolonging survival in others.

Unfortunately, these drugs are all highly toxic compounds that happen to slow the growth or sometimes kill tumour cells slightly more efficiently than normal cells. It is therefore difficult to achieve a high enough (therapeutic) dose to eliminate all the tumour cells without actually killing the patient. However, as cancer chemotherapy moves into the 21st century, the first of a new generation of 'designer' anti-cancer drugs has appeared, heralded by the introduction of Herceptin for breast cancer and Gleevec for some forms of leukaemia.

What makes these drugs rather special is that they have been designed to specifically target either individual molecules or growth-regulating pathways that are uniquely present on tumour cells. In theory at least, such drugs will prevent the growth or actually destroy tumour cells while sparing normal cells. Over 400 new drugs of this type are currently under development with many undergoing clinical trials. Although only a handful of these will ultimately prove to be good enough for clinical practice, the expectation is that over the next few years, these drugs and others in the pipeline, will dramatically impact on cancer survival statistics.

The development of these drugs is being made possible by the efforts of hundreds of research laboratories worldwide in both academia and the pharmaceutical industry in unravelling the molecular complexities of cancer cells. At the University of Essex, we are working closely with doctors in local hospitals to study some of the commonest cancer types such as breast and colon.

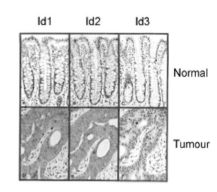

The central goal in this work is the identification and study of tumour 'markers' – often quite subtle molecular changes that distinguish tumour from normal cells. Such markers then provide the starting point for subsequent drug development. But tumour markers are not just important for drug development, they are also having a dramatic impact on the way that cancer is diagnosed. In the past, cancers have been classified by body part – breast, colon, and lung for example.

The spectrum of tumour markers displayed by cancer cells now provides a unique molecular signature that may be used to predict survival, response to treatment and to select appropriate treatment regimes tailored to the individual patient. As with the introduction of new designer anti-cancer drugs, it will be some years before the full impact of molecular diagnostics is felt in the clinic; making the transition with this technology from bench to bedside represents a formidable challenge.

John Norton

INFECTION OF CELLS BY INFLUENZA VIRUS

The influenza pandemic of 1918 killed 20 million people, almost 1% of the world's population at that time. Further less severe pandemics occurred in 1957 and in 1968. These pandemics arose through the appearance of new strains of the influenza virus to which humans had little immunological resistance and against which previously existing vaccines were ineffective.

Influenza is an enveloped virus, i.e. it is encased in a membrane similar to that which surrounds the cells in our body. Incorporated in the membrane are the "spike" proteins, so called because they can be seen as protruding spikes in electron micrographs. These include about 500 copies of haemagglutinin, a protein that binds to N-acetylneuraminic acid (also known as sialic acid) residues that are widely present on cell surfaces. Haemagglutinin is largely responsible for stimulating the immune system to produce antibodies that neutralise the virus. New viral strains are thought to arise from reasssortment of genes among animal and human influenza viruses.

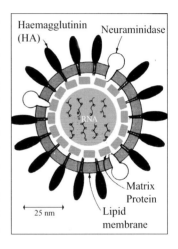

This process, known as antigenic shift, is responsible for influenza pandemics because the human population has not developed any immunity against the newly generated strain.

The life cycle of the virus begins when the haemagglutinin attaches to the surface of a cell. After binding, the virus hitches a ride on the cell's endocytic pathway, a natural mechanism for the ingestion of particles such as low density lipoproteins (LDL). The virus is taken into the cell bound to a small vesicle known as an endosome. The endosomes become acidified and this causes the haemagglutinin to undergo a dramatic change in its structure. A region of the haemagglutinin now brings the membranes of the virus and the endosome into close apposition such that they fuse together. In the process, the viral genome is injected into the cell's cytoplasm from where it is transported into the nucleus. New viral proteins are then synthesised and assemble at sites on the cell's surface membrane. The final stage in the life cycle, called budding, occurs when the virus particles are released from the cell.

At the University of Essex, we have used advanced fluorescence imaging techniques to visualise an important stage of the infection process, namely the fusion of the virus that occurs in acidic conditions. The virus particle is too small to be seen by conventional optical microscopy but it can be made to light up by incorporating fluorescent molecules in its membrane.

In the fluorescence microscope such particles appear as spots that can be recorded with an ultra-sensitive digital camera. At neutral pH, the virus simply binds to the surface of cells, such as red blood cells. If the pH is reduced to about pH5, however, the virus fuses with the cell membrane. Following fusion, the incorporated fluorescence molecules are free to diffuse throughout the cell's membrane so that the whole cell lights up. This provides a valuable method for investigating the mechanism of the fusion process.

Richard Cherry

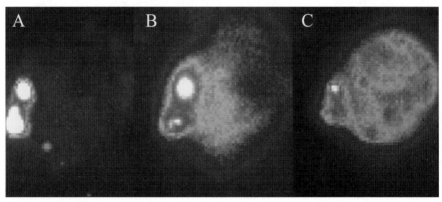

Fusion of an influenza virus with a red blood cell. In A, two virus particles (labeled with a fluorescent dye) have bound to the cell. After six minutes (B), the lower virus has fused and the dye is beginning to spread through the red cell membrane. After a further 19 minutes (C), the process is complete.

KISSING THE HAIRY MUZZLE OF A MOUSE

V iruses are unique entities on the boundary of life. They are intracellular parasites which need to enter and use the resources of cells to enable them to reproduce. This often leads to death of the cell. Death of a few cells can be tolerated in a multi-cellular organism and a virus infection may have little effect overall, or symptoms may be mild. The title of this article refers to a recommended cure, collected by Pliny the Elder (23-79AD), for the common cold, an example of a usually mild and short virus infection, although more serious consequences can follow in some cases. It is sometimes said that viruses live in balance with their host and often do not cause serious disease or death. After all, there is no advantage in killing the host, as this limits the number of individuals available for future infection and so reduces the opportunity of a virus to continue its own existence.

However, more virulent viruses do emerge. Changes in society such as increased travel, population growth and concentration into cities and encroachment into previously uninhabited area due to pressure on land, may be accelerating this process by allowing exposure to new viruses and their rapid spread in the human population. Climatic change, allowing the extension of the range of some biting insects which are involved in transmission of some viruses, is another important factor. Viruses are uniquely placed to respond to such changes, as they have a very rapid replication time (a matter of hours). They also tend to reproduce their genetic information rather imperfectly.

These factors drive rapid virus evolution, leading to the constant emergence of new variants, which could potentially infect new cell types or even hosts and so could go on to cause new diseases. Diseases such as AIDS and SARS are caused by viruses which previously circulated in animal populations, but have adapted to infect humans with devastating effect. The most virulent forms of influenza virus, such as that which killed over 20 million people in 1918/19, are also believed to originate in non-human populations, in this case birds. West Nile Virus, which causes serious brain infections, has recently been identified in the USA and is spreading rapidly there and is another virus where birds play a role in infection. Here, virus in the blood of infected birds can be passed to another bird when a mosquito feeds on both of them. This bird-mosquito-bird transmission route can be interrupted if the mosquito bites a human. Now, although the infection does not produce enough virus to infect another human or bird, it can cause serious, even fatal disease.

Thus, continued research on viruses is required to combat existing diseases and provide information which may be key to understanding viruses that may emerge in the future. Here at the University of Essex, we are studying picornaviruses. This name, comes from pico (which means small - they are amongst the smallest of all viruses) and RNA (the molecule the genetic information is made of). They have only 1/500,000th of the genetic information that humans have and encode only 10-12 proteins. Nonetheless, they are highly significant, as they include the rhinoviruses, the major cause of the common cold, and polioviruses, infection with which can give poliomyelitis, a permanent paralysis. This is a disease of such severity and frequency that it is the subject of a major WHO initiative, which aims to eradicate the disease in the next few years through mass vaccination campaigns. Foot-and-mouth disease, which had such a devastating economic and social impact on the UK in 2001, is caused by another picornavirus.

One of the viruses we are studying, coxsackievirus A9, is part of a group of viruses which can cause aseptic meningitis and may be involved in type 1 diabetes, which is becoming more frequent in Western Europe. Like all viruses, picornaviruses need to introduce their genetic information into cells and use the resources of the cell to make virus proteins and more copies of this genetic information, which will form new virus particles. We have identified a molecule on the cell surface which coxsackievirus A9 is able to recognise, to start the transfer of genetic material into the cell and also the region of the virus particle which is needed for this interaction. We will use this information to see how infection proceeds. The aim of this part of our work is to use our information to design therapeutics which are useful against a range of picornavirus infections and so reduce the impact of these important viruses. Hairy muzzled mice everywhere can then live in peace!

In addition, the interaction between a virus and the cell surface may cause signalling which changes the cell to make it more amenable to virus reproduction and we are also studying this process. We have found a protein in another virus we are studying, human parechovirus 1, which is involved in such a modification to the cell. This virus protein has a number of relatives in human cells and some of these seem to have a role in cancer, suggesting that viruses may also hold clues that can help our understanding of cell biology and non-viral human disease.

Glyn Stanway

TELOMERES: A PROGRAMME FOR AGEING?

There are many theories to explain the complex processes of ageing. Some invoke environmental factors that affect the functioning and efficiency of cells, while others implicate genetic programmes. One theory for ageing involves telomeres. It invokes elements of a genetic programme, although the programme could be modified by environmental insults such as xenobiotic toxins or ionising radiation.

Telomeres are the physical ends of linear chromosomes in eukaryotic organisms, including mammals. They have been compared to the plastic sleeves at the ends of shoelaces or the binding on the edge of a floor rug, there to prevent the ends or edges from fraying. The telomeres are specialised nucleoprotein complexes involved in the protection, replication, and stabilisation of the ends of chromosome. Telomeres usually contain lengths of tandemly repeated, simple DNA sequences (terminal repeats) composed of a guanine-rich strand and a cytosine-rich strand. These terminal repeats are highly conserved and all vertebrates appear to have the same sequence repeat in their telomeres – TTAGGG.

Telomerase is the reverse transcriptase that controls the extension of the telomeric repeat sequences. If telomerase activity is reduced or absent (as occurs in many differentiated cells or in ageing as the result of DNA copying errors), the telomeres will progressively shorten as the cells divide by mitosis, eventually resulting in their wearing down to mere stubs. The definitive chromosome genetic material will now start to `fray', much as a rug that has lost its binding will start to fray. In the cell this erosion will lead to cellular senescence as the telomeric sequences wear down to the point where they are not long enough to support the telomere-protein complex protecting the chromosomal ends and the chromosomes become dysfunctional or even become prone chromosome rearrangements in this situation.

It is suggested that telomeres act as a `clock' or a counter of cell mitoses. If the telomerase, which is found in germ cells and stem cells, adds telomere repeat sequences to the end of the DNA before each cell replication, then the life of that lineage of cells continues. Cell biologists have modified cultured human body cells *in vitro* so that they can make telomerase. These cells continue to divide for much longer than the usual lifespan of the cell line. Telomerase genes could be inserted into human cells *in vivo* to prevent ageing. However, it is worrying that most cancer cells have (re)gained the ability to make telomerase, so that they can divide indefinitely.

As with so much gerontological research, the picture is far from simple: the neatness of the telomere story is confounded by the fact that human telomeres are relatively short, despite human longevity, compared with short-lived mice where the telomeres are very long.

Richard Jurd

GENETIC DISORDERS AND THE BRAIN

Genetic disorders fall into two broad groups. One group contains inherited disorders, in which at least one parent will carry the gene or genes responsible for the condition. The other group contains chromosome abnormalities in which some genetic material is damaged, cracked or atypically organised during the process of early cell formation and division.

An example of an inherited genetic disorder which affects brain development is phenylketonuria [PKU]. Genes are organised in pairs, with one coming from each parent. Although the gene for PKU is relatively common in the population, it is a recessive trait which means that the child will only exhibit the condition if a PKU gene is inherited from each of the child's parents so that both genes in the pair are affected.

In PKU the child lacks an enzyme which is important for the metabolism of phenylalanine which is a components of protein food. As a consequence there is a build up of one of the derivatives of phenylalanine and the effect of this is to damage the process of myelination in the brain which is the growth of the coverings down nerve tracts which enable the nerve to carry messages rapidly. (The deterioration of this myelin sheath occurs in multiple sclerosis.)

In PKU, myelination of the late developing frontal lobes of the brain is particularly affected. If PKU is left untreated, the child will have severe intellectual difficulties and have very limited expectations in terms of the development of abilities, however PKU is an example of a genetic disorder whose outcome can be influenced by the environment. All children are given a blood test at birth called the Guthrie test, to test for PKU and for affected children, the diet is modified to restrict protein intake.

As a result, the effect on the brain is significantly reduced and the child can develop with normal intelligence, attend normal schools and eventually pursue normal adult employment. Subtle problems may remain which are minor in comparison to those of untreated children but are nevertheless the focus of much contemporary research as they may reflect subtle influences upon frontal lobe development.

There are 23 pairs of chromosomes with the last pair being either XX for a girl or XY for a boy. A number of different disorders which affect brain development can arise from abnormalities to these chromosomes. One example is Turner's syndrome [TS] in which there is absence or loss of material in the second X chromosome in girls. The children are of small stature and may be treated with growth hormone. They are also usually given hormone replacement therapy in adolescence so that they will develop normal adult female characteristics, however, they are not fertile as the ovaries although present at conception degenerate before birth. Without effective ovaries, they do not have eggs but they may be able to carry and give birth to a child with a donated egg that is fertilised.

Of interest to neuropsychologists, those with TS have a pattern of brain development which is associated with characteristic strengths and weaknesses in intellectual development. Intelligence in TS spans the normal range but they have difficulties with a number of spatial and perceptual tasks. In contrast, they have relative strength in language and may have reading, vocabulary and verbal memory skills which are higher than normal.

The disorder and its linked brain development is therefore associated with both specific disabilities and specific talents. A further issue of contemporary interest is whether the characteristics displayed by someone with TS are influenced by whether their intact X-chromosome comes from their mother or father.

Christine Temple

VISUALIZATION OF IMMUNOLOGICAL RECEPTORS BY MICROSCOPY AND IMAGING

E ver since microscopy was developed in the seventeenth century, scientists have been trying to depict and record their observations. Initially these had to be drawn by hand, usually by the scientists themselves, whose training included draughtsmanship. Drawing was replaced by photomicrography in the early twentieth century and more recently by computer-aided imaging. Each in turn has opened a new artistic universe. Molecules, intracellular organelles and receptors interactions can now be represented to help understand and explain how cells and molecules work.

Microscopy and imaging have been essential for the study of immunological receptors. All cells in the body carry transmembrane receptors. Receptors are used as 'markers' to designate cell types and are intrinsically related to the function of the cells. The identification of the cell receptors is made possible by the use of antibodies. Animals (in the early days rabbits and horses) inoculated with cells from another species would produce antibodies specific to the inoculated cells. In most cases the antibodies reacted with the predominant receptors of the cells initially inoculated.

In 1974, with the development of monoclonal antibodies, it became possible to use culture cells bioreactors to produce *in vitro* antibodies on a large scale that could be reactive against virtually any cell type or receptor. The binding of antibodies to a receptor is normally stable and with strong affinity. In humans such monoclonal antibodies have become invaluable tools to probe cells, tissues and body fluids in states of health and disease.

In order to reveal the presence of a given receptor antibodies are labelled with a fluorescent particle (eg fluorescein) and used to stain cells, which are mounted on a slide and examined under a microscope. Bright illumination excites the fluorescent particle which emits at a given wavelength (blue… green… red), and using a filter this can be captured by photography and enhanced or analysed by computer imaging. Over the past decade versions of this technique, first developed by the British scientist Albert Coons, have been widely applied in biomedical research.

Applications of this technique include detection and enumeration of cell types, quantification of receptors, and location of receptors in intracellular compartments. High-resolution microscopy has also allowed the determination of receptor associations by probing single cells with two or more antibodies coupled to fluorescent particles having different emission colours. Overall, these experiments have shown that receptors display mobility in the plane of the membrane and associate either with the same receptor or other receptors. These observations have unravelled the mode of action of receptors on cells and have contributed to our understanding of how immunological cells interact with each other.

A further development has been that of confocal fluorescent microscopy. This makes use of laser illumination to produce a series of optical sections or views of a single cell stained with a given antibody. An example of the use of this technique is given below. In this example cells (a rat-derived fibroblast cell line propagated *in vitro* under tissue culture conditions) were stained with a monoclonal antibody specific for histocompatibility receptors Class I. The antibody was tagged with the fluorescent particle fluorescein which emits green light upon excitation.

In Figure 1(a) the receptors can be seen on the surface of the cell.

In Figure 1(b) the cells were permeabilised with a mild detergent so the antibodies could penetrate the cells and stain the receptors in their intracellular compartments. The application of confocal microscopy and its variations have numerous applications for the study of immunological receptors since it provides high-resolution images with minimal sample manipulation.

The images in Figure 1 are not a visual record of the way the cells would look if we could see them but an encoded version that uses pseudo-colour to create an image that can aid the interpretation and understanding of the function of cells, their molecules and receptors. In this way a microscopic observation leads to a re-appraisal of nature. Science is, in this sense, not so far from art as is popularly believed. Like an artist, a scientist needs to be able to make an imaginative leap from ideas about the attributes of cells in a way that can make them compatible with what is visible to the eye. Once they have been decoded and rendered visible then, again, it is the imagination that has to help a scientist to understand how cells and molecules assemble and function in reality, how the system breaks down in disease, and how to correct anomalies in therapies and to enhance immunological responses.

Nelson Fernandez, Valerie Fraser, Ian Morrison and Richard Cherry

(a)   (b)

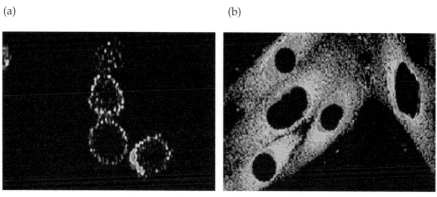

Figure 1.

Visualisation of histocompatibility complex class I receptors by high resolution confocal microscopy. In (a) the cells are optically "sliced" across the diameter by the laser illumination and the punctuate rings indicate localised surface staining. In (b), permeabilised cells show the presence of receptors throughout the cells except the nucleus (black holes).

THE IMPORTANCE OF KEEPING A COOL HEAD

A lack of oxygen to the brain at around the time of birth is responsible for brain damage or death in thousands of babies. Oxygen is required to generate the energy necessary for normal brain function. Indeed the brain is the organ in the body that is most critically dependent on a continuous supply of oxygen for its function. The brain receives its oxygen via the blood supply. There are two factors that can reduce the amount of oxygen reaching the brain of a human foetus. The first is that there is reduction in the amount of oxygen in the blood (called hypoxia). The second is that there is a reduction in blood flow to the brain (called ischaemia). A combination of hypoxia and/or ischaemia at around the time of birth is responsible for death or permanent brain injury in at least 1,000 term and premature infants each year in the UK. Perhaps the easiest situation to visualise that can lead to this tragic outcome is when the umbilical cord gets wrapped around the neck of the baby in the womb; however, there are several other situations in pregnancy that can lead to a lack of oxygen delivery to the foetal brain. The tragedy is that this occurs in otherwise normal babies that would be born with no brain damage at all.

Researchers at University College London Medical School have been leading the way in making non-invasive measurements of brain function in human infants. At the University of Essex we have been involved in assisting with the interpretation of these measurements. In particular we have investigated the role of overproduction of nitric oxide in initiating brain damage (see article a5) and at the development of *in vivo* markers of nitric oxide production to aid early diagnosis.

Previous research has shown that, although interruption to the oxygen supply commonly occurs during labour, the brain damage in these infants does not develop until many hours subsequent to their birth. At birth the brain appears normal. However, there is an increase in lactic acid in the brain evident on day two. This is the same molecule that makes your muscles "burn" during intense exercise and is evidence that the body's mitochondria are not consuming enough oxygen. This is not a problem in the muscle (an organ able to function without oxygen for long periods), but is potentially very serious in the brain (the most sensitive organ to oxygen deprivation). It is as if the lack of oxygen during labour generates a `time bomb' that slowly ticks away and eventually causes the brains to be irreversibly damaged one day after birth.

These findings raise the possibility that we could intervene with drugs or other treatments to prevent the damage from occurring, even after the baby is born. A `therapeutic window' may exist during which the brain may be saved from damage. However, attempts to find a pharmacological approach to the problem have so far met with only mixed success. Diagnosis of the "at risk" babies is difficult because at birth the brain appears normal. Many babies go through apparently traumatic labour with no ill effects.

There is, therefore, a reluctance on the part of drug companies to develop products that would have to be administered to apparently `healthy' babies. Even with treatment, many of these babies will go on to develop serious brain damage anyway (with the associated human and financial costs of lifetime medical care). How could it be proved that the drug itself did not contribute to the damage? It does not take an ambulance-chasing lawyer to realise that potential litigation costs (especially in the USA) do not make newborn babies a prime candidate for the development of aggressive neuroprotective drugs.

The solution to this quandary has come about from some unlikely sources. There are incidences of babies undergoing traumatic labour in situations where "high-tech" intensive care is not available (eg in developing countries). In these circumstances the baby's body temperature can drop dramatically (sometimes as low as 20°C). This hypothermia appears to protect the brain from damage. A similar effect is seen in some people who apparently miraculously survive with no brain damage following "drowning" in cold water, despite their heart stopping for a considerable period of time. Animal tests have revealed that severe drops in temperature are not required for this protection – in fact only a moderate 4°C decrease was necessary to provide significant protection from brain damage. These same tests also determined that no ill effects arose from this small degree of cooling, making it ethical to undergo a clinical trial in human babies. A small US company developed a cooling cap to keep the babies' head cool.

The results of this trial are just in and have exceeded expectations. "Keeping a cool head" works, even if the cooling is not applied till two hours after birth. Although it was not possible to prevent brain damage in all cases, significantly the trial showed that babies who would normally have a lifetime of disability are likely to have a significantly enhanced quality of life. Whilst many babies in special care will no doubt need the familiar incubators to keep their body warm, we may increasingly see a number of them with caps on to do the opposite to their heads!

Chris Cooper

HIGH DOSE VITAMIN THERAPY: SUPER-HEALTH, SUPERFLUOUS NUTRITIONAL SUPPLEMENTATION OR JUSTIFIABLE MEDICATION?

An increasing proportion of the UK population take single or multi-vitamin tablets regularly as nutritional supplements to ensure an adequate daily supply of essential vitamins. The recommended daily allowance (RDA) of vitamins is the dietary level to sustain normal growth and avoid associated vitamin deficiency disease – see Table 1. Two vitamins, vitamin C (ascorbic acid) and vitamin E (α-tocopherol), are often taken in amounts in marked excess of the RDA in the hope that this will to improved or "super-health". Until recently, there was no guidance on the safe upper levels of vitamins that may be taken as nutritional supplements. The European Union (EU) Food Supplements Directive 2002, implemented in UK law in July 2003, seeks to establish a recommended range (minimum to maximum) of vitamin supplement dose – although, as yet, definitive dose ranges have been set.

Table 1. Recommended daily allowances of "antioxidant" vitamins

Nutrient	Recommended Daily Allowance	
	Men	Women
Vitamin B$_1$/Thiamin (mg)	1.5	1.1
Vitamin C (mg)	60	60
Vitamin E (µg)	10	5

In May 2003, the UK Expert Group on Vitamins and Minerals produced a report with recommendations on the safe upper limits of vitamin supplements – although its remit did not cover assessment of the health benefits of high dose vitamin supplements. Generally, there is little evidence on the adverse effects of high doses of vitamins taken over many years but doses of vitamin C up to 1 gm per day for an adult (or 17 mg/kg/day) and doses of vitamin E up to 540 mg/day (or 9 mg/kg/day) are considered to be without adverse effect. The most famous proponent of high dose vitamin C consumption was Linus Pauling who won Nobel prizes for Chemistry (1954) and Peace (1962). In the latter part of his life, he took 3 - 40 g of vitamin C per day and risked adverse gastrointestinal effects such as abdominal pain and diarrhoea. He died at the age of 93 from prostate cancer. Why do people take high dose vitamin therapy? Is there a case for achieving a state of "super-health" – or at least prevention of illness? Are there illnesses where high dose vitamin therapy is a proven therapy? Research at the University of Essex suggests that a further vitamin, thiamine (vitamin B1) taken at high dose may be beneficial – particularly for people with diabetes.

High doses vitamin C (500 – 1000 mg/day) and vitamin E (67 – 270 mg) are taken primarily for an antioxidant effect. Proteins, nucleotides, lipids and carbohydrates in the body are exposed to low levels of hydrogen peroxide, hypochlorite and other oxidising agents. Unchecked, these oxidative processes damage cellular molecules which must then be repaired or replaced. Antioxidants slow down oxidative processes and protect against oxidative damage. Vitamin C is an antioxidant of the aqueous regions (cytosol) of cells and vitamin E an antioxidant of the lipid membrane regions of cells.

Claims that high dose vitamin C may prevent the common cold and cancer have not been proven in conducted clinical trials. Vitamin C may reduce the severity of symptoms of the common cold but extremely high doses are not required to achieve this since the body can absorb maximally only 200-400 mg/day. Evidence for a health benefit of high dose vitamin E supplements came from the Cambridge Heart Antioxidant Study (CHAOS) in 1996 where patients with established heart disease taking vitamin E (268 and 537 mg/day doses) for approximately two years had decreased risk of a heart attack (myocardial infarction). More recent and larger clinical trials have failed to provide support for this beneficial effect, however, and a further study with both vitamin E and C – the Heart Protection Study (2002) also failed to show a health benefit.

So what can thiamine do to help? The antioxidant effects of vitamin C and vitamin E are sustained in the body by regeneration of oxidised forms of the vitamins to the normal reduced forms by a tripeptide reducing agent, g-glutamylcysteinylglycine or glutathione (GSH). Glutathione itself has to be maintained in a reduced form which is achieved by the hexosemonophosphate pathway of glucose metabolism. A critical enzyme limiting the activity of this pathway is `transketolase'. The essential cofactor of transketolase is thiamine pyrophosphate – the major metabolite of thiamine. Without adequate thiamine, it is likely that vitamin C, vitamin E and glutathione itself cannot work to maximum efficiency. High transketolase activity is also associated with longevity in dietary restriction models of increasing lifespan. Thiamine pyrophosphate is also a co-factor of other enzymes essential for other aspects of glucose metabolism: pyruvate dehydrogenase and $\propto$-ketoglutarate dehydrogenase of the citric acid cycle.

So who can benefit from thiamine supplements? Thiamine therapy is conventionally only given to people suffering from alcoholism because high concentrations of alcohol decrease the intestinal absorption of thiamine into the body, and to communities who eat polished rice as a staple food and consequently have diminished dietary intake of thiamine. Recent evidence suggests that people with diabetes, kidney failure, heart disease and cirrhosis (alcohol-induced and other types) may benefit from high dose thiamine therapy – possibly up to 500 mg/day thiamine.

No significant stores of thiamine are retained in the body and so if the kidneys fail to reabsorb thiamine from filtered blood plasma efficiently, increased thiamine will be excreted in urine and thiamine deficiency ensues. Increased urinary elimination of thiamine occurs in diabetes. High dose thiamine has been shown to prevent damage to the kidney (nephropathy), eyes (retinopathy) and nerves (neuropathy) in diabetes experimentally, and neuropathy clinically – covered elsewhere in this booklet.

In kidney failure, dialysis therapy leads to increased losses of thiamine in the dialysis fluid. In heart disease, the use of therapeutic agents to decrease blood volume by increasing urine production leads to increased "wash out" of thiamine from the body; this may also apply to vitamin C. People with cirrhosis develop diabetes-like hyperglycaemia and thiamine can reverse this.

Thiamine, a vitamin considered little as a therapeutic agent other than for alcoholism, is now attracting a much greater following. It may be a vitamin where a health benefit of high dose therapy can indeed be achieved.

Paul Thornalley

SMART PILLS – BOON OR BANE FOR THE 21ST CENTURY?

Modern living puts great pressure on us all to meet its demands. Many of us increasingly depend on chemical 'props' in order to cope. Health foods and vitamins are being consumed in large quantities in an attempt to combat the spectre of disease and the rigors placed upon our bodies and minds by the daily routine. How many of us feel we must have numerous cups of coffee or tea to help us to keep alert and keep going until we gratefully settle down in our beds at the end of the day?

Performance enhancement, of one kind or another is becoming more and more important to succeed in the first world. Whilst a great variety of drugs have been, and are being, used by amateur and professional sports men and women with the conviction that their physical performance will be improved, we are about to move into an era where drugs that enhance mental performance are readily available to us.

The conditions and diseases of our increasingly aged populations have stimulated research into pharmacological agents to treat and alleviate them. One in five people over the age of 80 in the UK suffer from dementia. We now have drugs approved for the treatment of early stage Alzheimer's disease (donepezil, galantamine and rivastigmine) and Schizophrenia (ziprasidone and olanzapine) which have been shown to enhance the cognitive ability of the subjects. Although cognitive ability encompasses a variety of mental functions, ability to maintain concentration, retain memories in the short and long term and carry out intellectually demanding tasks are probably the more important features that are influenced by these drugs.

Some argue that the fact that the impaired mental functions of damaged brains may be ameliorated by these drugs does not necessarily mean that the mental functions of otherwise 'healthy 'people may be enhanced by their use. In fact, there are neuroscientists who are very sceptical about the whole idea of drug-induced cognitive enhancement of 'normal' brains. Nevertheless, studies reporting the cognitive enhancement of 'normal' brains are beginning to appear in the scientific literature.

So, we are presented with yet more moral and ethical dilemmas. Is it wrong to want to enhance our cognitive ability by using smart pills? Most official bodies that are required to address this question conclude that using smart pills to gain intellectual advantage is "cheating" and represents a divisive shortcut to the attainment of greater mental achievement. On the other hand, some bioethicists contend that it is desirable as long as the drugs are made available to all and not just the wealthy citizens of our society. However, we have not attained social justice in our education system where the wealthy are able to buy a better education for their children, so it seems unlikely that (presumably) expensive smart pills will be equally available to the poorest members of our society.

We mustn't forget that all drugs have side effects and health considerations must also influence the suitability of using smart pills. The so-called first generation of smart pills mentioned above has a long list of potential side effects and contraindications but they most commonly cause nausea/vomiting and diarrhoea. The second generation of smart pills is being designed to more specifically target biochemical components of mechanisms connected with cognition. Thus, it is assumed that problems of side effects will diminish.

Anecdotal evidence suggests that in America drugs such as methylphenidate (Ritalin), which are being increasingly prescribed for the treatment of attention deficit hyperactivity disorder (ADHD) in disruptive children, are being used by 'normal' schoolchildren, college students and adults. They do so in the belief that their ability to concentrate and to memorise facts will be enhanced. Thus, it is more than likely that such 'off label' use of drugs prescribed for cognitive enhancement of impaired brain function will increasingly be taken by 'normal' individuals in their quest for improved mental performance. Those of us with an e-mail account at our workplace are constantly bombarded on a daily basis with offers of a great variety of legal and illegal prescription drugs. It will not be long before the second generation of smart pills will be added to that list.

In a society where we are placing greater and greater pressure on our children and ourselves to produce excellent examination results and work to our maximum capacity, how will we be able to resist using these drugs? Neuroscientists suggest that our sense of self is in danger of being modified by the use of smart drugs. We need to enter into a debate as to whether or not their use will benefit society's mental health. As responsible scientists we must inform society of the facts and discredit the myths.

Gareth Jones

PSYCHOSOCIAL IMPACT OF NEW DRUG THERAPIES FOR HIV POSITIVE PEOPLE

The introduction and widespread use of highly active antiretroviral therapy (HAART) since 1996 has resulted in longer and healthier lives for HIV positive people in Europe, North America, and Australia. This has transformed HIV into a chronic condition requiring long-term management and care. One consequence of the success of HAART is that there are now more people living with HIV in developed countries than at any other time in the epidemic.

Not only has HAART had a dramatic impact on the physical health of HIV positive people but also on the psycho-social and health care needs of HIV positive people. In an attempt to understand better the social and psychological consequences of this dramatically changed situation, the British HIV Association commissioned the University of Essex to conduct a scoping exercise about the psychosocial impact of HAART in the UK.

In the UK, 2002 saw the largest increase ever in numbers of newly diagnosed HIV positive people in the UK. Men who have sex with men remain the largest group. The number of drug users currently being diagnosed with HIV is declining. Transmission via heterosexual sex is rising dramatically and most HIV infections acquired heterosexually are acquired in Africa. Rising numbers of all newly diagnosed groups are in London.

The changing epidemiology has created a very fragmented HIV population in the UK with diverse needs. There are migrant communities whose lives are often characterised by poverty and social exclusion. Poverty generally has a more profound impact on their everyday lives than HIV. Asylum seekers are particularly vulnerable especially since the introduction of dispersal which relocates migrants to areas which may lack a well-developed HIV service infrastructure.

There has been a shift from acute mental health problems associated with dying to chronic complex problems associated with living. HIV is no longer seen as a 'plague' but HIV-related stigma continues and this may lead to non-disclosure and lack of support. More HIV positive people are considering returning to work. There are many concerns that if they do so and then stop work, they may lose entitlement to the welfare benefits that they currently have. Poverty is a salient feature in the lives of a high proportion of the HIV-positive population in the UK.

Starting treatment is problematic for those who are healthy and feeling well. The treatment may well make them feel ill. This has been referred to as the 'treatment paradox'. The side-effects associated with HAART are problematic. In particular, lipodystrophy and lipoatrophy may change body shape which can lead to low self-esteem and serve as a visual marker of HIV. Also the health of some HIV positive people does not improve with HAART and some people still die.

There are logistical barriers that restrict access to HIV services especially for the most marginalised groups. HIV related stigma may deter HIV positive people from accessing services. Cultural difference may also deter those from ethnic minority groups accessing services that are mainly run by the ethnic majority and were originally targeted at gay men and drug users

Key challenges for the future are to co-ordinate good quality professional psycho-social support and counselling in a number of different agencies to meet the myriad of psycho-social needs. Additional mental health support geared towards HIV as a chronic illness affecting vulnerable populations is required. It is also important to ensure equity so that all people with HIV in the UK, whoever and wherever they are, have access to appropriate support.

Gill Green

BLOOD SUBSTITUTES

I n the UK, we take blood transfusions almost for granted. Willing donors voluntarily give blood and an efficient health service ensures that it is safe to transfuse into patients, with blood groups being matched and blood born diseases eliminated. It is true that with the advent of HIV and new variant CJD concern has grown but new and stringent testing has allayed fears. Many other countries do not enjoy this happy position, the transfusion service in many developing countries being in jeopardy.

What price then a blood substitute that can be guaranteed to be free from infection, needs no blood group matching, is easy to store and has a long shelf life? Such is the goal for scientists who over the last 20 years have been attempting to design a blood substitute. In fact this task is far too difficult and efforts have been concentrated on one important aspect of the function of blood, namely the transportation of oxygen from the lungs to the tissues. There are a number of strategies to achieve this and I consider here the design of a haemoglobin-based oxygen carrier.

Haemoglobin, the red protein in blood is a complex of four proteins, two so-called alpha chains and two beta - chains. In each of these is located a haem group, a flat, plate-like, organic molecule at the centre of which is an iron atom. It is at this iron atom that oxygen is reversibly bound.

How can we obtain enough haemoglobin that is guaranteed free of viruses and other infectious agencies? One way to approach this problem is to attempt to place the genetic information required to make human haemoglobin into another organism that does not bear the infections to which humans are susceptible.

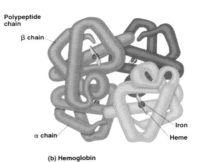

(b) Hemoglobin

Although haemoglobin is made of two copies of two different proteins and requires the insertion of a haem group into each protein it turns out that this task is quite easy. Many organisms can be induced to make Hb. Foremost amongst these is the bacterium E.coli, but yeast will also do it. In addition research is on going into whether it may be possible to induce some species of plants to make this human protein. This would certainly throw a different light on GM crops. The amount of human

Hb that E.coli can produce is impressive and by means of large scale fermentation, rather like that used in the brewing industry, it is probable that sufficient Hb could be produced to have an impact on world health, at least for use in some specific situations, eg trauma treatment and some surgery.

However it is not just the quantity of Hb that can be produced that is of concern, the properties of Hb must also be tuned and it is here that difficulties arise. If placed directly into the blood stream, ie not inside the red blood cell, Hb exhibits a range of undesirable characteristics. Firstly if the bloodstream is to have sufficient oxygen carrying capacity the amount of Hb present must be large. If this is not confined inside of the flexible but rugged red blood cell then the blood becomes very viscous and difficult for the heart to pump around he body. In addition this "free" Hb increases the osmotic pressure of the blood with the result that water is drawn from the cells surrounding the blood vessels. If unchecked this would lead to a disastrous and fatal loss of control of the body's water balance. The situation is made worse as free Hb has a tendency to dissociate into its constituent chains (dimers) that block and damage the kidneys.

Still further horrors await. Free Hb is able to react with and remove nitric oxide (NO) from the arterial wall. This small gaseous molecule has now been shown, surprisingly, to be a hormone that relaxes the arterial wall and thus controls blood pressure. Removal of NO thus increases blood pressure. Also because it contains an iron atom, possess a quasi-enzymatic activity that enables it to catalyse powerful oxidation reactions that form highly toxic products.

All of these problems would be solved if we could get Hb in a synthetic blood cell. This has been investigated using small lipid vesicles called liposomes as a substitute for the erythrocyte. These studies have, however, thrown up further problems that are still more difficult to solve. Instead each of the problems listed has been or is being addressed separately. Some remain intractable. For example, problems regarding osmotic pressure and the dissociation into dimers can be overcome by chemically coupling together the individual chains and then linking together large numbers of Hb molecules to produce stable aggregates that are not filtered by the kidney.

Problems associated with tuning the affinity of Hb for oxygen and the ability to bind NO have been partially solved through a very large programme of studies, largely conducted in the USA, involving genetically engineered Hb. In these the design of the protein, and hence its function, has been subtle altered by what is termed site-directed mutagenesis. This method relies on making slight but very specific changes to the genetic blueprint of Hb that is used to make this protein in *E.coli*.

A similar approach is at the centre of attempts aimed at reducing the ability of Hb to promote "oxidative stress". This problem is as yet unsolved but at the University of Essex we have an extensive research programme looking into this. To further this work we have joined a consortium of 14 laboratories across Europe in a project that is funded by the EU.

Mike Wilson

XENOTRANSPLANATION

Xenotransplantation is the use of organs and tissue from non-human animals for medical purposes in humans. The idea of using non-human animals in this way has been around for many years, and replacement of defective heart valves with pig heart valves is now routine. Since there is a shortage of organs for transplantation, xenotransplantation is advocated by some as a way of dealing with the problem.

Given the precedent of pig heart valves, it might seem that xenotranplantation was uncontroversial. In fact, it raises many issues of ethics and policy in biotechnology. Because of these concerns, there is currently a moratorium on xenotransplantation in the UK.

Virtually all attempts at a successful organ xenotransplant have ended in failure with the patients dying soon after the operation, although a woman did live for nine months with a chimpanzee kidney transplant in the US in 1964. All innovative medical interventions involve risks for patients. However, many people feel that in the case of xenotransplantation experimental patients need special protection (for example counselling before making a decision) to ensure that the consent they give to the procedure is genuine and unforced.

This need is especially important in the case of children, where it is parents who give consent. Parents will naturally strive to do all they can to save a dying child, and this can sometimes mean that they will be vulnerable to those who promise much. In 1984 for example the parents of Baby Fae were prepared to take her to the US for a baboon heart transplant, in an operation that had little chance of success. She died twenty days after the operation, and many felt that her death would have been better had the operation simply not taken place.

Xenotransplantation also raises public health risks. Some pathogens – disease causing organisms – can jump from species to species (influenza is a common example). Care can be taken in xenotransplantation to screen the source animals to ensure that they are free from known pathogens. But this is only part of the story. There may be unknown pathogens or pathogens that are harmless in the host animals but dangerous for human beings. In other words, it might be that transplanted organs could be the source of a major transmissible disease. Given the experience of BSE this fear has been of concern. For these reasons, it is common to suggest the monitoring of any patients were any operations to take place.

Unlike pig heart valves, any major organ transplant would involve genetic modification of the source animal to ensure that its tissue was compatible with the human immune system. (Even transplants from human to human require drugs that suppress the normal immune response.) There are significant currents of public opinion that exhibit disquiet about the practice of genetic modification in animals. In practice, there is unlikely to be an all or nothing response in public policy on this question, but those responsible for the regulation of xenotransplantation will want to ensure that the modifications in question do not harm the welfare of the source animals.

For some citizens, of course, the very idea of using non-human animals for purely human purposes is wrong. Those who believe strongly in the animal rights will argue that it is just as wrong to kill an animal to save a human life as it would be to kill another human being. This is a minority position in society, but it is one that is passionately held. As with all questions of deep morality (abortion would be another example), liberal democracies tend to enforce a principle of freedom of conscience on such matters. Whilst no one should be forced or pressured into having a xenotransplant if they object, nobody should be in a position to prevent others having one.

Does xenotransplanation have a future? The search is on for alternatives, including artificial organs. But no one can rule out the possibility that for some patients a xenotransplant may be the best option once the technique is perfected. As with any controversial biotechnology, a public choice cannot be avoided.

Albert Weale

FROM SMALLPOX TO MMR: DISEASES, PUBLIC AND PERSONAL RESPONSIBILITY IN VACCINATION DECISIONS

Despite the extraordinary advances in medicine over the past half century all infectious diseases have not been conquered. The Table lists four types of organism responsible for such diseases. Bacteria that produce most classical diseases are DNA-containing agents. The hereditary material in some viruses, such as those responsible for polio and influenza, is RNA. Viruses like the HIV pathogen are "retroviruses"; normally RNA-containing, when they enter the host cell they synthesize DNA from the host material and subsequent RNA and protein synthesis occurs as in the traditional bacterial case. The most mysterious group are the prions which are protein containing and switch the synthesis of a host protein from a native to a toxic form. The insidious brain-wasting disease, nCJD (new variant Creutzfeld-Jacob disease), appears to be of this type.

Table 1: Microbial infection types

Type	Examples	Replication mechanism	How the toxic protein is made
DNA	all bacterial	DNA makes DNA	DNA —> RNA —> protein
RNA	polio, flu	RNA makes RNA	RNA —> protein
retro	HIV, tumour retro	RNA makes DNA	DNA —> RNA —> protein
prion	BSE, nvCJD, scrapie	protein modifies protein	protein —> modified protein

The medical question then becomes: treatment or vaccination? In many cases once the disease is present there is no sure cure, even with classical bacterial infections. Vaccination as a preventative measure is the better route. For over 200 years since Jenner's discovery it has been generally accepted that vaccination against smallpox protects the individual against that disease in the community. Yet public acceptance of smallpox vaccination, especially for children, was slow, even against that hideous disease. The antivaccination league was one of the strongest social movements in late Victorian England, with many resisters fined or even imprisoned for refusing vaccination for their children. It recruited some famous supporters, most notably the playwright George Bernard Shaw and Alfred Russel Wallace, codiscoverer with Charles Darwin of the theory of evolution by natural selection.

How could Wallace doubt the biological reality of vaccination? Notwithstanding Pasteur's experiments, there was a neglect of microbes as components of the tree of life by Victorian and later evolutionists including Wallace himself. Wallace saw a "use for microbes in the scheme of life". In debate with John Tyndall on 'dust' and infection, he took the rosy viewpoint that disease is just nature's way of getting rid of the weak and wounded. When he did think of microbial evolution he used a "niche replacement model" between microorganisms - removal of one disease will simply give opportunities to others, possibly worse. The only sure route to public health, he said, was to improve housing and hygiene.

Alfred Russel Wallace (1822 - 1913)

Statistics were needed, but statistical methodology hardly existed. There was use and misuse of numbers by all sides in the controversy. Wallace emphasised overall trends rather than differences between vaccinated and unvaccinated populations. Communities embracing vaccination programmes were statistically often more susceptible to smallpox attacks than those who took alternative prophylactic measures, and smallpox deaths were more numerous in cities with vaccination programmes than in those without. His opponents cited the real differences between vaccinated and unvaccinated populations in single jurisdictions; but with legal compulsion it paid the infected to claim vaccination, and conversely, with their reputations to consider, it paid doctors to deny that the infected had been vaccinated. Even under the best circumstances vaccination was not risk free. And smallpox vaccination remains potentially dangerous even today.

Eventually, after a series of Royal Commissions, to which Wallace contributed, compulsory smallpox vaccination was abolished. My parents, followers of Bernard Shaw, refused me smallpox vaccination as a child although later it had to be done to allow me to cross the Atlantic. Older travellers may thus carry a residual immunity not possessed by those much younger. Smallpox later became the World Health Organisation's biggest challenge on the international scene. The WHO anti-smallpox campaign

using mass vaccination was one of the greatest achievements in the area of
public medicine. A resounding success, the last smallpox victims suffered in
the late 1970s.

A hundred years after Wallace's campaign, the combined vaccination of
children against mumps, measles and rubella (MMR) is being analogously
criticised. Wakefield's strongly opposed claims for a link between MMR
vaccination and autism and bowel syndromes included both medical
(pathological, individual) and epidemiological (global, societal) arguments;
his use of statistics in emphasising public trends rather than individual risks
echoes Wallace. Governmental responses, sometimes rather robust, raise the
question of freedom of choice again, as did the nineteenth-century
vaccination acts. Other diseases are on the increase: asthma, autism and
allergies. Are they, as Wallace might have argued, examples of niche
replacement linked to vaccination programmes? Measles is an unpleasant
disease but not in the same league as smallpox. What then, we might ask,
following Wallace, are the measles statistics? The Figure shows the decline in
measles in the twentieth century in the USA. Some conclusions are clear - an
early twentieth-century biennial oscillation of measles outbreaks had already
died down by the 1960s, before general vaccination started. Measles
mortality, serious in the early 20th century, declined steeply prior to such
programmes and is unaffected by them. Vaccination had its greatest effect in
diminishing occurrence of the disease to almost zero after it had already
fallen to very low levels.

**Figure 2. Measles statistics: USA 1912-1984 replotted from the web site
"Vaccination News".**

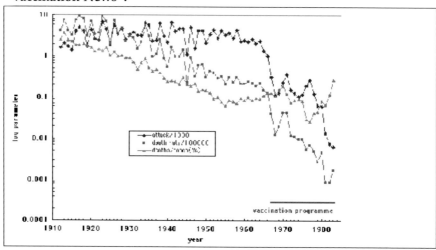

So what should the wise parent do? Calculation of risk – of disease and of medicine (iatrogenic) - is not easy. It will differ between common and uncommon diseases; between lethal and non-lethal diseases; between general (infectious) and local (contagious) diseases; and between diseases threatening everyone and those threatening only a specific subgroup. One of the three vaccines is anti-rubella. Previously given only to girls and women of child-bearing age, the disease is a threat to a foetus but not really to children or adults. A sink of rubella therefore remained amongst boys; they are asked to accept immunisation against something that does not threaten them but another social group.

We, selfishly, make calculations of personal benefits. Parents, more altruistically, make such calculations for their children. MMR vaccine is an undoubted benefit to the broad society although even here the possibility of partial immune protection encouraging appearance of resistant pathogen strains is a matter for the the group as well as the individual. MMR and other vaccines are also of benefit to the medical sector of society, directly for pharmaceutical companies, indirectly for medical professionals.

MMR vaccination possibly involves some small risk. The most advantageous personal strategy, and *a fortiori* the strategy to adopt in protecting one's offspring, is therefore to try to remain unvaccinated amidst a vaccinated herd - the 'defector' strategy of game theoreticians and the selfish option. But selfishness for one's children is not seen as morally reprehensible as self-selfishness. The advantage gained depends upon the several risks as well as the strategy followed by the "herd" itself. But in the UK the take-up of the MMR vaccine by parents hovers at the 85-90% level, too low, say epidemiologists, to control the spread of the diseases but interestingly somewhere near the Nash equilibrium strategies for the system with reasonable values for the payoffs.

Reluctance to allow medical treatment of one's children, however slight the evidence for danger, is undoubtedly linked unconsciously to other strategies involving social cooperation and defection in our evolutionary past. There are inevitable tensions between morality, politics and biology in assessing risk informally and socially, as well as formally and technically. But contrary to one famous prime ministerial remark, there is such a thing as society. On understanding that we must base our hopes for indirect parental altruism to win out, to society's benefit, in the long run.

Peter Nicholls

SNAKE VENOMS CAN BE GOOD FOR YOUR HEALTH

How can this be? Everyone knows that snake venoms can be lethal. Snake venom is a complex mixture of peptides and proteins. On injection into the prey, these interfere with the normal functioning of the nervous and circulatory systems to bring about immobilisation, if not death. However, research is showing that some peptides and proteins purified from venoms can be put to good use to treat various pathological conditions in humans.

Probably the first such example was teprotide, a small peptide isolated from the venom of the Brazilian arrowhead viper (*Bothrops jararaca*). Teprotide inhibits an enzyme called angiotensin-converting enzyme (ACE) that catalyses the formation of a very potent vasoconstrictor. Inhibition of the enzyme causes blood vessels to dilate with a resultant fall in blood pressure. Almost that action helps to subdue the prey and allows toxins in the venom to bring about their lethal effects. Human studies showed that teprotide was an effective treatment for hypertension, its only real drawback being that it had to be injected directly into the blood stream to avoid degradation in the gastrointestinal tract. Orally-active ACE inhibitors such as captopril and enalapril are then developed, and these are now used extensively to control hypertension and congestive heart failure, and are amongst the twenty most-prescribed medicines worldwide.

Another venom component that may be beneficial in treating cardiovascular disease is ancrod, an enzyme isolated from the venom of the Malaysian pit viper (*Agkistrodon rhodostoma*). Ancrod acts upon fibrinogen in the blood stream but unlike thrombin it does not produce a stable fibrin clot that could block the circulation. Instead it produces micro clots that are rapidly cleared from the blood stream. Ancrod reduces clot formation and so reduces the likelihood of lethal cardiovascular events such as stroke. About 80% of strokes are ischaemic where neurons are deprived of oxygen due to the formation of clots in the blood vessels within the brain and are the third-leading cause of death in UK. Ancrod is currently undergoing clinical trials for the treatment of acute ischaemic stroke.

A crucial phase in the complex sequence of events in blood clotting is the aggregation of platelets. The pain of untreated angina that precedes heart attack is due to the restriction of blood flow in cardiac blood vessels caused by clumps of platelets adhering to cholesterol plaques that have built up over time. Fibrinogen binds to specific receptors on the surfaces of the aggregated platelets and cross-links them. The cross-linked platelets then act as the focus around which the fibrin clot forms leading to the more severe pain of a heart attack due to blockage of delivery of oxygen to parts of the heart muscle. Small proteins called disintegrins that inhibit platelet aggregation have been found in many snake venoms. One of them, barbourin, isolated from the venom of southeastern pygmy rattlesnake, has been used as the lead compound to develop eptifibatide, a small cyclic peptide that unlike barbourin is relatively non-immunogenic and resistant to proteolytic degradation. Eptifibatide is now used for the treatment of severe cases of angina and certain types of myocardial infarction.

Other diseases such as cancer may be amenable to treatment with snake venom. For example, contortrostatin, a protein isolated from the venom of the southern copperhead viper is undergoing preclinical studies for the treatment of breast cancer. The protein appears to reduce the spread of the tumour by preventing the growth of the tiny blood vessels the tumour requires for nourishment. It causes a 60% reduction in the rate of growth of breast tumour in mice and a 90% reduction in metastasis to the lungs. Ovarian and prostate cancer cells are also affected *in vitro* which may mean that the protein may eventually be used to treat several types of cancer.

Each snake venom contains a mixture of toxins that produce various effects on injection into the prey. Viper venoms act mainly on blood components, blood cells and blood vessels and after 8 to 10 hours or so lead to death of the animal. Cobra and mamba venoms act mainly on the nerve centres of the animal producing death within 2 to 3 hours. The neurotoxins responsible produce total or partial stoppage of automatic lung and heart actions, rapidly inducing respiratory failure. In the future, molecules based on some of these toxins may be of therapeutic benefit. For example, dendrotoxins are neurotoxins present in mamba (*Dendroaspis*) venoms that block various types of K^+ channels in neuronal membranes and thereby increase communication between nerve cells. Chemically-modified dendrotoxins may be useful for the treatment of neurodegenerative conditions such as Alzheimer's disease which is the fourth-leading cause of death in industrialised countries.

Few poisons are as complicated as the snake venoms. They appear to have an effect on every organ system, and perhaps on every type of cell in the human body. This is not surprising when a single venom may contain 20 different toxins, 30 different enzymes, many different peptides and many other non-protein substances. Biochemical and pharmacological studies of snake venoms are proving to be very useful both scientifically and medically, but a lot more research remains to be done.

Graham Bailey

PILATES AS A SPECIFIC EXERCISE THERAPY FOR LOW BACK PAIN

Back pain (BP) is one of the most widely experienced health-related problems in the western world. The direct health care costs of BP within the United Kingdom have been estimated to be £1.6 billion per year in the late 1990s. However, this cost is increased dramatically when informal care and lost working days are taken into account. Viable and affordable treatments for BP and strategies to prevent it are urgently required.

Exercise therapy is widely used in rehabilitation, designed to target key areas of BP and thus increase strength and flexibility, decrease intensity of pain and reduce BP related disability. A good rehabilitation programme should increase confidence in the use of the spine and to overcome the fear of physical activity thus reducing disability.

Modified Pilates is currently being used by practitioners, as an active functional treatment for BP. BP has been shown to be associated with dysfunction and weakness of deeper abdominal muscles – the core muscles (transversus abdominis, multifidus, pelvic floor muscles and the diaphragm). Modified Pilates exercises are aimed at targeting these "core muscles" as well as improving muscular co-ordination in general. Pilates aims to lengthen and stretch the lumbar spine, increase the tone and strength of the "core muscles" and thereby alter the tilt of the pelvis, resulting in changes in posture of the lumbar spine and to improve the sensory-motor control of the trunk and the relationship to limb movements.

Anecdotal reports by practitioners and clients indicate that significant benefits do indeed exist, with increases in muscle strength and endurance, muscle co-ordination and sensory-motor control of balance and posture, leading to improvements in functional ability and return to normal daily living. These are important aspects for rehabilitation of patients with BP. Nevertheless, despite huge recommendations and referrals by GPs, to date there is no objective proof for Pilates as a suitable intervention for BP.

We conducted a pilot study to evaluate the effect of a programme of modified Pilates techniques for individuals with recurring non-specific BP. Following a six week intervention programme of Pilates (one class, two home based sessions) daily back pain decreased, there was a decrease in fear of activity at work and an increase in balance and flexibility of the lower back This study proves that a programme of modified Pilates techniques is an effective active exercise therapy for treatment of BP, which may be less costly than traditional therapies. However, further studies need to be performed to compare a Pilates programme with traditional types of intervention for rehabilitative treatment for BP.

Val Gladwell, Samantha Head and Ralph Beneke

NEW THERAPIES FOR DIABETES AND ASSOCIATED CHRONIC HEALTH PROBLEMS

Diabetes is a chronic disease in which the production of the hormone insulin is markedly decreased or insulin secretion and tissue responses to it are impaired. Insulin regulates the uptake and metabolism of sugars but also has effects on the metabolism of proteins and lipids. Diabetes is a syndrome characterised by chronic hyperglycaemia. The range of blood glucose concentration increases from 3 – 8 mM in normal human subjects to 7–30 mM in diabetic subjects; and even blood glucose concentrations of 50 mM have been found. Diabetes mellitus is classified into two main types: Type I and Type II.

Type 1 diabetes mellitus occurs most commonly in children and young adults and it is characterised by the rapid onset of symptoms, which include excessive drinking (polydipsia), the production of excess urine (polyuria), lethargy and weight loss. It accounts for 10% of diabetes mellitus worldwide. The most prevalent form of diabetes mellitus is Type II. It is an insidious disease, occurring in middle to old age, commonly associated with obesity. Recently, evidence is emerging that children with an unhealthy lifestyle (lack of exercise, eating readily absorbed, carbohydrate-rich `junk' foods) and clinically obese are at risk of developing Type II diabetes. The incidence of diabetes is increasing – it has been called `an epidemic in progress'. By 2010, it is predicted there will be 221 million diabetic patients worldwide.

Hyperglycemia in type 1 diabetes is controlled by insulin, quick release and fasting acting insulin injections at mealtimes, and slow release and longer acting insulin preparations at other times. In type II diabetes, hyperglycaemia is controlled by drugs that increase the secretion of insulin from the pancreas (sulfonylureas and meglitinides), increase glucose uptake into tissues (metformin and glitazones) and decrease uptake of dietary carbohydrates (acarbose). To prevent the development of diabetic complications, hyperglycaemia must be well-controlled. Careful control of blood pressure and blood cholesterol and lipids also decrease the risk of diabetic complications.

Diabetic complications

Abnormally high blood glucose, blood pressure and lipids in diabetes conspire as risk factors for the development of diabetic complications. Tissue damage is localised to cells that take up high amounts of glucose from blood plasma. This has profound impact on the eyes, kidneys and nerves. Over the course of 15 – 25 years, this causes blindness (retinopathy), renal failure (nephropathy), chronic pain, ulceration and limb amputation (related to neuropathy).

Diabetic retinopathy

Diabetes damages blood vessels throughout the body, including the fine blood vessels in the retina of the eye. This damage is called diabetic retinopathy. Initially retinal blood vessels start to leak, causing blood or fluid to seep into the retina. Later, retinal blood vessels close, cutting off nutrition supply to the retinal tissue and stimulating the growth of new blood vessels, bleeding and scar tissue. The bleeding and scar tissue can lead to blindness if not treated. Diabetic retinopathy is now the commonest cause of blindness amongst those of working age in the UK. After 20 years of diabetes, 87% of Type 1 and 53% of Type 2 diabetic patients have retinopathy - about a 25% of these have visual impairment.

Diabetic neuropathy

Diabetic neuropathy is a peripheral nerve disorder caused by diabetes. The symptoms are often slight at first - numbness, pain, or tingling in the feet or legs. After several years, this leads to weakening in the muscles of the feet. Other problems are indigestion, dizziness, bladder infections and impotence. The loss of sensation in the feet increases the risk of foot injuries to go unnoticed and develop into ulcers or lesions that become infected and, in severe cases, require limb amputation.

Diabetic nephropathy

Diabetic nephropathy is the kidney disease that occurs as a result of diabetes. It is a leading cause of kidney failure in the UK. After many years of diabetes the delicate filtering system in the kidney becomes destroyed, initially becoming leaky to large blood proteins such as albumin which are then lost in urine. Diabetic nephropathy progresses from mild to severe renal failure when dialysis is required. Diabetic nephropathy is a serious and common long-term complication of diabetes mellitus. It threatens the health and life of 20-25% of diabetic patients (50% of Type 1 patients and 20% of Type 2 patients).

Other diabetic complications

Diabetic patients also have increased risk of coronary heart disease (CHD) - a 2–3 fold increased risk in men and a 3–5 fold increase in women, relative to the non-diabetic population. There is also increased risk of cataract and perinatal mortality.

Mechanisms of hyperglycaemia-induced damage and proposed treatment

There are five main hypotheses about how hyperglycaemia causes diabetic complications. These are: increased flux through the polyol pathway, increased protein glycation, activation of protein kinase C (PKC), increased flux through the hexosamine pathway, and oxidative stress arising from mitochondrial dysfunction. There is no therapy to prevent the activation of these pathways specifically. Diabetic patients are encouraged to take antioxidants (vitamin E and vitamin C) to counter the effects of oxidative stress. Inhibitors of PKC are currently in clinical trial for the prevention of diabetic retinopathy. A further therapeutic approach of promise is high dose thiamine therapy – research by a group at the University of Essex.

Thiamine is an essential vitamin (vitamin B1). It is phosphorylated to thiamine pyrophosphate which is a cofactor of enzymes involved in glucose metabolism – transketolase, pyruvate dehydrogenase and a-ketoglutarate dehydrogenase. Maximizing the activity of transketolase activates the so-called "reductive pentosephosphate pathway" of glucose metabolism. This consumes intermediates of glucose metabolism, triosephosphates. Accumulation of triosephosphates and related metabolites is the driving force for the multiple pathways of biochemical dysfunction in the development of diabetic complications; preventing this may provide an effective therapy. High dose thiamine therapy has been shown to prevent diabetic neuropathy in clinically and diabetic nephropathy and retinopathy experimentally. Clinical trials for the prevention of diabetic retinopathy and nephropathy are planned for next year.

Naila Ahmed

EXERCISE AFTER TRANSPLANTATION SURGERY - THERAPY OR LUNACY?

Heart-, lung- and especially the combined heart- and lung-transplantation are extreme therapeutic interventions, which serve as a final resource for patients with fatal organ impairments. After a successful transplantation-surgery, the implanted organ is principally healthy given the rejection reaction can be suppressed sufficiently. However, any transplanted organ has not only been isolated from the vascular supply but also denervated. The latter is specifically important in the transplanted heart. The persisting denervation of the implanted heart causes an elevated resting heart rate, a delayed and decreased adaptive capacity of the heart rate to any sort of stress.

Other complications after transplantation-surgery are mostly consequences of the subsequent lifelong drug therapy to control rejection of the implanted tissue, to prevent infections and to treat the frequently developing severe hypertension with negative effects on all aspects of performance. Therefore, adequate exercise training is considered to offer an opportunity to improve numerous transplantation related physical, psychological and sociological problems.

Benefit of exercise training after transplantation

In heart-transplantation patients, exercise training is based on more than two decades of experience whilst training therapy after lung-transplantation is a rare experience of very few researchers. Beneficial effects of exercise training after transplantation of the heart are an increased performance capacity and consequently an improved tolerance of physical stress based on counter balancing effects with special respect to myopathy, osteoporosis and impairment of the cardio-vascular response such as an increase in the maximal heart rate and cardiac output as well as a potential decrease in the resting and exercise blood pressure.

Specific benefits for the transplanted lung are unproven, however, exercise induced adaptations of respiratory muscles have been discussed. Additionally exercise training is considered to facilitate the familiarization with the new organ and the newly gained physical options. The latter shall improve the acceptance of the new organ, body image and perception, confidence and therefore psychological stability, with relevance for the quality of life, decrease of risk factors and social (re-)integration.

Risks and problems of exercise training after transplantation

Post transplantation the adaptation to training and all recovery processes may be delayed. Severe rejection reactions are an absolute contraindication for exercise training whilst minor rejection problems may allow training with reduced exercise intensity and volume. In general any type of immunosuppressive and anti-hypertension drug therapy in spite of being absolutely essential is combined with a negative effect on the performance capacity and perception and may therefore require modifications in the training program.

Exercise testing and prescription

Knowledge of the individual performance capacity, acute response to physical stress and limitations are essential prerequisites of any kind of exercise prescription and training in patients after transplantation. Repetitive testing enables for the analysis of the performance development with special respect to changes in health status, medication and systematic modifications in the training programme.

A successful training program contains regular training sessions of 15 to 60 min activity, two to five times per week including endurance and resistance training but also any kind of coordinative elements. Shortly post transplantation most patients are not able to conduct such a program. Under the latter condition the increase of the sustainable training volume has priority compared to any increase in exercise intensity. Exercises with dynamic muscular work are preferable compared to static contractions. The relative mass of primarily engaged muscles should be increased gradually with increasing fitness level. Team sports and especially events with direct body contact require careful individual consideration.

Conclusions

Adequate exercise training is considered to improve numerous transplantation related physical, psychological and sociological problems. However to prevent any negative consequences for transplantation patients the exercise training needs to be carefully prescribed based on an objective analysis of the status of health, medication and performance capacity.

Ralph Beneke, Renate Leithäuser and Matthias Hütler

DRUG DESIGN AT HOME: HARNESSING THE POWER OF SLEEPING COMPUTERS

R andomly screening large numbers of molecules against a protein target in a laboratory is one approach to drug discovery that could best be compared to looking for a needle in a haystack. Virtual screening on the other hand is an exciting new approach that is attracting increasing levels of interest in Universities and in the pharmaceutical industry as a productive and cost-effective technology in the search for new drugs. Although the principles involved—the computational analysis of chemical databases to identify compounds appropriate for a given biological receptor (usually soluble enzymes)—have been pursued for several years in molecular modelling groups, the lack of inexpensive high-performance computing platforms has until recently been a major problem. It would take many years for a single computer to perform all the calculations needed to test all the drug-like molecules from a large database binding to a single protein target.

However, because 95% of the CPU power of an average PC is unused, there is much potential for harnessing this potential to benefit worthy causes. One such worthy cause is the 'Screensaver Lifesaver project' (www.chem.ox.ac.uk/curecancer.html), which currently uses the 'idle' CPU power of more than 2.6 million computers in more than 200 countries around the world; this is collaboration between the Universities of Oxford and Essex and several other institutions, with the University of Essex playing a major role in defining the binding sites of various cancer related target proteins. The screensaver, which can be downloaded for free from the internet (www.grid.com), facilitates calculations of the binding energy of different drug like molecules (from a database of 3.5 billion molecules) to the target proteins. While calculations on each of the molecules may take 20 minutes on a single PC, an excess of 320,000 years of CPU power has been harnessed from the volunteering PCs. Arrangements are in place for experimental testing of the highest scoring molecules.

We acknowledge the pioneering work of harnessing the power of sleeping PCs carried out by the SETI project team, a project to search for extra terrestrial intelligence (www.setiathome.ssl.berkeley.edu/).

George Psaroudakis and Christopher Reynolds

C1

HOW ACTIVE ARE WE?

A long with diet, physical activity is now known to be an important determinant of health and well-being. However, people living in both industrialised countries and urban settlements in developing countries have become increasingly sedentary in all aspects of daily life, including during leisure time, in traveling to and from work, and during work itself. Human metabolism and genetic make-up have been unable to adapt to the rate and magnitude of these changes in activity levels and the result has been an increase in both physical and mental health problems associated with inactivity (hypokinetic disorders). It is therefore important for the development of public health policy to have a clear picture of just how (in)active we are.

In Europe, there has been a dramatic fall in physical activity over the past 50 years with on average 2 MJ (500 kcal) less energy expenditure per day in adults aged 20-60 years. According to the National Audit Office, changes in life style over this period have led to a reduction in physical activity equivalent to the running of a marathon each week. Yet the public health consequences of these changes have not been widely discussed or accepted until very recently. The 2001 Eurodiet study states *"the importance of physical activity has been underestimated for many years by both doctors and policy-makers."*

Although similar trends have occurred across Europe and North America, the UK compares badly with many countries. Jobs themselves have become less physical, people are more likely to take the lift than walk the stairs, and adults and children are more likely to travel to work or school by car than to walk or bicycle. In the 1970s, 90% of primary school children in the UK walked to school; today 10% walk and 90% travel by car. The distance walked per year by each individual has fallen from 410 km yr-1 in 1975-76 to 298 km–1 in 1998-2000. Though walking has declined across the whole of the EU since 1970, only people in Greece walk less than Britons. Cycling varies from a low of 70 km yr-1 in Greece to a high of 850-900 km yr-1 in Denmark and the Netherlands, with Britons well below the average for all 15 EU countries (Table 1).

Table 1. Distances cycled and walked by people in Europe (data for 1995).

	Cycling km per person per year	Walking km per person per year
EU average	200	430
UK	77	415
Denmark	900	500
Netherlands	850	445
Germany	295	430
France	80	440
Greece	70	380

Our dependence on the car is further illustrated by the fact that the UK is one of only four EU countries in which bus and coach travel per person has declined since 1980 (the others are Germany, Finland and the Netherlands). The 20% fall in the UK compares unfavourably with a 40-80% increase in bus travel in Denmark, Italy, Spain and Portugal. Over the same period, car travel per person in the UK increased by 51%, and the road system has grown by 34,000 km since the early 1960s.

Home life has also become more sedentary, and though gym and fitness club membership has risen in the past 20 years there are some indications that people are becoming less likely to engage in organised sports. There have been falls in the provision of opportunities for physical exercise in schools, linked not least to sales of playing fields in the 1980s and 1990s. The proportion of young people spending two hours or more per week doing physical exercise fell from 46% in 1994 to 37% in 1999. The average young person also spent 26 hours per week watching television in the 1990s compared with 13 hours in the 1960s.

Physically inactive children become physically inactive adults, and in the UK only 32% of adults take 30 minutes of moderate exercise five times a week, the minimum recommended to maintain optimal health. This figure compares unfavourably with the 57% of Australians and 70% of Finns who achieve these recommended levels. Furthermore, only 47% of adults in the UK participate in sport more than 12 times a year, compared with the EU highs of 70% in Sweden and 80% in Finland, and lows of 18% in Italy and 25% in Spain. Consequently, some 63% of men and 75% of women in the UK do not take enough physical activity to benefit their health. In almost all activities (except swimming and yoga), female participation is lower than male. In the group aged 16-24 years, 42% of men and 68% of women are inactive, and these proportions rise steadily as people age. Again, this trend is not the same everywhere – in Sweden and Finland, in particular, participation in organised sport increases amongst older people. One of the major problems is that although 80% of people in the UK correctly believe that regular exercise is good for their health, a majority wrongly believe that they take enough exercise to stay fit.

Sport England has claimed that physical activity should now be considered *"one of the best buys in public health, providing physical, social and mental health benefits."* Moderate regular exercise reduces morbidity rates by 30-50%, having a particularly protective effect against maturity onset diabetes (type 2 diabetes), coronary artery disease, strokes and colon cancer, as well as reducing blood pressure and improving blood lipid and glucose profiles. Appropriate volumes of moderate exercise also enhance physical fitness which has a substantial influence on people's sense of well-being. The UK Health Education Authority recommends that *"individuals accumulate 30 minutes of moderate intensity physical activity at least 5 days of the week"*, and suggests that appropriate activities include brisk walking, cycling, and certain gardening activities, as well as more formal structured sports and leisure activities.

Jules Pretty, Murray Griffin and Martin Sellens

GOAL CONFLICTS AND HEALTHY CHOICES

W ouldn't it be better if we all followed a healthy life-style and lived longer and more healthy lives? Why it is that even if we do know what we should do, we don't do it? How many times has each of us sincerely intended to do something and yet failed to do it? It is a well-known fact that behaviour does not always follow wishes and intentions. It is an everyday experience that often even the best intentions do not translate into actions. This seems to be especially true for healthy choices; behaviours that if performed would ultimately lead to healthier outcomes.

Psychological research has identified a series of factors that may underlie this so-called intention-behaviour gap. For instance, it is known that if we make a specific plan of when and how we will behave as we say we intend to (an *implementation plan*), then it is much more likely that we will do it. However, comparatively little attention so far has been devoted to another potential reason why behaviour does not follow our best intentions: goal conflicts. Goal conflicts can freeze up the execution of behaviour and achievement of goals because the conflict interferes with action execution. People may give up trying to achieve a goal in the face of obstacles, may fail to act when opportunities present themselves, and may mobilize insufficient resources for effective goal achievement.

A first type of conflict is between two different goals (*Goal vs Goal conflict*). This occurs when there is an antagonistic relation between two (or more) different goals: the achievement of the target goal can be thwarted by the simultaneous existence of other goals that create conflicts for resources and time. For instance, Michael would like to run three times a week, but he also likes to stay 'cosily' at home or to spend time with his friends. Therefore, whenever he contemplates the decision to put on his running shoes, and go out for a run, he may give up because he prefers to go out with his friends for a pint. If two goals tend to conflict for the same resources and time, one of the two may be not achieved, even with the best intentions.

A second possible type of conflict is between behaviours and goals (*Behaviour vs Goal conflict*). We have different wishes and desires. One may desire to achieve a first class mark, yet without desiring to study enough. In other words, we may have a certain desire to achieve a goal, but without a corresponding desire to behave in a way that will enable us to achieve the goal. This type of conflict can therefore be defined as a discrepancy of desires at a behavioural and goal level. For instance, Anna has a strong desire to get healthier (*goal*) but no desire (or a markedly weaker one) to exercise three times a week (*behaviour*) in order to achieve the goal.

A third possible type of conflict is among implicit and explicit evaluations (*Implicit vs Explicit conflict*). An explicit evaluation (or *attitude*) is when somebody expresses a preference for some target object or action. For instance, Mark thinks that exercising three times a week is good, healthy and pleasant. By contrast, an implicit evaluation is not expressed directly and does not require that one is aware of it. It is based on how quickly positive words (eg love, good) are associated with stimuli corresponding to the target action (eg run, jogging). In other words, implicit evaluations are reflected in the strength of the association between valence and concept: the stronger the association, the quicker it is to associate good and exercise.

Of course, the same reasoning holds for negative implicit evaluations. These implicit evaluations can be measured using sophisticated computer tasks. To summarise, the important point that differentiates implicit from explicit evaluations is that the former are based on speed of response in carefully specified indirect tasks (one is never asked to say what he or she thinks about a certain object or action), whereas the latter are based on stated likes and dislikes. Coming back to goal conflicts, the third type of conflict can therefore be defined as the discrepancy of evaluation (attitude) at an implicit and explicit level. For instance, John has a positive explicit attitude towards exercising three times a week, but he also has a negative implicit attitude. Therefore, he may fail to notice good opportunities to exercise or perhaps adopt a procrastination strategy ("I will do it next time").

Although all three types of goal conflict appear likely to interfere with action execution, and therefore partly to explain the intention-behaviour gap, so far little research has investigated them. Further studies will be needed to establish if, and which of, these types of goal conflict are responsible for people failing to make healthy behavioural choices despite declarations of good intent. The next step will be to establish how to intervene so as to resolve the goal conflict and therefore increase the likelihood of making healthy behavioural choices. There is still a long way to go, but the personal and public heath outcomes of changing behaviour in this way will be well worth the journey!

Marco Perugini

IS EXERCISE BAD FOR YOUR HEALTH?

There is no doubt that, in general terms, exercise is beneficial for health. For example, it is well established that a lack of exercise is a major risk factor contributing to the development of cardiovascular disease, obesity, type II diabetes and "metabolic syndrome", a pre-diabetic condition involving reduced insulin sensitivity and poor glucose control. (See c5).

However, those with an aversion to exercise sometimes justify their inactivity by pointing out incidents of sudden death during athletic activity, even among the very young, citing the frequency of sports-related injury, and relating anecdotes about athletes always having colds. There have also been celebrated cases of unidentified viral illnesses among the highly trained (eg Sebastian Coe before the 1988 Olympics). Undiagnosed illness would certainly be expected to impair performance at the highest levels of competition, and might account for the high profile `failure' of Paula Radcliffe in the women's marathon at the 2004 Athens Olympics.

The risk of sudden death through participation in sport is vanishingly small and far outweighed by health risks of being sedentary. Of course, it is indisputable that you are more likely to sustain an injury playing football, or rock climbing, than watching TV, but every human activity carries risks as well as benefits and it is perhaps more useful to consider if, on balance, exercise increases or decreases the likelihood of becoming ill.

As early as 1918, it was reported in the Boston Medical Journal that most cases in an outbreak of pneumonia in a boy's school were among athletes. Later, in the 1950s epidemiologists noted that intense physical activity during the incubation period of an infection with the polio virus increased the severity of the resulting paralysis. It is commonly supposed that endurance athletes are particularly susceptible to illnesses such as infectious mononucleosis (glandular fever) and upper respiratory tract infections, and there are some data to support this presumption. For example, among participants in the 1987 Los Angeles marathon, in the 2 months prior to the event the incidence of colds and 'flu in those training more that 60 miles a week was double that in those training less than 20 miles a week. After the event those that had participated were five times more likely to suffer illness than those had trained but did not compete.

This evidence strongly suggests that we shouldn't exercise vigorously if we suspect we are "coming down with something", and that large volumes of intense exercise (heavy training) increase susceptibility to viral illness. But there is another side to the coin. Moderate training and participation in shorter races has a negligible effect on rates of infection, and may be protective. Epidemiological studies have suggested that exercise training prior to exposure to infective agents, including both viruses and bacteria, decreases subsequent infection rates and the severity of the illness. Brisk walking for 40 minutes a day, 5 days a week, halved the incidence of viral upper respiratory infections in a population of sedentary middle aged women.

The balance of evidence therefore suggests that the old adage moderation in all things might also apply to exercise. It has been proposed that the relationship between exercise and susceptibility to infection is best described by a `J-curve'. In other words, susceptibility is relatively high if no exercise, or too much exercise is taken, but at its lowest with moderate levels of physical activity. Furthermore, it is now believed that there is a period of enhanced vulnerability to infection in the few hours following intense exercise and this has been referred to as the `open window effect'.

These observations are all consistent with what we now know about the effect of exercise on our hormones and our immune system. Exercise is a form of stress, and the body responds to the levels of stress by producing hormones that, in turn, produce physiological changes to enable us better to cope with that stress. This is part of the "general adaptation syndrome", or GAS, that has evolved to give us the best possible chance of survival in an unpredictable world. Moderate amounts of intermittent stress, including regular exercise, promote the activity of our immune system (and, incidentally, also promote the growth of muscles and strengthen the heart). On the other hand, continuous, or high levels of stress, including heavy training schedules, can impair the function of the immune system. This means that we become easy targets for disease producing micro-organisms. Interestingly, recent work has suggested that we might be able to reduce the damaging effects of chronic stress by ensuring that we take in adequate amounts of carbohydrate in our diet, a nice link between the complementary notions of healthy eating and healthy levels of exercise.

So, is exercise bad for your health? The answer is neither a simple yes nor a perverse no, but even so the take home message is clear. Don't be a couch potato, but also, don't overdo it. Moderation may sound unexciting, but, for both individual and public health, it is usually the best policy.

Martin Sellens

IS BREATHING DANGEROUS? THE MITOCHONDRIAL THEORY OF AGEING

W e breathe to take in oxygen from the air. Our cells use this oxygen to oxidise the hydrogen that is present in chemical combination in our food, thus forming water; ie

Eq. 1
$$4H + O_2 = 2H_2O$$

This reaction is very similar to that between gaseous hydrogen (H_2) and oxygen and is a reaction that gives out a lot of energy, so much in fact that we will shortly use it to fuel our cars once we have run out of petrol to oxidise. This reaction was discovered some billions of years ago by biological systems, once oxygen had entered the atmosphere formed from the processes of photosynthesis. Because oxygen is so reactive it is both a molecule that is essential for our lives but one that is also dangerous and it has to be handled carefully. In fact when oxygen first appeared in the atmosphere it was the biggest pollutant ever, killing some 99.9% of all life on the earth's surface. Most cells can now utilise oxygen to derive great benefit by releasing the energy available in the oxidation of hydrogen (Eq 1). But control of this reaction is not perfect and mistakes are made leading to cellular damage and disease, a process often called "oxidative stress".

The reaction shown in Eq. 1 takes place in the mitochondrion and this is the organelle that is particularly at risk if the reaction is not handled properly. The reaction, although simple to write is difficult to do and can easily lead to side reactions in which "Reactive oxygen species" (ROS) are formed. These species include the superoxide anion radical ($O_2^{\cdot-}$), hydrogen peroxide (H_2O_2) and the hydroxyl radical ($OH^{\cdot-}$). These species can react with components of the mitochondrion and lead to damage and loss of function. One of the components most at risk and the one that when damaged leads to the most dramatic consequences is the mitochondrial DNA. In fact it has been the proposed that the whole process of ageing is a consequence of lifelong accumulation of damage to our mitochondrial DNA (mtDNA). We are as old as our mitochondria.

This mitochondrial theory of ageing has recently received strong support from experiments conducted in Sweden. How was this achieved? Well the theory states that throughout your life oxidative stress damages the mitochondrial DNA. As the mtDNA is not repaired well (unlike nuclear DNA) and as the mtDNA codes for the machinery that captures the energy released from Eq 1 in a form your cells can use, then as time goes on our ability to use this energy declines. We become less able to repair ourselves, to work our muscles, to keep our brain cells active, to defend ourselves from infection etc etc. In short we become old. This process eventually leads to pathological loss of function and death. Some evidence for this idea comes from the fact that if we take small muscle biopsies from people of different ages then we find that the older the person the more random damage we find in the mitochondrial DNA. So damaged DNA and age are certainly correlated. But are they causally linked? Perhaps just by living a long time you accumulate damage but this may not have a functional consequence.

In order to clarify this position the Swedish group, based in Stockholm, did a very clever experiment. The details are complex but in essence what they did was to produce rats that had introduced random errors in their mtDNA as this was being made. Thus rats were born that had randomly damaged mtDNA. The question was "Do these rats age very quickly?" The results were spectacular. The increase in mtDNA damage was associated with reduced lifespan and premature onset of ageing-related characteristics, such as weight loss, reduced subcutaneous fat, alopecia (hair loss), kyphosis (curvature of the spine), osteoporosis, anaemia, reduced fertility and heart enlargement. In other words the rats were old before their time! These results thus provide a strong causative link between mtDNA changes (mutations) and ageing in mammals.

What can we do to protect our mtDNA from oxidative damage and to stave off the ageing process? Well at the moment not too much, although a balanced diet rich in antioxidants such as vitamins C and E and selenium (see article by Fryer) and eaten from an early age seems sensible as these help to remove the ROS. There is one dietary regime one might try that rests on the following reasoning. If it is side reactions from Eq 1 that lead to ROS, mt DNA damage and hence ageing, then perhaps we could live longer if we limited the extent of the reaction. How to do this? Well the hydrogen needed comes from our food, so what happens if one eats less? The answer is also dramatic. For a large number of species including mammals it is the case that life span can be greatly increased, up to 50%, by following a diet limited in calories. This calorific restriction must, however, be very severe and although it seems to work, no one is likely to want to follow such a life-long regime. You may live longer but would you want to?

Alternatively one may try adding something rather than subtracting most of the food. As stated above antioxidants may help. What else? Drugs may become available that stop the reaction of Eq 1 running excessively. This would allow you to eat what you want but the hydrogen in the food would not be so available to fuel Eq1. So far compounds that achieve this, such as 2-deoxy-D-glucose, are toxic and in any case it seems morally reprehensible, unless there is a good medical reason, to take a compound that allows you to satisfy an appetite but without using the calories it contains, especially when millions starve for the want of such food.

Another interesting possibility is to increase the concentration of enzymes that protect against ROS. This has been achieved by increasing the concentration of the enzyme that removes $O_2\cdot^-$, in a strain of mice. Similarly, mice have been produced that have, in their mitochondria, elevated levels of catalase, an enzyme that removes the ROS H_2O_2. In both cases these mice have significantly longer lives.

Recently oxidative damage to mitochondrial DNA has been reported to be fourfold higher in males than in females. Mitochondria from females produce significantly less hydrogen peroxide and, amongst other differences, are reported to have higher levels of superoxide dismutase. Thus the mitochondrial theory of aging has been proposed to explain why females live longer than males.

Although other factors are no doubt important (cell signalling and apoptosis for example) the evidence now seems very strong that damage to mtDNA by ROS is at the root of long-term loss of function of the energy transduction machinery of the cell. This causes that change in us that we call ageing. It also leads to neuronal death and to dementias of various sorts. Altogether a bad thing! So although we cannot live without it, breathing is in fact dangerous. The best we can do presently is to lead a healthy active life and to eat a balanced diet in moderation. Eat up your greens! Your great grandmother certainly knew this.

Mike Wilson

CARDIAC HEALTH: HOW MUCH PHYSICAL ACTIVITY IS ENOUGH?

S moking is no longer the most dangerous life style risk factor for death from heart disease in the UK. Recent research presented by the British Heart Foundation reports that 37% of deaths from coronary heart disease (CHD) in the UK are related to inactivity whereas only 19% are related to smoking. Looked at from the opposite perspective, inactivity is also the most prevalent risk factor for the development of CHD. In 1999 an estimated 70% of women and 60% of men in the UK were not sufficiently active to achieve the health benefits that are known to be associated with physical activity. Therefore it is clearly essential for the health of the nation and of the NHS budget that ways can be found to persuade people to exercise.

Equally important is that we should have some clear idea as to just how much exercise is sufficient to lower the risk of succumbing to CHD or to contribute to the treatment of pre-existing heart disease. Armed with this information it should be possible to promote the idea amongst health professionals that the prescription of exercise (the "green prescription") should be a central plank in a public health strategy to prevent and treat coronary artery disease.

The first challenge lies in getting people who are physically inactive to begin, and continue to adhere to, physical activity programmes. We all know that physical activity is good for us but often the setting and the types of physical activity on offer don't seem to fit our needs. And then there's the issue of the accessibility of most formal exercise programmes. They seem never to be at the right time or in the right place or for that matter at the right cost. All these factors represent barriers to taking up physical activity in the first place, and then to persevering with it after the first flush of enthusiasm has worn off.

A new approach to overcoming these barriers has been the development of exercise programmes that are not based around gyms but that involve less formal and structured "green exercise", such as guided walks and opportunities for gardening or physical conservation work. Many individuals who suffer from heart disease don't fit the typical profile of the fitness centre user and they suffer from a form of exercise phobia known as `lycraphobia'. That is they don't like going to fitness centres because only fit people with well-sculptured bodies go there. At the University of Essex we have set up a new kind of cardiac rehabilitation clinic (The Phoenix Club www.the-phoenix-club.com/) that offers "green exercise" opportunities in a supportive environment, and is also helping us to evaluate the physical and mental health benefits of this kind of exercise.

One of the things we would particularly like to know is how much (or little) exercise can be tolerated by, and be of benefit to, individuals with a very low physical activity capacity. There is still some debate as to how much physical activity is enough to produce health benefits. Estimates of the total duration range from 6 hours a week to as little as 1 hour a week. It has been suggested that leisure time physical activity (LTPA) of even relatively low intensity, such as walking or housework, and for as little as 1 hour per week, decreases the risk of CHD and has beneficial effects on the inflammatory response. As excessive inflammatory responses are associated with the development of CHD this may represent one mechanism by which LTPA reduces coronary risk.

Finally, there is the question of how risky physical activity is for "at risk" patients. There have been well-publicised instances of even apparently fit individuals dying during exercise. However, crossing the road or eating a steak are also "risky" activities that are associated with benefits and it is the balance of risks and benefits that needs to be considered. It has been estimated that, even for moderate-high risk patients, remaining physically inactive is actually between 2 and 100 times more risky than embarking on a programme of physical activity. So we can be confident that providing opportunities for physical activity for both physically impaired and apparently healthy individuals will have a positive impact on the health of the nation. And for those suffering from diseases of inactivity, there is clearly nothing worse than continuing to do nothing!

Jerry Shearman

THE ROLE OF EXERCISE IN WEIGHT REGULATION

B oth the media and health professionals agree that the UK is in the grip of an epidemic of obesity that is also afflicting much of the developed world. This has serious implications for national budgets, with the estimated cost to the UK economy already running at £2.5 billion a year, and it also has a hidden personal cost in terms of quality of life for those hauling round the burden of an excess of stored energy. Looking on obesity as a disorder of energy storage focuses on the simple but uncomfortable truth that we only become obese if we habitually take in more energy as food than we expend in our daily activities. It follows then, that if we wish to avoid putting on weight (as fat) we need to balance our energy budget, and if we wish to lose weight we must spend some of our stored energy reserves by using more energy than we consume. This can be achieved by eating fewer calories, by exercising more, or by a combination of the two.

Eating fewer calories sounds like the easy option, but the dieting industry thrives on the depressing fact that it rarely works over the long term. The problem is that operating an energy deficit indefinitely will lead inevitably to lethargy, infertility, decrease in functional capacity and ultimately death. The body recognizes this situation as potentially life threatening and adopts a survival strategy that involves minimizing energy expenditure and reducing muscle as well as fat mass. If you have less muscle, you use less energy, and require less food. Dieting alone is therefore counter-productive. By contrast, increasing energy expenditure by exercising means that you can indulge cautiously in the basic human pleasure of eating, improve your chances of avoiding the curses of coronary heart disease and cancer, and increase the quantity of energy-hungry muscle tissue at the same time as you are losing those unwelcome fat deposits. Of course, the fastest results are obtained by a combination of moderate calorie restriction and exercise, a two-pronged strategy that most health professionals actively promote.

Just staying alive costs energy, and this basal metabolic rate (or BMR) amounts to between 1,000 and 2,000 kcal per day for most adults. The actual value depends mainly on fat free body mass because fat is relatively inactive, whereas muscle and other tissues require energy even when they are "resting". When muscle contracts, its energy requirements increase dramatically, so activity that uses lots of muscle, such as walking or running is a good way to use calories. Because these activities are weight bearing, their energy cost depends on body mass, but a useful approximation is that either walking or running a mile uses about 100 kcal. By contrast, cycling a mile only uses about 40 kcal because body mass is supported by the bicycle. In all activities, the rate of energy expenditure is higher as the activity becomes more intense. So running a marathon in 3 h uses a similar amount of energy to walking it in 9 h, but the rate of energy expenditure is three times as high. It follows that the same benefit for weight loss can be gained by exercising gently for long periods of time, or vigorously for a more limited period. For most people with a busy lifestyle, half an hour of running is probably a more realistic option than a 90 min stroll. And there is an unexpected bonus of hard exercise that is also worth having.

After vigorous exercise energy expenditure is elevated for up to several hours. This phenomenon is known as EPOC, or excess post-exercise energy expenditure, and it is a consequence of the disruption that heavy exercise causes to many of the bodies systems. The beating of the heart, and the contraction of the respiratory muscles consume energy, and both of these remain elevated after exercise ceases. Furthermore, tissues are warmed up by the heat released during exercise, and warm tissues burn more energy. Depleted stores of energy need to be replenished and stress hormones, which increase metabolic rate, are released in proportion to the intensity of the exercise. Finally, the minor tissue damage that is normal during heavy exercise has to be repaired. All these energy costs are in addition to those incurred by the exercise itself and might be considered to represent a free gift in terms of weight loss. But is the free gift worth having, given that vigorous exercise can be uncomfortable?

Work in the Centre for Sports and Exercise Science at the University of Essex has examined the effect of different durations and intensities of exercise on the amount of EPOC. In cycling exercise, doubling the intensity (taking half the time to cover the same distance) increased the duration of EPOC by three fold (to more that 2 h) and increased the extra post-exercise energy cost by four fold, to over 50 kcal (see Fig 1). This represents about 15% of the cost of the actual exercise, or in supermarket jargon, "an extra 15% free!"

It also turns out that, if you exercise at a relatively low intensity, EPOC increases disproportionately with exercise duration. For example, EPOC is more than three times greater after exercising for 30 min than it is after exercising for 10 min. We have also found that EPOC is slightly greater after running than after doing the same amount of work cycling. So, we have found that working quite hard for 30 min, either on a bicycle or running, can provide a free gift of about 50 kcal energy expenditure. Although this isn't very much when considered against the total of 2-3,000 kcal expended

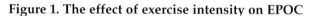

a day by a moderately active adult, and would be more than offset by an extra Mars bar (280 kcal), accumulated over a year an energy deficit of just 50 kcal per day translates to burning off about 2 kg fat and losing rather more than that in body mass.

Overall then, EPOC can make a small, but potentially significant contribution to the expenditure side of the energy budget. There is also a cardio-vascular health benefit from exercise that increases when intensity is moderate to intense. The take-home message then, is that if you have a restricted time for exercise, you will get most benefit by working hard. Not only does this increase the energy you spend during the exercise, but it also comes with a worthwhile free gift of EPOC!

Figure 1. The effect of exercise intensity on EPOC

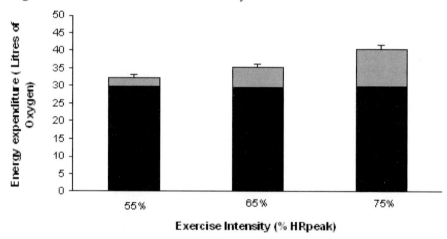

Total oxygen consumption (a measure of energy expenditure) was measured following a fixed amount of work but at different exercise intensities. EPOC is the gray area and increased disproportionately with intensity. The black area is the oxygen that would have been consumed during the same period but without the effect of exercise (ie resting energy expenditure).

Martin Sellens and Vasilios Voutselas

MEASURING PHYSICAL ACTIVITY WITH TIME DIARIES

The 2000/01 National Time Use Study collected two diaries of daily activities on a weekday and a weekend day from 11,667 people aged 8 or older living in a randomly-selected sample of British households. The findings of this study illuminated both the extent and the context in which people engage in six categories of physical activity: sports and exercise; productive exercise (such as gardening); walking dogs; cycling and other walking; physically active housework; and physically active care. At the University of Essex, we are performing research which considers the affects of a number of important factors on average daily minutes of physical activity. These factors include the type of day, diary quality, time spent watching television and using a computer, perception of time pressure, possession and use of cars, self-assessed health status, employment status, home ownership, sex, age, marital status, whether the household includes a child aged less than 8, education, ethnicity, and population density.

The data indicate that a proportion of Britons – especially those who are young or full-time employees - lead sedentary lifestyles. On an average day, 15% of Britons undertake no physical activity lasting at least ten minutes. While total minutes of daily exercise decrease as people watch more television and spend more minutes using computers, the combined effect of all computer use and television viewing yields a smaller reduction in total exercise time than other lifestyle choices, such as the proportion of travel to work or school time which people undertake in a car.

Young people in the current decade perform less physical activity than their counterparts in the 1960s, largely as young people today often avoid active housework and travel more regularly in cars than by self-powered means. School and working-aged people cut back their daily exercise by half on school and work days.

This research challenges some common stereotypes. Women are as active as men. Older people lead active lives, performing over two hours of physical activity on an average day. Men's activity levels remain roughly stable from age 65 to 89. Older women's activity levels decline steadily, but at a shallow slope – amounting to around 7 minutes of daily physical activity over each five year interval between 65 and 84. Even after the age of 90, British people on average still are doing more than an hour of daily physical activity. The present debates about retirement that have focussed on expanding the proportion of older people in the workforce to help pay for pensions and the medical needs of the ageing UK population may have to develop a broader focus. Health services and leisure industries will need to cater for the active elderly as well as for the dependent elderly.

Changing levels of physical activity will take time. It might be more realistic to define progress in the short-term by reducing the growth of car dependence or increasing the proportion of people who walk to work and school on at least occasional days.

Kimberly Fisher

Average Total Physically Active Time in Minutes for Men and Women in Older Age

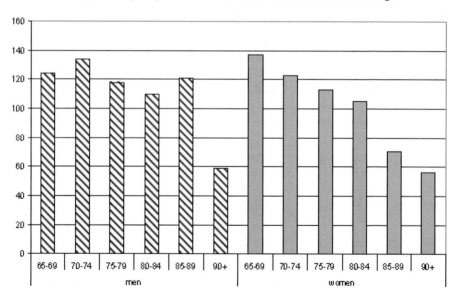

Source: Office for National Statistics (London), National Time Use Study, 2000/01

EXERCISE TESTING IN THE PAEDIATRIC POPULATION (ARE CHILDREN JUST SMALL ADULTS?)

The energy we need to fuel daily activities is released from nutrients in food (mainly carbohydrates and fat) by processes that are collectively referred to as metabolism. If energy requirements are not excessive, then the metabolism of nutrients involves oxidizing them using the oxygen in the air we breathe. This process is called *aerobic metabolism.* During intense exercise that can be sustained only for periods of about 10 s to 3 minutes, most of the energy requirements are met by another metabolic process that does not require oxygen (*anaerobic metabolism*). Although anaerobic metabolism can release energy quickly, it also produces a substance called lactic acid (lactate) that rapidly causes fatigue and therefore limits the duration of exercise at high intensity. It has been claimed by numerous researchers that the relative contributions of anaerobic and aerobic metabolism to energy production change during growth and maturation. In many of these studies this change has been detected by determining the maximum workload that can be maintained without lactate levels rising significantly; the workload at *maximal lactate steady state* (MLSS). However, claims that MLSS changes during development are based on a comparison of findings between separate studies on either adults or children, and these studies have used methodologies that differ in important details. Consequently it is possible that reported differences between children and adults are simply due to methodological inconsistencies. Because of this uncertainty, the paediatric exercise science group at the University of Essex decided to investigate how the MLSS changes across age groups using a carefully controlled, constant methodology.

Some 73 healthy male subjects aged between 9 and 32 yrs volunteered to take part in the study. MLSS and workload at MLSS were measured by the subjects undertaking a series of exercise tests in which they cycled at different constant loads. The concentration of lactate was measured in a sequence of blood samples taken throughout the tests. We also measured the maximal workload that the subjects could achieve during an incremental load test, and worked out the proportion of this maximum workload at which MLSS occurred. The overall results of these studies are shown in Table 1. MLSS (Fig. 1), and the percentage of maximum workload at which MLSS occurs do not change with age. On the other hand, the workload at MLSS (Fig. 2) and the maximal workload both significantly increased as age increased, as would be expected on the basis of increases in muscle mass (children are small adults).

Previous claims that MLSS is lower in children than in adults therefore appear to reflect methodological differences between the studies. This illustrates the dangers of using the results from independent studies to draw conclusions about developmental changes. On the other hand, the finding that the MLSS is independent of age does support the theory that lower performance in some kinds of exercise in children compared with adults may reflect maturation related changes in neuromuscular factors and is probably not due to changes in exercise metabolism. In other words, from the perspective of exercise metabolism, perhaps it is reasonable to consider that, after all, children are just small adults.

Table 1. MLSS and MLSS workload measured during constant load tests, maximal workload determined at the end of an incremental load test, and MLSS-intensity (MLSS-workload as a percentage of maximal workload) in a population of 9-32 year old males.

Caroline Angus, Renate Leithäuser and Ralph Beneke

N = 73	Mean ± SD	Minimum	Maximum
MLSS (mmol·L^{-1})	4.4 ± 1.1	2.3	7.5
MLSS-workload (W)	187.3 ± 57.2	65	310
Maximal workload (W)	275.9 ± 77.1	100	425
MLSS-intensity (%)	67.5 ± 6.7	50	84

Fig.1: Maximal lactate steady state (MLSS) related to age.

Fig. 2: MLSS workload related to age.

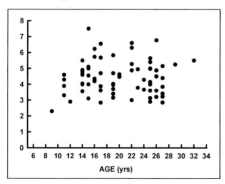

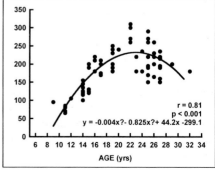

DOES TRAINING HAVE TO HURT TO WORK?

"No gain without pain". Is this just a macho mantra chanted by sadistic coaches and their athletes, or is it true that training has to hurt to work? To some extent the statement is supported by the fundamental and widely accepted principles of training. For training to be effective it should be progressive, specific to the activity, personalised to the individual's current state of fitness and potential to respond, and it should involve overload. Finally, and rather depressingly, it is reversible, providing the rationale for the second training aphorism "use it or lose it". Progressive and overload are the two principles that suggest that training has necessarily to involve discomfort. They acknowledge that the purpose of training is to induce adaptation in the athlete that will enable him/her to achieve ever-greater work-loads, whether that be in terms of endurance or power. Biological systems have the ability to respond to stress by adaptation.

Thus, for example, the skeleton responds to the tiny deformations that result from muscles contracting and from the effects of gravity by laying down more bone. The bones of tennis players are heavier and denser in the arm that wields the racquet. Consequently they become better able to withstand increased stress without fracturing. Conversely, if muscles are immobilised, or the effects of gravity reduced by bed rest or space flight, then the skeleton loses some of its mineral matrix and becomes weakened, resulting ultimately in osteoporosis. Similarly, muscles adapt to the frequent production of maximal force by developing more contractile protein and growing in diameter. Thus what was originally a maximal force becomes sub-maximal, and the muscle is less likely to be damaged, or to become fatigued, when required to produce it. Herein is the rationale for the need for training to be progressive. As adaptation occurs, so the training effect (stimulus to adapt) of a particular dose of exercise becomes weaker. To maintain improvement, the training must therefore become progressively harder.

Of course, the hard work of training is uncomfortable while it is going on, and to add to the sum of human suffering, the discomfort often persists as post-exercise soreness. The immediate soreness is probably due to the stimulation of pain receptors by stretching and might not reflect cellular damage. However, longer-term muscle soreness (delayed onset muscle soreness, or DOMS) that accompanies hard training or unaccustomed exercise is largely due to microscopic damage of the muscle cells and connective tissue. The damage provokes a local inflammatory reaction that ensures that cells of the immune system are attracted to the damaged area to begin the process of cleaning up. Inflammation also results in the production of growth factors that stimulate the process of repair. Thus, the damage and soreness might be necessary companions of repair and adaptation.

Delayed onset muscle soreness (DOMS) is particularly intense after exercise that involves the muscles producing tension as they are forcibly lengthened. Such "contractions" are referred to as being "eccentric". This kind of muscular work is common in sports that involve rapid deceleration and turning, and also in downhill running, and DOMS in the front of the thighs is a familiar sensation to footballers returning to pre-season training, to novice squash players and to hill walkers who are a little "rusty". The soreness is accompanied by weakness and DOMS can make descending stairs a precarious as well as an uncomfortable business.

Although soreness can be intense and inconvenient, perhaps it is a prerequisite for adaptation since it reflects the normal healing processes that result in the repair of the damaged tissue and enhancement of its function. Certainly it has been shown that strength training is more effective when it comprises eccentric contractions such as the controlled lowering of heavy weights. These observations suggests the following train of logic. Eccentric muscle contractions produce muscle damage, the resultant inflammatory response results in DOMS, and eccentric muscle contractions are also particularly effective at producing a training effect. Ergo inflammation and pain are necessary for training to occur.

We have looked at this possibility at the University of Essex and have some evidence to support the link between inflammation and adaptation to eccentric exercise, though we have not looked directly at the training effect. In addition to strength improvement following eccentric exercise, there is another way in which the muscle adapts. A single bout of eccentric exercise produces DOMS, but a subsequent bout of identical intensity and duration produces much less soreness. This phenomenon is referred to as "the repeat bout effect". The muscle (or possibly the nerve endings that produce the sensation of soreness) has adapted so that the same stimulus produces less stress. We wanted to find out if the repeat bout effect (adaptation) was mediated by inflammation, so we treated one group of subjects with ibuprofen, a drug that suppresses the inflammatory response, and another group of subjects with a placebo (a calcium tablet used to treat osteoporosis). The subjects then did a strenuous bout of eccentric exercise of the upper arm muscles. As expected, the ibuprofen group had less soreness in the muscles over the following few days. About 4 weeks later the subjects repeated the exercise bout without drugs and we measured their muscle soreness over the subsequent week. Surprisingly, the group that had taken ibuprofen had *more* soreness, supporting the idea that suppressing inflammation prevented adaptation to training as measured by DOMS.

Our results have therefore provided some support for the idea that pain (inflammation) may be necessary if training is to produce adaptation and others have come to a similar conclusion. This raises some interesting issues. If inflammation mediates the training effect athletes should embrace the inflammatory response. They should avoid taking anti-inflammatories and Paula Radcliffe's strategy of taking ice-baths after training to suppress inflammation might be misguided. On the other hand, ice baths might only suppress some of the consequences inflammation, such as the dilation of blood vessels and might also be acting as a local anaesthetic without inhibiting the production of the chemical messengers that induce muscle adaptation; at present we do not know as the mechanism of ice treatment has not yet been fully investigated. There is also the intriguing possibility that cell and molecular biologists might identify the signals, produced during the inflammatory response, which are responsible for the adaptation to exercise. If this were achieved then it might be possible to get some of the benefits of training by taking the appropriate "training factors". Of course, this would be no more ethically acceptable that dosing up on steroids or other illegal substances, but it might have medical applications in the treatment of muscle wasting diseases.

So where does all this leave us, and the athlete striving to achieve their full potential by optimising training? In truth, the possible link between inflammation and the training effect has not yet been proven, but there is ample evidence that training has to be hard, and at least uncomfortable, to produce maximal gains. Perhaps the grimaces and grunts of the exercise junkie are an inevitable accompaniment to the search for optimum performance. Perhaps the coach is right to urge his athletes on with the assurance that there is no gain without pain.

Martin Sellens

THE WARMER PERFORMER

The generally accepted practice of athletes warming-up prior to competition is commonplace across sporting arenas. Historically many coaches have prescribed warm-up to their athletes to prevent injury and/or improve performance even though the evidence that it is effective has been mainly anecdotal. However, there is now a growing body of scientific evidence to support the practice. Warm-up has been found to improve performance in short term power events, intermediate duration events (>30 secs but <5 minutes) and some endurance-based events but there is still a lack of information as to the best warm-up for each event. In addition the effect of changing such variables as the duration and intensity of warm-up, the length of the recovery period between the warm-up and competition, the active/passive nature of the warm-up and the specificity of the warm-up to the event is not yet known. There is also still little direct evidence that warm-up has a protective effect against injury.

The mechanism by which warm-up appears to exert an effect varies depending on the nature of the task. For short-term explosive power-based events an increased muscle temperature may be partly responsible for the improvement in performance. The warm-up, despite needing to be intense enough to elicit an increased temperature, should not be so intense as to induce metabolic fatigue (excessive production of lactic acid) and requires an adequate recovery period so that the high-energy phosphate stores (ATP and creatine phosphate) are fully replete. It is currently therefore suggested that warm-up should last for 10-20 minutes at no more than 40-60% of maximum oxygen uptake. A recovery period of 5 to 15 minutes should precede competition depending on environmental conditions so that muscle temperature remains elevated but high-energy phosphate stores are restored.

Evidence that warm-up improves performance in longer duration events is more limited. Many studies have focussed on the physiological response to exercise following warm-up and the results have often indicated (but not always directly measured) an improved tolerance to heavy exercise. For example warm up has been found to spare the immediate high-energy phosphate stores, reduce lactic acid production and reduce oxygen deficit (indicating that energy is being produced aerobically from the onset of exercise). These findings have been supported by studies at the University of Essex. We found that a warm-up typically used by middle-distance runners resulted in an increased aerobic and decreased anaerobic contribution to a middle-distance run, but did not significantly improve performance. Elsewhere a recent study has found that prior heavy exercise that caused an increase in blood lactate levels, with 10 minutes of recovery, enhanced performance during subsequent high intensity exercise (at 100% to 120% of the work rate at maximal oxygen consumption). The mechanism for the improved performance has yet to be established but might be due to increases in oxygen availability, aerobic enzyme activity and substrate availability and possibly to changes in motor-unit recruitment. As the effect is likely to be within the active muscles it can be inferred that the warm-up should be specific to the musculature required for competition and not generic in nature.

For longer duration events it is currently suggested that a warm-up at approximately 70% of maximal oxygen uptake for 10 minutes produces beneficial metabolic changes without significantly reducing muscle glycogen stores or high-energy phosphates. Such a warm up does not induce metabolic fatigue (cause by lactic acid build up) or induce thermoregulatory strain and should be followed by a recovery of up to 5 minutes.

Interestingly, increased muscle temperature does not seem to be a requirement for producing performance improvements except in short-term maximal power events. An increase in core temperature may even be detrimental for endurance exercise undertaken in the heat by contributing to fatigue. Athletes competing in endurance events in the 2004 Athens Olympics, where the average temperature was 31°C, might have been be expected to benefit from 'pre-cooling' rather than 'warming-up'. Studies have shown that whole-body pre-cooling results in an increased capacity for endurance exercise and may exert its effect via the central nervous system.

So the current advice is to carry on using a warm-up unless you're an endurance athlete competing in hot conditions – in which case try cooling down. However, the experience of Paula Radcliffe, who followed this suggestion by wearing an ice vest prior to the marathon at the Athens Olympics, but failed to complete the race, shows that getting the warm up, or the pre-cooling, right is no guarantee of success.

Anne Wittekind

MUSCLE BLOOD FLOW AND THE RESPONSE TO EXERCISE

A dequate distribution of blood flow to skeletal muscle is vital to be able to perform any type of exercise and this places an increased demand on the cardiovascular system. At rest muscle blood flow averages 5-10 ml per minute in every 100 g of muscle but this has been shown to rise to 150-500 ml per minute during high intensity exercise. The increases in blood flow to skeletal muscle during exercise are directly related to the four- to five-fold increase in cardiac output.

Cardiac output is the total volume of blood pumped by the left ventricle per min or the product of heart rate and stroke volume (HR x SV). For a trained male athlete with an average resting heart rate of 50 beats per min and a stroke volume of 100 ml per beat, this gives a cardiac output of 5 L.min^{-1} at rest. An individual's cardiac output will vary according to their gender and training status. An untrained male may achieve a cardiac output of 22 L.min^{-1} compared with a trained male attaining 35 L.min^{-1} during high intensity exercise. At rest approximately 15-20% of cardiac output is distributed to the skeletal muscle. However, during near-maximal exercise 85-90% of cardiac output is distributed to the cardiac and skeletal muscles.

During exercise blood is also redirected away from areas where it is not essential to those areas that are active. Therefore, vascular resistance (constriction of the vessels) increases in skin and other inactive tissues and vascular conductance (dilation of the vessels) increases in the skeletal muscles. This ensures that adequate supplies of oxygen and nutrients are received by the working muscles, in order to be able to sustain the exercise. Therefore, adequate blood flow to exercising skeletal muscles is provided by simultaneous increases in i) cardiac output and venous return; ii) vascular resistance in viscera, skin and other inactive tissues; and iii) vascular conductance in the skeletal muscles.

The measurement of muscle blood flow is important to understand the physiological changes that occur in muscles during exercise. Currently there are several invasive and non-invasive methods available, but many of these techniques are cumbersome and not practical to use in exercise testing conditions. One of the latest techniques currently being used at the University of Essex is that of near infrared spectroscopy (NIRS). NIRS is an optical technique that allows the measurement of changes in the volume and oxygenation state of blood within the muscle. Early studies used the NIRS method to calculate cerebral blood flow in sick newborn infants. This method has now been applied to calculate resting forearm blood flow in adults. Forearm blood flow calculated from NIRS was shown to give comparable values to those obtained by the established technique of strain gauge plethysmography with a small mean difference of $0.14 \text{ ml}.100\text{g}^{-1}.\text{min}^{-1}$ between the methods.

Some questions still remain about the control of muscle blood flow during exercise. In the past, studies have investigated the benefits of using a one-legged training regime as a rehabilitative tool, in order to prevent a loss in aerobic fitness or strength following injury to a limb. It appears that there may be a cross-transfer effect of fitness benefits between the trained and untrained (injured) sides following a one-legged exercise training programme. However, no theory exists to explain the underlying mechanisms. At the University of Essex we have used the near infrared spectroscopy technique to measure changes in muscle blood volume during a one-legged exercise test, which allows us to examine changes occurring in an exercising and non-exercising limb simultaneously.

The figure shows that during one-legged exercise an initial decrease in blood volume only occurs in the exercising leg. After the initial fall at the onset of exercise, blood volume rises throughout the test. In the non-exercising leg blood volume rises immediately exercise begins. Both legs show a blood volume rise during recovery.

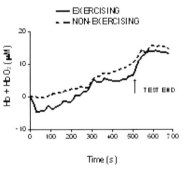

We found that increases in muscle blood volume are almost identical in both the exercising and resting legs following a one-legged exercise test. Although some increase in blood volume in the non-exercising leg would be expected, it appears that the trigger to increase blood volume may come from a local message in the exercising leg and the effect is expressed equally in both limbs.

This study suggests that during one-legged exercise the non-exercising muscle is not resting. Large increases in blood volume occur in the non-exercising leg. These changes may contribute to the underlying mechanism of the cross-transfer effect. These results may have implications for injured athletes; by exercising the uninjured limb during rehabilitation, an athlete may be able to prevent deterioration in muscle function in the injured limb by exploiting the cross transfer effect.

Caroline Angus

YOUNG PEOPLE, DRUGS AND OFFENDING

I t is now well accepted that drug use and offending are linked, and that combining drug use and offending may increase the likelihood of becoming drug dependent and/or of becoming a persistent offender. We aimed to find out more about these links by exploring patterns of drug use and patterns of offending in 293 young people who were clients of Youth Offending Teams (YOTs) in England and Wales.

We asked the young people a range of questions about their drug use, offending and other aspects of their lives. Those who took part were mostly male (81%; as are most YOT clients), and mostly white (83%). All but one were under 18, and just over half (52%) were aged 15 or 16. Although one-third (33%) were still at school, 44% had left or been excluded before the age of 16. Importantly, the group was highly delinquent – most had committed multiple types of offences repeatedly. Over 20% reported at least 20 offences in the previous year, including shoplifting, selling stolen goods, taking a car without consent and drug dealing.

The young people's use of substances was very high. As figure 1 shows, over 85% had used cannabis, alcohol and tobacco. Fewer than 20% had used heroin or crack cocaine – although this rate is still high for such a young group.

Figure 1: Substance use in 293 young offenders.

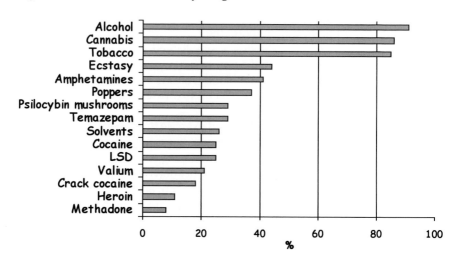

When we explored the relationship between patterns of drug use and offending, it was alcohol, cannabis and tobacco that predicted offending more than other drugs. However, shoplifting was related to addictive type drugs such as heroin and crack cocaine, whereas stealing from cars and beating people up were related to stimulants and multiple drug use.

Substance use and offending were both predicted by other factors, such as disliking and being excluded from school, poor coping mechanisms and expecting to be in trouble again. Most striking though were the life difficulties many of the young people had faced. As Figure 2 shows, more than half had experienced the death of a close friend or relative in the previous two years, and nearly one-quarter had been a victim of crime themselves.

Figure 2: Life difficulties and events in 293 young offenders.

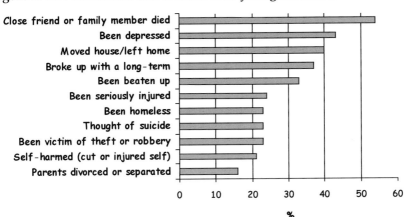

The fact that most young offenders use cannabis and alcohol extensively means that interventions need to address these substances as well as drugs such as heroin and crack cocaine that are more often targeted. Some key factors are related to both substance misuse and offending, and a vicious circle might develop whereby drugs and offending are used to cope with life's difficulties – making these worse, and confirming young people's expectations of getting into trouble again. Young people need to be taught positive coping mechanisms, including for dealing with past events and trauma.

Many schools adopt a low- or zero- tolerance approach to drug use. This may not be helpful as it encourages young people to conceal rather than deal with their drug use, and can lead to the exclusion of those who are caught – even though they are not necessarily those who use drugs most.

Louise Marsland and Richard Hammersley

THE VIAGRA STORY

I t is not often that a drug name becomes so familiar that everyone in the world knows it. Indeed in the case of Viagra its generic (chemical) name, sildenafil citrate, is probably almost as well known as the commercial name – especially to those of us who have struggled to avoid internet spamming by those who feel we need assistance in our sex life (there is a more serious side to this problem that I will return to later in this article). In the case of Viagra, the story of its discovery is even more interesting, and certainly less predictable, than the phenomenon of its entry into the cultural lexicon of everyday life. With Viagra it was not so much a case of kicking the baby out with the bath water, as the bath water itself being kept, the baby being of no use.

What do these cryptic comments mean? All drugs have side effects. Most serious side effects are picked up in cell testing, animal testing or clinical trials (with the result that the drug is then withdrawn). However, drugs are highly active biochemicals and most will have some minor secondary side effects in addition to their primary therapeutic effect. Although occasionally they only become noticeable when the compound enters clinical use, side effects are usually recognised early in the drug development process.

A decision is then taken as to whether the side effects are worth tolerating because of the benefits the drug produces in the patient – if the benefits are great, significant side effects might be acceptable. For example, serious discomfort is an acceptable (if undesirable) side effect of the strong drugs used in cancer chemotherapy whereas this would not be the case for a drug used to treat headache.

The drug Viagra was designed to treat angina by delivering increased levels of the messenger molecule nitric oxide (NO) to improve blood flow in the heart. Unlike the nitro-glycerine that helped Alfred Nobel, Viagra does not work by delivering nitric oxide directly. Instead it acts later in the NO signalling pathway. To understand how it works we need to think how signalling works in the body. All signalling pathways need a mechanism to turn them off as well as turn them on. What our body does is the sum of all the signals (messages) being sent at a particular time. If signalling pathways could never be turned off the body would always be turned on and we would only have one state, not the almost infinite variety we need to survive in an ever changing internal and external environment. In the case of the NO pathway one of the "stop signal" messages is provided by an enzyme, called a phosphodiesterase, that breaks down the second messenger, cyclic GMP, to an inactive form. The drug company Pfizer designed Viagra to inhibit this enzyme's activity, and hence make the NO signal "last longer". They hoped to increase the blood flow to the heart and hence alleviate the dangerous consequences of an angina attack (akin to a mini heart attack).

However, the initial Viagra drug trials in angina patients were not successful. The drug was about to be withdrawn when Welsh GPs reported an interesting side effect from another trial. In an attempt to improve the drug's potency higher doses were being tested in clinical trials on healthy volunteers (in this case the good citizens of Merthyr Tydfil). At these higher doses the volunteers reported increased penile erections as a side effect of the drug and Pfizer wasted no time in re-branding Viagra as a drug "designed" to prevent erectile dysfunction. Following successful clinical trials the Viagra phenomenon was born, generating millions of pounds for Pfizer and millions of emails for the rest of us.

Oh and about those emails. I once met someone who used to work in sales for Pfizer. I said rather flippantly that it must have been an easy job. Of course, it isn't – the main problem being that many men with erectile dysfunction, an essentially treatable condition that can have serious effects on their lives, are too embarrassed to see their GP about it. This is one reason for the arrival of hucksters and conmen on the web attempting to sell real, or fake, versions of Viagra to us all in the hope of the one in a million "hit" that makes their emails worthwhile. But buyer beware. Apart from not knowing whether what you are buying is actually Viagra, nitric oxide is involved in so many different vital physiological functions that it is potentially a risky business taking a drug that interferes with its normal production without medical supervision.

And the reason there was this desirable side effect? The body has several different types of phosphodiesterase. Viagra is designed to inhibit one, PDE5, that is present at high concentrations in the penis. Obvious when you know it, but the Viagra phenomenon might never have happened but for a group of thirty priapic Welshmen from Merthyr Tydfil. Now you know who to really blame for your e-mail spam…

Research in levels of nitric oxide in the body at the University of Essex

Nitric oxide research in the Department of Biological Sciences looks at ways of affecting nitric oxide levels in the body. In this case, unlike Viagra, the intention is to *decrease* NO levels in organs where its production is "out of control", for example in the liver and kidney during septic shock.

The prevention of NO overproduction in these disease states is being addressed by research, in collaboration with pharmaceutical companies, that aims to design and test specific inhibitors of the enzyme that makes NO, nitric oxide synthase. Of course, we will be hoping that we can avoid making patients impotent.

The Viagra Story

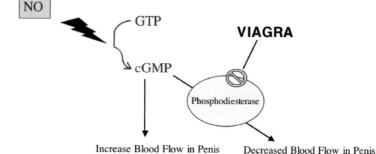

Nitric oxide levels increase on arousal and raise levels of the second messenger, cGMP, which then induces a rise in blood flow in the penis. An enzyme, phosphodiesterase, decreases cGMP levels and has the opposite effect. Viagra inhibits the phosphodiesterase activity, causing the effects of cGMP to be longer lasting.

Chris Cooper

TEENAGE BIRTHS AND THEIR CONSEQUENCES

UNICEF estimates that about 250,000 young women will give birth before they reach their 20th birthday this year. Of the developed countries, the USA has the highest teenage birth rate while Britain has the highest rate in Europe with about 11% of women giving birth before the age of 20. At the same time, the average age of first birth is increasing, which is usually attributed to a combination of extended periods in education, increasing numbers of women who decide to remain childless, technological advances that help extend childbearing years and a simultaneous increase in the average age of first marriage. This means that a teenage birth is, increasingly, seen as a pathological life event that has negative consequences for the mother, by way of reduced chances for human capital accumulation, and for the child, by way of a restricted developmental environment.

Numerous studies have shown that women who give birth as a teenager suffer from a broad range of socio-economic disadvantages later in life when compared to women who start childbearing later. The conundrum is that many of the women who give birth as teenagers come from disadvantaged backgrounds and, as such, are at more risk for adverse outcomes later in life whether or not they have a child in young adulthood. The key question is: what additional negative effects does the birth of a child have on later life circumstances, taking into account the background of the women who have an early birth? The characteristics that increase the chances of a teenage birth reflect disadvantages in the young woman's home and family, and in their own development and temperament.

The usual differences between women who were teenage mothers and those who gave birth later may suggest, but do not identify, any potential causal effects of the teenage birth on outcomes later in life. In the studies conducted at the Institute for Social and Economic Research at the University of Essex, a statistical technique has been used that, arguably, brings us closer to identifying causal effects from the data available. Roughly speaking, the assumption is that by confining the analysis to young women who became pregnant as a teenager, a comparison of the later outcomes for those who actually had a baby with those who had a spontaneous miscarriage provides a truer measure of the effect of having a baby. This provides a measure of the average impact of a teenage birth among those women having one, which allows for the fact that not all women will have the same outcome.

Using this technique we analysed data from the British 1970 Birth Cohort Study and found that a teenage birth has little or no impact on a woman's qualifications, employment or pay at age 30, or on the probability that she has a live-in partner. These results contrast with previous studies, which did not have a control group of women who had had miscarriages. However, a teenage birth significantly increases the probability that a woman's partner at age 30, if she has one, has no post-secondary education and her partner is also more likely to be unemployed.

These effects are large: compared to postponing childbearing beyond her teens, the probability that the teenage mother's partner has post-secondary education is about 20 percentage points lower, as is the probability that he has a job. Therefore, women who have a teenage birth appear to fare worse in the 'marriage market' in the sense that they partner with men who are poorly qualified and more likely to suffer unemployment. Having a teenage birth also substantially reduces the probability that a woman and her family will be homeowners at age 30.

Differences between ethnic groups in Britain were also studied, using ten years of data from the Labour Force Survey. The focus was on whether or not a woman was in a working family (defined as one in which one of the adults worked at least 16 hours per week) in the years following the birth. Among white women, postponing childbearing appeared to increase the probability of being in a working family.

However, Figure 1 shows that this advantage of postponing childbearing (the disadvantages of a teenage birth) is much lower among mothers from the Caribbean, African and Indian ethnic groups. In these groups the impact of postponing childbearing is only half as large as for whites. There was no evidence of disadvantages associated with a teenage birth among Pakistanis and Bangladeshis. This seems to

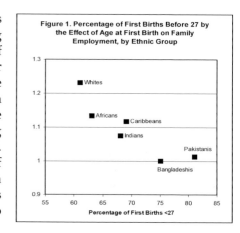

Figure 1. Percentage of First Births Before 27 by the Effect of Age at First Birth on Family Employment, by Ethnic Group

support the hypothesis that higher penalties associated with young motherhood are faced by women in cultures (in this case, the white population) where early births are unconventional.

So we can see that there are some long-term negative consequences of having a teenage birth for the mother, but they are not as wide-ranging as other research has suggested. It is acknowledged that young mothers are usually in a worse position than women who start childbearing later, but this mainly reflects the fact that those who become young mothers are already a disadvantaged group of women.

Our research measures the consequences of the birth after controlling for this fact. The primary consequence for mothers is that women having a teenage birth fare worse in the 'marriage market' in the sense that they partner with men who are poorly qualified and more likely to suffer unemployment. This has adverse consequences for their standard of living into their thirties and forties.

It is not clear how any policy might negate the marriage market consequences of teenage births, but our results do suggest that reducing teenage motherhood would have positive payoffs in terms of the future standard of living of the mothers and their children. There is, however, considerable diversity in outcomes. Some mothers are less affected by early childbearing than others. One manifestation of this is the difference in the impact of early motherhood on living standards among minority ethnic groups. It has a much larger negative impact among whites than among other groups, and no effect at all on Pakistanis and Bangladeshis – both communities with very high rates of teenage parenting.

David Pevalin and Karen Robson

STIGMA AND MENTAL HEALTH

My area of research interest is the sociology of mental health. I have been working on this for the past five years and have developed a sociological understanding of the place of mental health and 'illness'. My specific interest lies in the social *stigma* which often accompanies mental 'illness'. Stigma can be defined as a mark of shame or discredit. The key point is that because someone has a psychiatric diagnosis they may be stopped from fully participating in civil society. Yet there may be no basis for this exclusion, as they might be perfectly able to participate fully. It is the stigma attached to their 'illness' which leads others to exclude them.

My research is not concerned with looking for examples of people being stigmatised. I take stigmatisation as a starting point and look for evidence of what people do to combat these stigmatising processes. Stigma can occur at many different levels and through many different processes. My specific focus for these investigations is on the discourses that the people use. A discourse can loosely be defined as a 'collection of statements that describe an object'. I am looking for discourses about stigmatisation of people because they have a psychiatric diagnosis.

Much of the stigmatisation of mental health can be attributed to the prevailing medical model. Broadly speaking, the medical model regards all illness as biologically caused, whereas sociologists would argue that there are social causes of illness. If biology is taken as the sole cause, then, people may come to be seen as nothing more than repositories of pathology. This becomes problematic when we consider mental health because often the condition or illness is not solely identifiable as an illness. For example, a psychiatrist might feel that Barry is schizophrenic because of an imbalance of chemicals in his brain. Barry may feel he is emotionally troubled because of his traumatic childhood. Barry's explanation is social, whilst the psychiatrist's is biological.

My research considers people with psychiatric diagnoses in terms of how they relate themselves to this medical model. In this piece I want to consider two ways of relating to this model. Specifically, service users as psychiatric patients, and as survivors of psychiatric treatment. The table highlights these different types and examples of the discourses that may accompany them.

Type Discourse

Psychiatric patient	⟶	I am a schizophrenic
Survivor of treatment	⟶	I am a voice hearer

People who can be typified as psychiatric patients can be shown, through an analysis of their talk, to endorse this medical model and to consequently limit the degree to which they can counter the stigma. A person who utilises the patient discourse would be seen as passive recipient of treatment who works under the maxim that 'doctor knows best'. As such, they are more likely to be seen as a repository of pathology and less likely to be seen as a whole person. If they are seen as an illness they are less able to resist the stigmatisation of a diagnosis, because they are already excluded from society.

This becomes clearer if we consider the opposite end of the spectrum, the survivor. From the table, we can see that survivors reject the medical explanation, to the extent that they offer a non-medical discourse to describe their situation. As a result, they can challenge the stigma that accompanies the diagnosis. A key point in this process is around the ownership of the discourses used to describe them. In much the same way that the term 'nigger' has been reclaimed by black Americans, survivors reclaim talk about themselves and re-interpret this talk to offer a discourse which is not framed in a bio-medical context. Another example of this would be survivors talking about themselves as *'experiencing emotional distress'*, as opposed to the far more common term *'suffering from mental illness'* (someone identified as a patient may use this second term).

By challenging and resisting a medical explanation, survivors offer a different social space in which it is possible to talk about and consider different explanations for emotional distress (or mental illness). This is one component of the many different ways in which users of mental health services can be seen to be organising themselves and resisting the misplaced and misguided stigma that all too often accompanies mental illness.

Ewen Speed

EXERCISE AND MENTAL HEALTH

There a many ways to explore the relationship between mental health and exercise, but here I consider self-esteem and depression.

Self Esteem

Most mental health problems seem related to reduced self-esteem either as a consequence or a cause of the illness. So:

- If we could fix self-esteem we could perhaps fix the underlying problem.
- If we could fix self-esteem we could use that as a marker to help us to see if we are helping the underlying problem.
- If we could fix self-esteem then that would be a good thing in itself.

Self-esteem can be defined as an awareness of good possessed by self. Self-esteem is a self-rating of how well the self is doing. This worth is dictated by both the individual and the primary culture in which we operate. So it is both a personal thing based on the things that we value most, and a societal thing, based on the things which those around us value the most. The personal is the most important and many things may contribute to it. The symptoms of low self-esteem include depression, anxiety, neuroses, suicidal ideation, sense of hopelessness, lack of assertiveness, and low perceived personal control. Clearly the consequences are likely to be negative.

How can we fix self-esteem in the context of sport and exercise?

One way is to engage in aerobic exercise. This is exercise that raises heart rates. The characteristics of effective exercise are cardiovascular activity, exercise frequency, and programme duration. An important question is who benefits? For children and adolescents, exercise is an effective medium for developing positive self-esteem. It is very good for those with low self-esteem and can also encourage mastery and self-development. For middle-aged adults it is also very important, and it probably is for older adults too but little research has been done on this age group.

There seems evidence to support the idea that physical activity has a positive effect on depression. One sticking point is defining clinical depression. The problem is that many people say they have clinical depression (emphasising the clinical bit) to make sure that people understand that they are more than just fed up. In truth, you are clinically depressed if you go and see your doctor and they evoke an intervention, i.e. give you time off work, prescribe drugs, tell you to go and see a counsellor or therapist or something. This is important as many of the studies cited as evidence that exercise beats depression were not with clinically depressed patients.

Epidemiological evidence
There have been several important studies:
i)   one found that fitness levels were lower for psychiatric patients than non-hospitalised controls. Patients who had short (up to 61 days) hospital stays had higher levels of muscular endurance on admission than those who stayed longer (at least one year) even though they had similar initial levels of depression. So, does lack of exercise cause depression, does depression cause lack of exercise and will increasing fitness speed up recovery?
ii) Another over eight years showed that women who did little or no activity were twice as likely to develop depression as those who engaged in "much" or "moderate" activity.
iii) Another baseline, nine years later and a further nine years later study found a relationship between inactivity and depression. The relative risk of depression was greater for both men and women.
iv) And finally, it was found that men 23-27 years of age who engaged in three hours or more of sporting activity had a 27% reduction in the risk of developing depression compared to those who did an hour or less.

There is some evidence for a dose response – those who expended 2,500 kcal or more per week were 28% less at risk of developing clinically recognisable depression than those expending less than a 1000kcal per week. And those who expended between 1000 and 2499 had a 17% risk reduction compared to those in the least active group.

Thus, we believe that exercise may be an important treatment for depression but the research is somewhat equivocal. Exercise programmes can reduce clinically defined depression, and this can happen as quickly as 4-6 weeks. However, there needs to be more work on adjunctive drugs treatment, and there is a need to conduct long term follow ups.

So if you feel that you lack self-esteem or feel depressed then you should certainly participate in physical activity. It certainly will not harm your mental health and will probably help it.

Murray Griffin

REFUGEES AND MENTAL HEALTH

Refugees are persons who have sought asylum in another country because there was a 'well-founded fear of being persecuted' in their own country 'for reasons of race, religion, nationality, membership of a particular social group or political opinion' (International Refugee Convention, 1951, article 1A.2).

According to 2004 United Nations statistics, there are now over 19 million such people. News media highlight only a small faction of the conflict spots in the world that force people to abandon their homes; yet the issue is much bigger that we think and it has a strong impact on most countries in the world today.

However, it is important to emphasise that although the causes of forced migration should be condemned (i.e. brutal regimes, uncontained political and military conflicts), the consequences should not be taken as being exclusively negative. Regardless of the difficulties people face in being uprooted, their move to a new country may also open up new opportunities (material as well as psychological). Equally, although the receiving countries often find it difficult to respond appropriately to the presence of refugees, at the same time, they may also benefit from the refugees' vitality, resourcefulness and resilience.

Arriving in a new country, often after repeated traumatic experiences, refugees face a multiplicity of difficulties including financial, medical, educational and social. It is widely believed that refugees are 'traumatised' individuals and as such they have severe mental health problems. Although forced migration inevitably implies a great deal of mental anguish, this does not mean that all refugees suffer from mental health problems of pathological kinds.

The best way to expressed this is in terms of 'normal reactions to abnormal circumstances'. What is of paramount importance for mental health workers is to achieve a sensitive balance between attending to the multiplicity of actual psychological difficulties refugees experience and avoiding either pathologising human suffering or psychologising the political dimensions involved.

It should not be ignored that we have an enormous potential to deal effectively with unpredictable turns in our lives, especially when we have supportive resources within families and communities. Being exposed to adversity does not always affect negatively all the functions of individuals; certain capacities may remain intact and resilient. Moreover, the very exposure to adversity may offer unique opportunities for the activation of many positive responses, including increased stamina and resolution, new modes of creativity, breakthrough of impasses, revitalised energy and zest for life, new priorities in life, discovery of new meaning, and so on.

At the same time, the psychological implications of involuntary loss of home should not be underestimated. These may bring about varying degrees of disorientation with regard to personal and collective identities, roles, and inter-relationships. In addition to the host of losses refugees experience, there are also many losses that are not so consciously experienced but they leave a sense of a painful and inexplicable gap in the person. These less tangible losses include the loss of familiarity with smells, tastes, sounds, and architectural and natural landscapes.

A new Masters degree at the University of Essex assists all workers with refugees to introduce therapeutic elements in their work by sensitising them to a balanced approach with regard to the mental health needs of refugees.

Renos Papadopoulos

ASSESSMENT OF DIVERSION FOR MENTALLY DISORDERED OFFENDERS (MDOS) APPEARING AT COURT

There is a long and well-documented association between crime and mental illness. A high proportion of offenders have various co-existing forms of mental health problems such as mental illness, personality disorder, drug and alcohol dependence. A number of studies have reported a disproportionate number of people with severe mental illness involved in the criminal justice system and the 1991 Reed Report advised that schemes should be set up to divert MDOs to health and social services either at first point of contact with police, while held in custody, at court or in prison.

By 1999, over 150 schemes had been established throughout the country in response. At the University of Essex, NHS research funding supported a follow-up study of individuals who underwent psychiatric assessment by one such scheme – a Criminal Justice Mental Health Team (CJMHT) – operating in Essex.

At assessment, many people were identified with substance misuse problems, as homeless and with a history of psychiatric contact. Diversion was effective in terms of identifying mental illness among those with *severe* mental illness and facilitating their mental health care. However, most of the people assessed by the CJMHT in our study had problems that were of *insufficient severity* to merit diversion to statutory psychiatric care.

The study mapped service contact, housing and offending of clients in the year following assessment and compared this to the year prior to assessment and found that there was no noticeable change in their circumstances. Thus assessment by the CJMHT brought few discernible advantages for the majority of clients. This was also the perception of the clients who were interviewed. The majority of clients who were ineligible for statutory sector support had high rates of substance misuse problems, re-offended, and remained homeless or vulnerably housed. Interviews with clients suggested that over the study period, local community services were limited in what they could offer. Furthermore, lack of a fixed abode together with rigid appointment-based systems and lengthy waiting times hampered engagement with services.

Overall, the lack of a systematic approach to the needs of clients with minor mental health problems, associated or not with substance misuse, together with inappropriate appointment-based systems which increase inaccessibility for some potential clients with chaotic lifestyles, leaves a great deal of unmet need. The CJMHT provides a professional and dedicated liaison and assessment service. However, as a result of a lack of services to which they can refer the majority of their clients, contact with the CJMHT is currently a missed opportunity to begin a process of 'enabling' engagement with alternatives to the 'treadmill' of problems > offending > treatment or prison > return to the streets > and > repetition of this pattern once again.

Gill Green, Rose Smith and Nigel South

'TO BE INNU IS TO BE A HUNTER': THE HEALTH AND MENTAL HEALTH CONSEQUENCES OF FORCED CHANGES TO THE INNU WAY OF LIFE

The Innu are Algonquian speaking people of the Labrador-Quebec peninsula. Until the mid 20th century, they were permanent nomadic hunters ranging over an area the size of France. In the boreal forests and tundra of the interior of the peninsula they hunted caribou, including the vast George River herd, as well as bears, marten, lynx, fox, beaver, otter, muskrat, partridges, ptarmigan, ducks, geese, several varieties of fish and occasionally seals in the bays of the coastal areas.

Among Native North Americans, the Innu are unusual in that their hunting way of life has survived so long. This is, in part, because their land was by-passed on the westward expansion of settlements over the last few centuries. It is unsuitable for agriculture and, hence, was seen as of little use to settlers. Although the Innu were impacted by contact with European missionaries and fur traders, it was their absorption into Canada that precipitated a massive change in their fortunes. The eventual result of government efforts was the sedentarization of the nomadic Innu into villages in Labrador and Quebec. Sedentarization inevitably diminished the relationship of the Innu to *Nitassinan*, their land.

The severing of the links with the land has coincided with a massive transformation of the Innu. Within a short space of time, they have gone from being a healthy, vibrant people, surviving one of the most demanding physical environments on the planet to a deeply traumatised people. Since their sedentarization, the Innu settled in the Labrador villages of Utshimassits and Sheshatshiu have suffered extremely high rates of suicide, alcohol abuse, solvent abuse and sexual abuse. Each time I return to the villages I hear that things are "worse than ever."

To provide a rough idea of the vast gulf between the life and death experiences of the Innu and Canadians as a whole, I went through the death registers in the two villages to find out the ages at which people were dying. From 1975 to 1995, more than half of all deaths in Innu communities were of people aged under 30; this was the case for only five percent of

Canadians. Conversely, while at least eighty percent of Canadian and Newfoundland deaths were over 60, only a quarter of Innu deaths were in this age range – ages to which people are expected to live in G-8 countries. For the Innu and other Aboriginal peoples, the surfeit of untimely deaths represent a complex interplay of physical and mental health problems. The sudden irruption of hitherto unknown illnesses such as obesity, cancer, heart disease and diabetes, the latter affecting at least half of the Innu in the two Labrador villages, obviously affects how people think and behave.

As a sociologist, I have been preoccupied with explaining why the health of the Innu has declined so rapidly. My research has circulated around a number of social and political factors. The most important of these is the loss of connection with the land. The land is what provided Innu people with meaning, purpose and identity. "To be Innu is to be a hunter" is a frequently heard refrain among the elders of the villages. The immersion of the Innu into Canadian schools, based on the presumption that the Innu needed to be transformed into whites, has undermined the authority of the parents and precipitated a loss of confidence in the Innu way of life. This process has been aided by the government authorised sale of Innu land for industrial projects, which is experienced as a humiliation by many of the people.

Other drastic changes to the health of the Innu have been caused by biological factors such as the rapid change of diet and physical activity. A diet of wild animals, fish, mammals and berries has been supplanted by store-bought foods, which are almost exclusively mass-produced processed foods, and, more recently fast foods. This has coincided with an upsurge in diet-related diseases. While Northern peoples such as the Innu have been consuming wild foods, the incidences of obesity, diabetes and cardiovascular diseases have been relatively rare. It has been suggested that this is due to the high content of omega-3 fatty acids and antioxidants in the traditional diet. There is further evidence that the sudden shift from diets derived from hunting, fishing and gathering to those based on store-bought foods is an important risk factor linked with the deterioration in the mental health of circumpolar peoples. For example, the decline in consumption of omega-3 fatty acids has important implications for neuronal and brain development, function and health, and this has been linked to increased levels of aggression, depression and suicide.

There is no simple way to alleviate the physical and mental health problems of the Innu. However, one line of research suggests that an important determinant of psychological resilience is cultural continuity. In the mid 1990s, an Innu association of hunting families called Tshikapisk established an Innu 'school' in the country for Innu youth desperately caught up in cycles of depression and dysfunction within the village. With the help of many hunting families, the programme taught young Innu the history of their people, the geography of their lands and the practical skills needed to live in the country. This assisted in both the transmission of Innu skills and the strengthening of Innu identity among the youth.

As a result, those who set up the projects argue that the young people who participated in the programme became some of the healthiest and strongest individuals in the communities. According to the organisers, several spontaneous initiatives of the Innu to expose gas-sniffing youth to country life also resulted in vastly enhanced self-esteem and confidence. In all of their meetings and conversations on this matter, no one mentioned an instance in which a gas sniffing child from the community continued to abuse the substance when they were placed in the very different environment of the country.

Colin Samson

MENTAL AND EMOTIONAL HEALTH NEEDS IN RURAL COMMUNITIES

There is an assumption that rural communities are idylls, with rural life commonly portrayed as consisting of friendly people who have time to talk to one another. Life in the village consists of summer fetes or, in the winter, community singing in the village hall. The reality may be somewhat different. In recent years, rural communities have experienced a combination of depopulation by traditional rural folk and newcomers who often live in the village, but do not contribute its life. Isolation may be a problem for those regarded as mentally healthy, and it is significantly worse for those who have mental health problems.

Uttlesford is a small rural district in the west of the county of Essex. It consists of charming and picturesque villages, representing the best in 'chocolate box' images. Some 70,000 inhabitants live within the district, with about 38% within three areas. The remaining inhabitants live in a large number of villages and hamlets. The Department of Health and Human Sciences at the University of Essex was invited to carry out a survey of emotional and mental health needs within the district. The study involved questionnaires and interviews with members of the general public, people already using mental health services and the people who provided services.

The study supported the finding of other national and international studies. People with mental and emotional health needs in rural communities experienced a lack of transport, choice and information coupled with a fear of stigmatisation. There was a circular problem in operation whereby people could not get to use services because of transport and consequently services did not develop because of a low level of uptake leading to limited choice.

An interesting facet of the district was the public perception of services. Statutorily provided (primarily NHS) services were planned around district and county boundaries. But this did not accord with people's perceptions about where they lived. Whilst people in Saffron Walden live in Essex, they felt part of Cambridgeshire and would orient themselves to Cambridge for shopping and services. Access to information was a problem to many users in rural communities such as Uttlesford. People talked about the difficulty of accessing basic information about support services for mental and emotional health within the area. There was also a stigma associated with using services that were perceived as mental health related.

The research has had a number of unforeseen benefits. In January 2004, a conference involving 70 service users and service providers took place to discuss the issue of rural isolation in Uttlesford. The event presented the opportunity for organisations working in the district to work more closely together to reduce the impact of emotional and mental health problems in rural communities such as Uttlesford.

Peter Martin

PSYCHOLOGICAL BENEFITS OF SPORTS MASSAGE

The origins of massage can be traced back to China in about 2600 BC, where it is mentioned in the earliest known medical text the *Nei Ching*. Hippocrates, the patriarch of modern medicine, advocated the use of massage as a remedy for sports and war injuries. Indeed contemporary massage is still used to treat injuries and is a recognized form of physiotherapy. Recently massage has become popular among athletes, not only in preventing and treating injuries, but also in the belief that it can enhance exercise performance. But research has so far failed to uncover any convincing evidence that massage enhances athletic performance, leading many to conclude that pre-performance massage is an indulgence. Nevertheless, the prevalence of this indulgent behaviour among athletes has led other researchers to explore the psychological effects of massage.

Massage has the potential to alter various aspects of psychological state. Researchers have reported improved anxiety, self-feeling and activeness following massage, while demonstrating reduced perception of fatigue and increased perception of recovery. The most convincing evidence was reported by an investigation of the effect of various types of exercise on mood using the profile of mood state questionnaire (POMS).

Researchers took 183 university students and compared their mood states before and after 30-minutes of rest (N = 56), massage (N = 40), swimming (N = 39), jogging (N = 47), racquetball (N = 52), or tennis (N = 45). The mood state changes observed in running and massage conditions, resembled the 'iceberg' profile of elite athletes, i.e. high levels of vigour and low levels of tension, depression, anger, fatigue, and confusion. It has been speculated that such massage-induced mood changes might enhance athletic performance.

At the University of Essex, we are exploring selected psychological responses to massage and the prospect of enhanced athletic performance. Preliminary research has shown a significant reduction in tension and vigour POMS following massage, and improved total work and average power output in a 30-second Wingate Anaerobic cycling test (WAnT). The post-massage mood-state changes in our study were not consistent with earlier findings, which may suggest an indirect relationship between massage and mood state that is probably mediated by a range of other factors. Indeed, we have demonstrated that different mood state outcomes can be provoked by varying the type and intensity of the massage protocol. In addition to extrinsic factors, the relationship between massage and mood state may also be mediated by intrinsic psychological factors such as an athlete's personality, beliefs about massage, pre-massage mood state, self-awareness, pain tolerance and sensitivity. The research efforts at the University of Essex are currently exploring these issues further, in order to predict more accurately how the mood state of specific individuals will change in response to particular types of massage treatment.

Research concerning the effects of massage on exercise performance is limited and has produced varied results. Massage seems to be most effective at enhancing performance in short-duration exercise tests that have accurate scales of measuring performance and a high-degree of test-retest reliability. Our preliminary research supports this hypothesis, since increases in WAnT mean power and total work were observed following massage. The relationship between massage-induced mood states and exercise performance is not yet fully understood, although it is speculated that any mood state changes rapidly diminish from the onset of exercise.

With increasing exercise duration, massage-induced positive mood states are gradually superseded by other exercise-induced psychological states, therefore limiting performance effects. Furthermore, the time elapsed between treatment and exercise may limit the impact of massage on performance, since mood-changes are psychological *states* that given time will return to baseline levels. The timing of pre-performance massage and the duration of any subsequent exercise test may therefore be critical to performance outcome.

The popularity of sports massage continues to grow within the athletic community even though there is a lack of supportive empirical evidence. At the University of Essex we are exploring the relationship between the psychological effects of massage and exercise performance. Our research has indicated that massage provokes positive changes in mood state that may facilitate the performance of short-duration high-intensity exercise. This relationship seems to be mediated by a number of other factors including the psychological profile of the athlete, the nature of the performance task, and the timing and type of massage used. With further research, we hope to improve our understanding of these relationships so that pre-performance massage can be tailored to optimise exercise performance.

Dominic Micklewright

CAN YOU THINK YOURSELF FIT?

S adly the answer to this is no, but thinking about sport can greatly improve your performance. This is particularly true if you use the right kind of thinking – and that is mental rehearsal or visualisation. The interesting thing about this is we know it works but we do not know why. Visualisation is mentally practising a particular sporting activity. For throwing a Javelin, the athlete imagines: picking up the javelin; running forward; moving their arm backwards; throwing their arm forwards; letting go; stepping forward; stopping; watching the flight of the javelin; seeing it hit the ground; turning round; and walking away.

Elite performers use imagery extensively. Various researchers have shown that more than 90% of elite performers and their coaches use imagery and that elite athletes are more proficient than non-elite athletes. There is, however, a distinction made between imagery and mental rehearsal. Imagery is defined as a symbolic sensory experience which may occur in any sensory mode and is seen as a mental process or a mode of thought. Mental rehearsal, though, is the employment of imagery mentally to practice an act – so it is seen as a technique rather than just a mental process. We have found that using mental rehearsal is better than no practice at all, but it is better still to combine it with physical practice. So for example practicing swinging a golf club (without trying to hit a ball) is better than either no practice or just thinking about hitting the ball.

There are some things that make the mental rehearsal more or less effective and we call these mediators. There are three of these. The first, Imagery ability looks at how able an individual is at forming vivid images and whether they can control them. This ability has been shown to influence the effects of mental rehearsal on performance and to help distinguish between elite and non-elite, and successful and less-successful sports performers. It seems important to point out that it is perfectly possible to learn to be good at imagery (ie learn to both do it and to control it).

The second mediator is Imagery perspective which distinguishes between internal and external imagery. External imagery is where an individual perceives themselves from the perspective of an external observer, whereas internal imagery is where the person images being in their body experiencing the sensations which might be expected in the actual situation. Which is best? Some researchers support the idea that internal imagery is best because it allies the perceptual and kinaesthetic (i.e. knowing where your body is in space) experience of performance. Many sports performers to use a combination of both.

The third mediator is Imagery outcome i.e. imaging the end of a race or competition. Research has shown that mental rehearsal involving negative outcomes degrades performance. That is if you practice losing then you will lose. Some researchers suggest that negative imagery negatively affects performance because it harms confidence and motivation. The opposite should be true too. So, if you imagine successful outcomes then you should do better and there is some evidence for this.

This last point is especially important since it asks the "why does it work" question. There are three theories.

Psychoneuromuscular theory

This idea says that the body runs the performance programme but with the gain turned down. So EMG activity (a measure of the electrical stimulation of muscles) which mirrors the EMG activity that occurs when the task is performed should be recorded during mental rehearsal, but at a lower level of intensity. This is tricky to do but there has been some success.

Symbolic learning theory

The idea here is that mental rehearsal allows the performer to practice the cognitive aspects of the task – things like task strategies, spatial and temporal sequences. If this is true then mental rehearsal should be important for new skill acquisition. Some researchers though hold the opposite view i.e. that mental rehearsal is most useful when the performer is familiar with the task (the argument being that we cannot use imagery until we know what to image). Again there is evidence to support the symbolic learning theory.

Bio-informational theory

Some think that symbolic learning theory is too simplistic, and put forward the idea that an image is a "functionally organised set of propositions stored by the brain". Imagery is divided into propositions about stimulus and about response with relevant physiological components to both. This is an interesting and quite new idea but some researchers think this sounds more like a description than an explanation. No doubt further study would clear this up.

All of which seems to leave us with the conclusion that: we know it works but we do not know why.

Murray Griffin

GREEN EXERCISE – THE MENTAL AND PHYSICAL HEALTH BENEFITS OF PHYSICAL ACTIVITY

Two of the primary determinants of physical and mental health, leading to increases in life expectancy, are now acknowledged to be diet and physical activity. Ironically, just as food shortages have been largely conquered in industrialised countries, so diets have become a major public health cost. On average, people now consume more food calories than they burn, and consume types of food constituents that are making them ill. The costs of diet-related illness (coronary heart disease, strokes, obesity, maturity onset diabetes mellitus, gall-stones, osteoporosis and a third of cancers) now exceed those of tobacco use.

Physical activity greatly reduces the risk of dying from coronary heart disease, and also reduces the risk of developing diabetes, hypertension and colon cancer. It enhances mental health, fosters healthy muscles and bones, and helps maintain health and independence in older adults. We use the term `activity transition' to describe the changes in modern societies in the past 2-3 generations, with people no longer active in the workplace, nor in traveling to and from work, nor during leisure time.

The primary role played by diet and physical activity in emotional and physical well-being is complemented by secondary roles played by connections to nature and social communities. An innate connectedness to nature is the core principle in the `biophilia hypothesis', which suggests that closeness to nature increases well-being as well as the likelihood of understanding of and care for nature, and its rediscovery can lead to transformations in people and nature. It also suggests that disconnections are harmful – both to individuals and to societies and cultures at large.

There is a well-established literature that shows that the physical and social features of the environment affect behaviour, interpersonal relationships and actual mental states, as well as shape relations with nature. People seem to prefer natural environments to other settings, and the benefits go beyond just enjoyment. The contexts include the effectiveness of wildernesses in contributing to spiritually beneficial recreation and leisure experiences; the healing value of hospital gardens or of nature views from hospital or gaol windows; the benefits of nature areas in urban settlements; and the psychological benefits of companion animals and pets.

Yet an important challenge remains. Intuition, experience and some evidence support that notion that nature contact should be seen as a positive health intervention, yet health professionals have not widely adopted horticulture, wilderness, nature or animal therapy.

Regular physical activity positively affects mental well-being and self-esteem. High self-esteem is important as it is seen as a key indicator of emotional stability, and adjustment to life demands is one of the strongest predictors of subjective well-being. The symptoms of low self-esteem include depression, anxiety, neuroses, suicidal ideation, sense of hopelessness, lack of assertiveness, and low perceived personal control. Evidence suggests that aerobic exercise can improve self-esteem as well as have an antidepressant effect. There is good evidence to support the idea that physical activity has a positive effect on self-esteem and depression. We conclude that exercise programmes can reduce clinically-defined depression, and that this can happen as quickly as 4-6 weeks.

We believe, therefore, there is a synergistic benefit in adopting physical activities whilst at the same time being directly exposed to nature. We call this `green exercise'.

Many people already appreciate the benefits of protecting the environment, undertaking physical activity, and combining the two. Despite the daily disconnections between a predominantly urban population and nature, and the increase in sedentary lifestyles imposed or adopted by the majority of the population, people still express their values in a variety of direct and indirect ways, through i) membership of environmental and wildlife organisations; ii) visits to the countryside and the growth in national and international eco-tourism; and iii) membership of gymnasiums and of sports and outdoor organisations.

Green exercise is likely to have important public and environmental health consequences. A fitter and emotionally more content population costs the economy less. Increasing the support for and access to a wide range of green exercise activities for all sectors of society will produce substantial public health benefits. There are many policy options, including gyms at GP surgeries, healthy walks projects, exercise on prescription, healthy school environments and travel to school projects, green views in hospitals, protection and support for city farms and community gardens, less anonymous food (with substantial health benefits if there are increases in fruit and vegetable consumption), and more support for ecotourism, outdoor leisure activities, and visits to the countryside. These, though, still remain on the margins of public health, environmental and agricultural policy.

If everyone ate five pieces of fruit and vegetable per day, and engaged in 30 minutes of moderate physical activity five times per week, and ensured that calorie burning matched consumption in food and drink, then a significant proportion of the annual £10 billion costs of obesity, coronary heart disease and physical inactivity could be avoided. If these benefits are also achieved through activities that provoke long-term changes in attitudes to nature and the environment across society, then the possibilities for transformations and actions to support sustainability outcomes will be all the more likely to occur.

Jules Pretty, Murray Griffin, Martin Sellens, Rachel Hine and Jo Peacock

DIETING AND WATCHING WHAT YOU EAT

A At any one time, the majority of young women are 'dieting'. Harmful practices include fasting, excessive exercising, laxative abuse and vomiting, which may be related to a higher incidence of eating disorders. However, much of the information on dieting is based on self-report surveys where respondents describe their dieting behaviour using categories of dieting predefined by the researchers. Generally, it is assumed that respondents and researchers share a common definition of the behaviours that constitute 'dieting'.

Dieting is a complex activity that can occur for short or long periods, can be intense or moderate and can have various objectives. People may restrain their food intake to improve their appearance, to lose weight, to maintain weight rather than gaining it, to enable them to wear special clothes (e.g. for a wedding or a beach holiday), to reduce their fat intake or to otherwise improve their health. As there is a considerable time lag between dietary restraint and its valued effects, most restraint must be controlled by what people expect to happen – on the basis of past experience and other people's advice – rather than actual effectiveness. There is also the paradox that concern is expressed about the high prevalence of 'dieting' amongst normal weight people while, at the same time, obesity researchers are concerned about the low success rates of weight loss diets and the very rapid increase in obesity rates over the past 20 years.

Little attention has been given to 'healthy' eating behaviour patterns and 'healthy' attitudes related to eating in the general population. A study by Nichter *et al.* in 1995 is an exception. In this study attitudes related to eating and weight control were investigated in 231 adolescent females. Ethnographic interviews were conducted that allowed for close attention to the language used by these adolescents, which resulted in a modification of the description and analysis of weight related behaviours. The findings were inconsistent with the majority of past surveys that have tended to report negative behaviours related to dieting. Instead a majority of the sample reported healthy, positive attitudes related to eating and weight control.

Furthermore, dieting episodes, as described in food diaries and recounted in telephone interviews, were less frequent and less severe than reported in past surveys. Across the sample, only 9% of days were 'dieting' days. On the basis of this work, it has been suggested that 'dieting' can be distinguished from 'watching what you eat'. The latter involves generally monitoring weight, healthy eating and food intake and, sometimes, 'dieting' as required. It does not generally involve being restrained or obsessive about diet in unhealthy ways.

To what extent has 'dieting' been confused with 'watching what you eat'? We surveyed 153 women undergraduates. Figure 1 shows what they reported. Almost half watched what they ate and dieted occasionally, while only 17% dieted most or all of the time, which was less than the percentage who watched what they ate but never dieted (26%). If the study had put all 'dieting' behaviour together then at least 65% of these women would have been classed as 'dieting', which is misleading, but consistent with the rates reported in other studies.

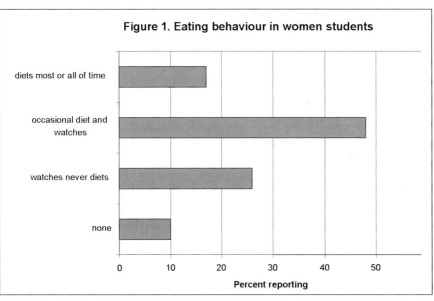

Figure 1. Eating behaviour in women students

This suggests that watching what you eat is more common than dieting and that it is misleading to confuse the two. Watching what you eat to some extent may be necessary to ensure healthy eating and avoid weight gain in a world where we are surrounded by an abundance of palatable food.

Marie Reid, Richard Hammersley and Jaynie Rance

OUR CHANGING DIET

Since hominids diverged from the apes, we have passed some 300,000 generations as hunter-gatherers, the last 600 of which have seen us come to rely mainly on agricultural systems for our food. In the last two generations, the diets of most people in industrialised countries, and of an increasing number of those in developing countries, have undergone enormous changes. On average, people now consume more food calories than they burn, and increasingly they consume types of food, such as those containing simple sugars and an excess of salt, that are making them ill.

The average UK diet has changed greatly in the past fifty years (Table 1). According to the National Food Survey published by Defra, which has been collecting data on weekly consumption of foods since 1942, the average Briton now consumes less milk/cream, eggs, vegetables, bread, direct sugar, fish and fats, and more cheese, fresh fruit, cereals and meat than in the 1940s. Consumption of sugar, meat, eggs, milk/cream and fats rose until the 1970s, and has since fallen.

Of particular concern for public health is the 34% fall in vegetable consumption over 50 years, and the 59% decline in fish consumption. On the other hand, the consumption of fresh fruit has increased by 129% since the 1940s – though this still leaves UK consumption the third lowest in the EU (fruit consumption ranges from 400 g/day in Greece to 100 g/day in Ireland). Vegetable consumption in Europe ranges from 440 g/day in Greece, to 60 g/day in Iceland, with a value of 280 g/day in the UK.

Table 1. Changes in per capita weekly diet for UK, 1942-2000

Foods	1942-1949 average (g per person per week)	1974-1976 average (g per person per week)	1998-2000 average (g per person per week)	Change from 1940s to 1998-2000 (%)
Milk/cream products	2455	2899	2038	-17%
Cheese	73	106	106	+45%
Eggs (number)	2.42	4.1	1.72	-41%
Fresh fruit	316	504	724	+129%
Vegetables	3026	2324	1986	-34%
Bread	1741	948	726	-58%
Cereals (not bread)	645	680	757	+17%
Sugar (direct)	269	345	110	-59%
Fish	242	126	144	-59%
All fats and oils	251	314	189	-25%
All meats	727	1042	940	+29%

Source: National Food Survey

These changes in diet have occurred far too quickly for human physiology to adapt through the process of evolution, and diet-related illness now has severe and costly public health consequences. According to the comprehensive Eurodiet study, in the second half of the twentieth century *"most of Europe has seen a very substantial increase in a number of chronic diseases in adult life. These become worse with age and are multifactorial. The principal factors, however, are diet and inactivity in coronary heart disease, strokes, obesity, maturity onset diabetes mellitus, gall-stones, osteoporosis and several cancers."*

Worse still, the Eurodiet study concludes that *"disabilities associated with high intakes of saturated fat and inadequate intakes of vegetable and fruit, together with a sedentary lifestyle, exceed the cost of tobacco use"*. Some problems arise from nutritional deficiencies of iron, iodine, folic acid, vitamin D and omega-3 polyunsaturated fatty acids, but most are due to excess consumption of energy and fat (causing obesity), sodium as salt (high blood pressure), saturated and trans fats (heart disease) and refined sugars (diabetes and dental caries). Highly energy-dense diets rich in sugars are nearly as conducive to over-consumption of energy as are diets containing excessive amounts of fatty foods. Consequently, many low fat alternatives provide an illusion of `healthfulness' as they are high in sugar.

Diet is thought to be a factor in 30% of cases of cancer in developed countries. The strongest association between diet and cancer is provided by the positive relationship between the consumption of vegetables and fruit and a reduction in the risk of cancers of the digestive and respiratory tracts, with some epidemiological evidence of an association between intake of salt and gastric cancer. Low fibre content, vitamin and mineral insufficiency, high meat consumption and excessive alcohol intake have also been implicated as risk factors for cancer.

Jules Pretty, Murray Griffin and Martin Sellens

e₃

EATING AND DRINKING FOR OPTIMUM PERFORMANCE

C orrect nutrition is vital, not only for health, but also for optimum physical and mental performance. A healthy balanced diet is therefore particularly important for an athlete, who also requires nutrients to regenerate body tissues and to provide fuel for the many bodily processes that operate in overdrive during exercise. The difference between the nutritional requirements of an athlete and a sedentary person is mainly the total amount of energy they need. The energy expenditure of a sedentary adult is about 2000-2800 kcal per day. This increases by 500 to >1000 kcal for every hour of exercise, depending on the size and physical fitness of the individual, and the type and intensity of the exercise. This increase in energy expenditure must be balanced by a corresponding increase in energy intake by increasing food consumption.

It is generally recommended that athletes should consume 60-70% of their total energy intake in the form of carbohydrates, 12% as protein, and the remainder as fat. However, expressing these guidelines in percentage terms is not helpful for an athlete as it does not indicate how much they should be eating. Instead, recommendations are easier to understand if they are stated in relation to body weight. For instance, the recommended daily protein intake for an endurance athlete is 1.0–1.2 g per kg of body weight. An endurance athlete who is training daily at a moderate to high intensity should consume 7-12 g of carbohydrate per kg of body weight every day. A high carbohydrate diet is recommended for athletes participating in endurance and multiple sprint sports as performance is generally limited by carbohydrate availability. It is the only nutrient that can fuel intense exercise for a prolonged period, but its stores are comparatively small.

In order to ensure that the correct balance of macronutrients (carbohydrates, protein and fat) and micronutrients (vitamins and minerals) is being consumed, the athlete should carefully monitor his or her dietary intake. The 24-h recall and the three-day food record are the most frequently used methods. However it is important to recognise their limitations. The 24-h recall method may not reflect the usual diet, and both methods may underestimate portion sizes and/or omit some food items. Athletes also tend to over-report low intakes and to under-report high intakes. To ensure that nutritional practices are optimum, it is also important to monitor body weight and body composition over time.

Optimum nutrition will vary between sports and between individual athletes, and depends on factors such as exercise intensity, exercise duration, environmental conditions, and training and nutritional status. Frequency of competition is also important. A common strategy to improve performance in endurance events is carbohydrate loading. Carbohydrate loading involves undertaking a prolonged training session to use up carbohydrate stores in the muscles, then eating a high carbohydrate, high total energy-content diet, and tapering the training volume for about 3-5 days prior to competition. This seems to work for endurance events such as running a marathon or competing in a triathlon but the practice is not recommended for sports such as football or rugby where there may be one or two games per week. For these sports it is better simply to consume a high carbohydrate diet on a daily basis.

There is a continuing debate as to whether supplements are beneficial for performance. It is generally accepted that vitamin and mineral supplementation should not be necessary if the athlete is eating a healthy balanced diet. However, supplementation with iron and calcium might be justified for female athletes because they can be particularly susceptible to anaemia and the development of osteoporosis. Although supplement use appears to be widespread amongst athletes, only a few supplements (notably caffeine, creatine and bicarbonate) have been shown to improve certain aspects of performance in controlled experiments under laboratory conditions. Caution must be advised if an athlete is considering taking any supplement because it may not improve performance, it may be harmful, and/or it may contain illegal substances.

Another important component of a healthy balanced diet is fluid. As a general rule, fluid intake (in both food and drinks) should balance fluid losses on a daily basis. Guidelines suggest a daily intake equivalent to approximately 4% of body weight in adults. For a 68 kg person, this amounts to 2.7 L/day. The amount of fluid required increases when exercising, and an additional intake of 1 ml fluid for every kcal expended during exercise is recommended. Thus, adequate hydration is vital before, during and after exercise.

Why is it important to drink during exercise? When exercise is prolonged, and especially in the heat, an athlete can become dehydrated. This is because excess heat, produced as a by product of energy transfer during exercise, and taken up from the environment, is predominantly lost by sweating. Sweat rates of 1-2 litres per hour are commonplace in endurance athletes and this represents a weight loss of about 1-2 kg per hour, or 1.5-3%

of body weight for a 68 kg person. The physiological consequences of dehydration are serious, as for every litre of water lost, heart rate increases by 8 beats per minute, cardiac output decreases by 1 L/min and core temperature increases by 0.3° C. Therefore, it is important that athletes try to drink fluids at approximately the same rate that they are losing water through sweating. This can be monitored by measuring body mass before and after exercise.

The best fluid to ingest is a carbohydrate-electrolyte solution containing 4-8% carbohydrate, which provides the body with both fluid and fuel. The American College of Sports Medicine recommends that individuals drink about 500 ml of fluid about 2 hours before exercising, and then drink early and regularly during a bout of exercise. If the exercise lasts longer than 1 hour, it is recommended that carbohydrates are ingested at a rate of 30-60 g per hour in order to provide both fluid and fuel at adequate rates.

When significant sweat losses have occurred during exercise, it is vital that both the fluid and electrolyte losses are replaced during recovery. Rehydration is most effective when the athlete drinks a dilute glucose solution containing sodium chloride and the volume ingested should be about 150% of the weight lost during exercise. Another important consideration during recovery from exhaustive exercise is the replenishment of the body's limited glycogen stores, ready for the next bout of exercise. In order to do this, it is advised that 50 g of mostly moderate to high glycaemic carbohydrates (those which increase blood glucose concentration the greatest) should be ingested every 2 hours. A total of 600 g carbohydrate should be ingested over 24 hours.

Nutrition should not be overlooked when training and competing, as when all other factors are equal, what you eat and drink can make the difference between winning and losing.

Ceri Nicholas

JUNK FOOD AND THE OBESITY EPIDEMIC

T he UK has one of the fastest growing rates of obesity in adults in the developed world. This is also echoed by the continued rise in obesity in children. In fact, between 1995 and 2002 the prevalence of obesity in children has almost doubled and currently 6% of boys and 9% girls in England are obese. Nearly a quarter of all children are either overweight or obese; this includes children as young as two years old. The trends suggest that as these children grow up they will become the overweight and obese adults of the future. Being overweight or obese increases the risk of developing a number of diseases and conditions, such as Coronary Heart Disease (CHD), Type II diabetes and some cancers.

Obviously exercise is crucial in tackling the obesity epidemic and it is necessary to identify how we can introduce more physical activity into children's lifestyles; for example by encouraging more children to walk or cycle to school. However, we must also discourage them from too much sedentary behaviour such as watching TV and playing computer games as there appears to be a link between obesity and increased TV viewing time.

In order to understand the link between obesity and physical activity patterns we need to be able to measure how much activity children are getting. The Paediatric Exercise Science research group at the University of Essex has recently investigated the methods used to collect information about physical activity levels in children and is developing a new self-report activity diary that will increase the accuracy of the information collected, particularly in young children.

A well balanced diet is essential for good health. However, less than half of all children are eating the recommended five portions of fruit and vegetables a day. It is evident that the type and quantity of food that children eat has changed markedly in recent years. There has been a significant rise in the amount of high fat, high sugar and high salt foods that children consume on a regular basis and perhaps some of the blame for this should be directed at the food industry.

The so-called "big five" food companies, that manufacture the majority of sugared breakfast cereals, soft drinks, confectionery, savoury snacks and fast food, aggressively target children in their advertising campaigns. These manufacturers try to directly influence children's food choices and their efforts seem to be working. Children now get approximately 20% of their energy from sugar, and up to 25% of this sugar comes from soft-drinks.

Consideration has been given to whether food and drink advertising should be banned during peak TV viewing time, particularly when it is aimed at children under the age of 12 who are less able to distinguish between programmes and advertisments. At present a ban has been ruled out, but many commentators believe that the number of advertisments promoting unhealthy foods is disproportionate and this issue needs to be considered carefully.

More recently some confectionery manufacturers have pledged to stop producing "king size" versions of chocolate bars in a move to address the problem of obesity. While this is to be welcomed, perhaps one needs to consider whether the real problem is super-sizing or simply the number of chocolate bars children are consuming. The problem is also heightened by the availability of vending machines selling these products in schools.

Some food manufacturers, particularly in the US, have offered their products to be given as rewards for academic performance, but these tend to be snack foods high in fat or sugar. Other "sponsorship" schemes involve collecting food wrappers that can be exchanged for educational or sports equipment. However, the manufacturers associated with these campaigns are often one of the *big five* and this covert advertising could be said to be contradictory to the healthy eating messages many schools are now trying to promote.

Currently, the Paediatric Exercise Science research group at the University of Essex is surveying the levels of childhood overweight and obesity in the region and investigating the suggested relationship between fatness and fitness. Decreased cardiorespiratory fitness may be an independent risk factor for coronary heart disease that is linked with increased body fat and sedentary behaviour. However, there can be no doubt that, as well as encouraging an active lifestyle, promoting healthy eating behaviour will also be vital to avoid a public health catastrophe when today's "junk food" children become tomorrow's obese adults.

Caroline Angus and Jules Pretty

THE HEALTH BENEFITS OF WILD FOODS IN LABRADOR

The nutrition transition is a well-established phenomenon in both industrialised and developing countries. It involves a shift from diets based on locally-derived foods to diets high in cereal, refined sugars, fats and salt. As a result, diet-related illness now has severe public health consequences in most industrialized countries. This is certainly true in the USA, where the cost of obesity (about $117 billion per year) has now overtaken the public health cost of smoking (about $79 billion).

For the most recently settled hunter-gatherer societies, such as the Innu, the nutrition transition has occurred directly (and abruptly) from wild foods to modern refined (and often junk) foods. In the Arctic and Subarctic regions, indigenous peoples' diets have made a change from foods that are nutrient-dense, with high levels of protein, fat (especially omega-3 fatty acids), and antioxidants (eg selenium), but low in carbohydrates, to diets high in carbohydrates and saturated fats and low in essential nutrients such as omega-3 fatty acids.

Among older Innu there is a widespread view that store-bought food is unhealthy and makes people ill. This was evident almost as soon as the previously nomadic Innu were settled in static communities. Father Frank Peters quoted Innu at the new Davis Inlet village in 1972 as saying, *"In the store is always food. But when we eat that food, we are still hungry. It is not the same as caribou meat; it is not Indian food."* Before settlement, the Innu were remarkably healthy, with very few cardiovascular or lung problems, and good dental health. The major causes of mortality were infant illnesses and trauma from accidents.

A wide range of wild foods are still consumed by all indigenous peoples in Canada, with more than 50 species of animals and birds regular in diets, including caribou, moose, rabbit, muskrat, beaver, porcupine, muskox, squirrel, lynx, fish, duck, geese, ptarmigan and grouse, together with a variety of fish, marine mammals, berries, wild rhubarb, wild onions and Labrador tea. While Northern peoples have been consuming these foods, obesity, diabetes and cardiovascular diseases have been relatively rare. It has been suggested that this is partly due to the high content of omega-3 fatty acids and antioxidants in the traditional diet.

Although now very common among hunting peoples who have been required to adopt a sedentary way of life, degenerative diseases such as diabetes, coronary heart disease and cancer have been relatively rare in hunter gatherers. As well as having an active lifestyle that involves more energy expenditure, hunter-gatherer diets comprise foods that are more fibrous, have a high protein to fat ratio and lack the high amounts of sugar, salt, saturated fats and high calories characteristic of many diets of people in industrialised societies. There is much to learn from the hunter-gatherer diets and lifestyles in terms of health promotion.

Why are the problems of diet transition particularly acute for indigenous people like the Innu? Once there has been a lifestyle change brought about by settlement, then indigenous people have no constant access to wild food throughout the year, and so come to rely on store-bought food derived from distant agricultural systems. This becomes a health problem because hunted and gathered wild foods are very different in nutrient content and density than bought foods. Table 1 shows the energy, protein, fat and key vitamin content of eight types of wild and domestic meat and fish.

Table 1. Nutrient content for wild-caught and store-bought foods

Food	Energy kcal $100g^{-1}$	Protein g $100g^{-1}$	Total fat g $100g^{-1}$	Saturated fat g $100g^{-1}$	Iron mg $100g^{-1}$	Vitamin C mg $100g^{-1}$
Caribou	167	29.8	4.42	1.7	6.17	3
Pheasant	247	32.4	12.1	3.5	1.43	2.3
Beaver	212	34.9	6.96	2.1	10.0	3
Rabbit (wild)	173	33.0	3.51	1.1	4.85	0
Moose	134	29.3	0.97	0.29	4.22	5
Duck	123	19.9	0.97	1.32	4.51	6.2
Salmon	184	27.4	7.50	1.59	0.71	1
Trout	150	22.9	5.80	1.52	0.38	2
Mean country foods	173	28.7	5.69	1.64	4.03	2.8
Luncheon meat	334	12.5	30.3	10.8	0.72	5 1
Bologna beef & pork	304	15.2	24.6	9.7	1.21	0.8
Pork loin chops	247	27.9	14.5	5.3	1.05	0.8
Beef, braised	342	26.9	25.7	10.2	3.04	0
Steak	256	28.0	15.2	6.1	3.04	0
Beef corned	249	26.9	15.2	6.2	2.10	0
Beef/pork frankfurter	320	11.1	28.9	10.7	1.10	0
Pork sausage	369	19.2	30.8	10.8	1.1	3.8
Mean store foods	302	20.9	23.2	8.7	1.68	0.81

For this sample, store-bought food has 70% more energy content than wild food (302 kcal 100g^{-1} compared with 173 kcal 100g^{-1}), 37% less protein (20.9g compared with 28.7g), and more than four times as much fat (23.2g compared with 5.7g), of which 8.7 g are saturated fats. These saturated fats are known to be an important risk factor in coronary heart disease and also contribute to the accumulation of body fat.

How do these foods compare with a typical "junk" food meal? One meal of a cheeseburger with fries, each of some 170g in weight, would supply about 52g fat (of which 16g are saturated), 31g of protein, and a total of 1025 kcal (35% of the daily recommended total for adult males and 47% for women). By contrast, a 340g meal of caribou meat would supply 15g of fat (of which 5.8g are saturated), 101g of protein, and 568 kcal. Clearly, a plate of caribou steak is the healthy Innu option!

Colin Samson and Jules Pretty

INCREASING ANTIOXIDANTS IN CROPS – HEALTHIER FOODS

An increasing body of evidence indicates that antioxidants in fruit and vegetables are crucially important for human health. Ascorbic acid (vitamin C),α-tocopherol (vitamin E), carotenes (precursors of vitamin A) and a range of phenolic compounds are common antioxidant constituents of green vegetables, which when taken in the diet can potentially reduce levels of oxidative damage to human cells and consequently assist in the prevention cancers and heart disease.

Concerns are growing because there is evidence that levels of these compounds are becoming lower than optimal for human health requirements in many food crops grown using conventional agricultural and horticultural practices. Although levels of vitamins and phenolics in vegetables can be increased by genetic manipulation, the widespread consumption of genetically-engineered crops, even after commercial consents are granted for cultivation in the European Union, is likely to be limited by public attitudes towards these foods. Fortunately, alternative methods for improving the vitamin and phenolic content of vegetables offer considerable promise for dietary improvements.

It is well established from a range of studies over many years that levels of ascorbic acid, α-tocopherol, carotenes and phenolics in leaves can all increase dramatically when plants are exposed to environmental stress. For example, water stress has been shown to increase ascorbate and α-tocopherol levels by up to 5- and 20-fold, respectively. Also, different agronomic practices have been found to modify the levels of vitamins and phenolics in crops. Crops grown with organic and sustainable agricultural practices have been found to have considerably elevated ascorbic acid and phenolic contents. Consequently, there is considerable potential for improvement in the food quality of vegetables by manipulating the crop environment and horticultural practice.

A particularly attractive approach to producing vegetables with improved antioxidant contents is to use water stress to induce additional synthesis of vitamins and phenolics. Plant response to water deficiency involves a host of complex processes. However, two well-described main responses are reductions in leaf growth and photosynthetic rate. In many crop species the reduction in photosynthetic rate with mild water deficits is commonly due to reductions in CO_2 supply into the leaf because of reduced stomatal aperture.

In high light the loss of photosynthetic activity can result in excess absorbed light and lead to photoreduction of oxygen with ensuing generation of reactive oxygen species. It is now well established that leaves respond to the onset of such potential photo-oxidative stresses by inducing synthesis of antioxidants, such as ascorbic acid, α-tocopherol, carotenes and phenolics, which will protect the leaf from oxidative damage. Consequently, growing plants under water stress conditions can increase the contents of vitamins and phenolics in the leaves.

From a food production standpoint the losses in crop yield resulting from severe water stresses will more than offset the gain in food quality. However, when exposed to mild water stresses plants can perceive the change in soil water status and modify their metabolism to increase the levels of vitamins and phenolics, presumably to deal with the possibility of the stress becoming increasingly severe in the future. Such metabolic changes in response to mild water stress can occur prior to decreases in photosynthetic productivity and growth, which are associated with greater water stress.

Consequently, it should be possible, with the careful modification of the watering regimes used in crop cultivation practices, to improve the antioxidant content of leaf vegetables without a significant loss of crop productivity. This is an important future goal for plant scientists and the food industry.

Neil Baker and Phil Mullineaux

VITAMIN E AND NERVES OF STEEL

A ntioxidant supplements are big business today. Hardly a week goes by without another claim being made about their 'supposed' benefits to health. This is especially true of vitamin E. Away from the anti-wrinkle skin cream adverts and the glossy magazines, are there *really* any genuine, clinically proven medical applications for Vitamin E? Fortunately, there are and they are to be found in the treatment of a handful of relatively unknown (and in some cases, hereditary) defects of fat absorption and transport. Left untreated, this group of diseases leads to a very specific form of neurodegeneration, unmasking the essential function of the antioxidant within the nervous system and giving tantalising clues to the origins of other illnesses.

Vitamin E (specifically, α-tocopherol) is a small, fat-soluble molecule carried in the blood by lipoproteins, from where it is delivered to all other tissues. It is the major antioxidant that protects cell membranes from oxidative deterioration. Chronic vitamin E deficiency, in which the α-tocopherol level in the blood remains either very low or undetectable, is exceptionally rare and is associated with a characteristic, progressive neurological syndrome. A form of ataxia (meaning 'inco-ordination') develops, with disturbances in gait, sensory loss in the limbs, muscle weakness, degeneration of peripheral nerves, the spinal chord and brain stem.

Severe vitamin E deficiency is only ever seen secondary to other illnesses associated with the abnormal uptake of dietary fats or their transport within the blood (abetalipoproteinaemia), an inability to solubilize fats (cholestatic liver disease), and in conditions that result in inflammatory obstruction of the gut (Crohn's disease, cystic fibrosis and in premature, very low birth weight babies that develop enterocolitis).

Additionally, a very rare hereditary 'ataxia with vitamin E deficiency' (AVED) can occur due to the presence of a defective α-tocopherol transfer protein in the liver, which is essential for maintaining the circulating vitamin E levels within the normal range. The spectrum of symptoms characteristic of a vitamin E deficiency usually appear in the first few months or years of life in cholestatic liver disease but take at least ten years to develop in abetalipoproteinaemia and AVED and up to two decades in Crohn's disease and so both the mature and developing nervous systems are at risk from hypovitaminosis E. The ataxia originating from the vitamin E deficiency attributable to these illnesses is treatable with high dose oral tocopherol supplements in various forms. In the special case of cholestasis, a water-soluble form of ∝-tocopherol is used that bypasses the need for the bile salts. If the supplements are started at a very early age, development of neurological abnormalities is preventable and in older patients, they can stop further deterioration.

Understanding the effects of a vitamin E deficiency upon the nervous system has proved important for another reason. The neurological problems that develop in AVED bear an uncanny resemblance to those seen in a major inherited neurodegenerative illness. Friedreich's ataxia (FRDA) is the most common of the hereditary ataxias, affecting 1 in 50,000 people and with a carrier rate of 1 in 120 in European populations. In fact, it wasn't until the genes for the two ataxias were found to be on separate chromosomes (8 and 9, respectively) that it was realised that AVED was a distinct disease entity in its own right at the genetic level. Previously, AVED cases were diagnosed as FRDA. But there are subtle differences between them. In the case of FRDA, plasma levels of vitamin E are usually normal whereas in AVED they are very low. AVED is treatable with vitamin E whereas FRDA is not.

FRDA is almost always fatal. Patients often have additional symptoms (a cardiomyopathy and diabetes or glucose intolerance) that do not appear in AVED. But somewhere in the disease mechanism, ∝-tocopherol and/or lipid peroxidation had to be central to both illnesses. This issue was resolved when it was discovered that the chromosome 9 gene codes for 'frataxin' (the *Fr*iedreich's *atax*ia prote*in*), a regulator of iron import into mitochondria. Mutated frataxin leads to mitochondrial iron overload and it had long been known that vitamin E inhibits iron-induced lipid peroxidation.

On the one hand, in AVED patients, nerve mitochondria do not get a supply of the antioxidant (because it is not put into general circulation) but their mitochondrial iron is bound up in a harmless form. Conversely, in FRDA patients, the vitamin E supply is normal but large quantities of iron are loose in a dangerous, catalytic form that overwhelms the antioxidant protection. Either way, the outcome is more or less the same and mitochondria become poisoned by relentless oxidative stress. Why are nerves and muscles in AVED and additionally the heart and the pancreatic islets in FRDA affected, but nowhere else to the same extent? All of these tissues are highly-metabolic with a continuously heavy energy demand.

When their mitochondrial ATP output begins to decline, then so will they. But why should heart failure and diabetes be additional symptoms seen in FRDA but not AVED patients? One likely explanation is that because the mitochondrial oxidative stress burden is far greater in FRDA than in AVED, the threshold for mitochondrial decline is far lower and so other highly metabolic tissues also become susceptible.

The link between the two illnesses and vitamin E has given some hope of treatments for FRDA. From the oxidative stress perspective, two therapeutic targets have been identified. The first is to tackle the mitochondrial iron overload by searching for a suitable 'chelator' compound that can safely bind and inactivate the redox-active iron. The second involves trying to limit the runaway lipid peroxidation in mitochondrial membranes by administering small, fat-soluble antioxidants with vastly improved vitamin E-like properties.

One such compound, idebenone, has already shown promise by reducing the extent of damage to heart muscle in FRDA patients and further international clinical trials are currently underway. The hope is that if it could be started early enough in young patients, then a combination of chelation and antioxidant therapy might be able to at least slow the degenerative symptoms of FRDA. Vitamin E is definitely a lot more than just a fashionable health supplement.

Mike Fryer

WHY DO WE NEED SELENIUM IN OUR DIETS?

I n 1817, the Swedish chemist Jons Berzelius isolated a new, pale yellowish-white element. He named it 'selenium', after Selênê, the Greek goddess of the moon, because its colour reminded him of moonlight. For more than a century afterwards, the element was condemned to be little more than just a curiosity by biologists and chemists alike, but all of this was to change in the mid-1930s when a selenium deficiency was found to be responsible for a number of serious infertility, heart and muscle-wasting syndromes of livestock. After a great deal of searching, two decades later it was identified as the essential dietary component present in Torula yeast extracts that could prevent liver necrosis in rats.

But it was only as recently as 1973 that the importance of selenium to human health finally took off with the discovery that the glutathione peroxidases (GPXs), a family of antioxidant enzymes, were actually selenoproteins. We now know that selenocysteine is the 21st amino acid, has its own transfer-RNA molecule and is incorporated into some 35 or so selenoproteins. They are by no means all antioxidant enzymes and many of their functions are still largely shrouded in mystery.

A selenium deficiency is bad for the heart. In regions of China where crops and animals are raised on selenium-poor soils, a low dietary intake of this micronutrient plays a role in the development of both an endemic form of heart failure affecting mainly young people (Keshan disease) as well as a type of arthritis (Kashin-Beck syndrome) and in the West, patients who receive their sustenance solely from nutritional fluid (total parenteral nutrition) because they cannot digest or absorb solid food, develop an almost identical degenerative heart condition that can be traced to insufficient selenium intake. All of these conditions are selenium-responsive. In the immune system, selenium has important stimulatory properties and up-regulates cytokine signalling molecules such as interleukin-2, as well as clonal expansion, lymphocyte development to cytotoxic T cells and their ability to destroy tumours.

Time and again, epidemiological studies undertaken over the last two and a half decades have shown that good selenium status is correlated with a reduced risk of cancer. The anticarcinogenic properties of selenium are not just attributable to immunostimulation alone, but also to compounds such as methyl selenol, which interfere with tumour cell metabolism, starve cancerous cells of their blood supply and induce transformed cells to undergo apoptosis.

Over the last decade, selenium has been found to exert a subtle yet major influence upon host-virus interactions. Selenium deficiency is a driving force for viral mutations and a co-factor in emerging infectious diseases. Coxsackievirus infection is partly-responsible for Keshan disease. How could this normally harmless virus, which infects 20 million Americans annually and causes nothing more than minor cold symptoms, have been transformed by a selenium deficiency into a lethal, fast-reproducing form that attacks heart muscle in Chinese children? It was found that during selenium deficiency, the GPX activity of someone simultaneously harbouring a benign form of coxsackievirus was not strong enough to protect the viral genome from mutating into a much more aggressive form. Worse still, the lethally-mutated virus could easily infect another person who was eating a selenium-replete diet.

In theory, it takes only one selenium-deficient person or animal to produce a new family of virus mutants. The implications are enormous. If it is true of coxsackieviruses, which are common-or-garden RNA viruses, it might just as easily apply to many other RNA viruses such as influenza and help to explain the flu pandemics that have swept across the world several times over the past century and were responsible for the death of millions. Birds are the normal reservoir of infection for influenza virus and new strains originate in ducks and chickens which are intensively farmed on a large scale in China and South East Asia and it may be no coincidence that the soils here are poor in selenium. The virus makes a trans-species jump from birds via pigs to humans and in the process, its virulence is massively enhanced. In 2001, it was proven that a selenium deficiency in mice infected with the mild 'Bangkok' strain of influenza not only impaired their immunity but more worryingly, changed the pathogenicity of the virus into a much more dangerous form.

Perhaps just as disturbing is the fact that in the viral 'hot zone' in Zaire where HIV first crossed-over to humans and new outbreaks of Ebola regularly emerge, the soils contain little selenium and deficiency is very widespread both in the population and in the wildlife and domestic animals that live there (Ebola's natural reservoir of infection may be bats). Viruses such as HIV usurp the host's selenium supply to their own ends by diverting the micronutrient to viral selenoproteins instead of host proteins. The loss of CD4-T cells in HIV infection very closely mirrors a steady reduction in plasma selenium concentration, even in the very early stages when it cannot have arisen from malnutrition or malabsorption alone. When all of the selenium supply within the infected host cell has been used up, the virus reproduces and infects other nearby cells to satisfy its need for more of the micronutrient. As an HIV patient's selenium is progressively hijacked by the virus, general immunity finally collapses, leading to life-threatening, secondary opportunistic infections. Selenium supplementation 'buys time' in AIDS patients firstly by boosting immunity but mainly because the virus gains a constant supply of selenium, allowing it to establish a more stable, slow-replicating, low level infection. Ebola kills 75% of the people it infects within three weeks. Part of the speed and lethality of this virus may be because it, too, possesses genes dependent upon selenium, the difference being that the requirement for a selenium supply is ten times greater than that of HIV. Consequently, if the selenium levels in an Ebola-infected cell are low, the virus exhausts the supply more rapidly. It must replicate fast in order to escape the dying cell and quickly procure another selenium source, propagating infection that spreads from cell to cell throughout the body and causing massive tissue hemorrhaging in the process.

In terms of general health, selenium deficiency contributes to cardiovascular disease. Lowered antioxidant and anti-inflammatory GPX activity predisposes to the formation of plaques which can furr-up arteries because low density lipoproteins are more prone to oxidation, platelet cells aggregate and stick to blood vessel walls which, in turn, are stimulated to produce vasoconstrictive compounds. The kidney contains the highest levels of selenium in the body and is the major site of synthesis of (extracellular) plasma GPX which helps to maintain the antioxidant capacity of the blood. This declines during the course of renal failure and is partly responsible for the fact that haemodialysis patients suffer an incidence of atherosclerosis several orders of magnitude greater than the general population as well as more infections.

The rate of neurotransmitter secretion within the brain is influenced by selenium, which is known to affect mood and depression. GPX is the main peroxide-removing enzyme of brain tissue, which contains little catalase. Consequently, many forms of dementia that are thought to involve oxidative stress in their pathologies (such as Alzheimer's disease), may be accelerated by a lack of selenium. In human reproduction, certain forms of recurrent miscarriage as well as male infertility have been linked to a selenium deficiency. The nutrient is required for testosterone synthesis and the GPX which protects developing sperm from oxidative damage is later polymerised into a major structural component of the mid-piece, without which mature sperm are unable to swim normally and males become sterile. Over the last decade, clinical trials have also shown selenium administration to be a strikingly effective treatment in necrotising pancreatitis (a free radical-mediated disease) with remarkable reductions in mortality down from 89% to zero, as well as some potential to slow age-related macular degeneration.

Meat, fish, eggs and grain are all good sources of selenium in a balanced diet. Kidney and brazil nuts are especially rich. However, low protein foods such as fruit and vegetables contain far less. Levels of selenium in the food supply depend on where it was grown and so European intakes fall well below those in the USA, where the soils contain more selenium. Since the importation of North American and Canadian wheat (which used to be a substantial source of our dietary selenium as bread and cereals) was discontinued, our intake (29-39 mg/day based on 1997 MAFF data) and status has markedly declined and now falls far short of the UK Reference Nutrient Intake (the level required to maximise GPX activity in the plasma) of 75 mg/day for men and 60 mg/day for women. This downward trend has been present in British diets for the last quarter of a century. Many dietary supplementation trials (using high selenium yeast extracts, which contain readily bioavailable selenomethionine) are currently underway to investigate the impact of correction of this dietary short-fall.

Mike Fryer

 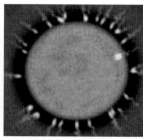 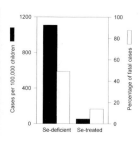

Left: Selenium deficiency leads to mutations in the flu virus genome that increase its virulence and may contribute to new pandemics. (*electron micrograph reproduced courtesy of Linda M. Stannard, University of Cape Town*). **Middle:** Selenium deficiency is responsible for certain types of miscarriage and leads to sterility in males as sperm become immotile. The sperm GPX is a truly remarkable protein. It changes its character completely from being a soluble antioxidant enzyme that protects the developing sperm in the early stages to an insoluble polymer that forms a structural component essential for swimming in mature sperm. **Right:** Dramatic reduction in the incidence of Keshan disease following daily oral treatment of children with sodium selenite between the years 1974-1977.

HUMAN IMMUNONUTRITION AND THE SEARCH FOR AN IMMUNOTHERAPEUTIC DIET

Since ancient times it has been known that opportunistic infections occur more frequently in malnourished people. In developing countries reduced resistance to infections increases the rate of infant mortality and morbidity. It is also known that malnourished hospital patients are prone to infections due to the suppression of the immune system – often a secondary effect of illness. More extreme examples of the effect of poor nutrition on the immune system occur in anorexia nervosa, in hunger strikers, during prolonged starvation, in severe self-imposed dieting, and in acute illnesses such as cancer and AIDS.

Thus there is a direct relationship between immune function and the nutritional status of a person. Immunity is defined as the ability of an individual to combat environmental pathogens. Immunological processes are also involved in the fight against cancer. The "immunosurveillance theory" postulates that neoplasias (cancers) occur throughout life and are kept at bay by the immune system. The paradox is that, although a vigorous immune system is essential for good health, if it is too reactive, or normal controls break down, then autoimmunity, immune reactivity to "self", can be the undesirable result. The immune system is active throughout life but declines with age: ageing consequently brings an increase in autoimmune diseases, malignancies and opportunistic infections.

Nutrition is essential to build up a good immune system. It contributes to haematopoiesis (the process whereby the blood cells are formed from the bone marrow) and the formation of the tissues of the immune system. The immune system contains millions of cells with specific functions including the release of small molecular weight proteins such as cytokines. The synthesis of antibody molecules (the most powerful weapons of the immune system) requires the assembly of a high molecular weight protein that is expressed both attached to the lymphocyte membrane (on the principal cells responsible for immune responses) and released into the bloodstream as soluble proteins.

In recent years immunonutrition has emerged as a new branch of medicine. It is particularly important at the two ends of the lifespan – fetal life, infancy and childhood (Paediatric immunonutrition) and in old age (Geriatric immunonutrition). With the advent of 'molecular targeting' therapies it is now possible to use the immune system as a 'therapeutic tool box' throughout life. Examples exist in the treatment of a variety of illnesses, and also in preventative medicine for the maintenance of the person's well being in the absence of disease. The advantage of a well though-out immunnutrition programme is two-fold (a) there are no side effects and (b) it is a form of self-medication without a drug prescription and its side effects.

The new frontier and futures of immunonutrition lie in the application of selective and combinatorial micronutrients. These include vitamins, minerals, and related cofactors. Examples of micronutrients with known effects on the immune system include vitamins A, B, E, and C, minerals (selenium, copper, chromium, iron and zinc), and amino-acids such as arginine and glutamine. Recently, it has been shown that ingestion of these micronutrients from natural sources rather in the form of tablets increases gastrointestinal absorption, arguing against the consumption of vitamins in the form of tablets. Evidence is also accumulating on the usefulness of phytonutrients (herb-derived substances) that boost the immune system. There is also anecdotal and scientific evidence that omega-3 fatty acids and their derivatives (all found in fish oils) enhance immunity as well as protecting the heart and acting as anti-inflammatory agents.

Research in the area of micronutrient immunonutrition is still in its infancy. Only few properly designed randomised, placebo-controlled double-blind studies have been performed and in most cases the mechanisms underlying the effects of immuno-nutrients are still not understood.

Maintaining the correct balance of micronutrient and calorie intake must be the goal of a good 'immunotherapeutic diet' and this can be 'tailor-made' to an individual person. Recent data using animal models, including non-human primates, have shown that a low-calorie diet (without starvation) appears to benefit the immune system and to increase longevity. A well balanced diet without excess calories (and, of course, a sensible amount of exercise).....surely the simplest of prescriptions for a healthy immune system and a healthy life.

Nelson Fernandez

INDUSTRIALISED AGRICULTURE AND FOOD-BORNE ILLNESSES

Having mostly conquered hunger in industrialised countries, it is a sad irony that food is now a major source of ill-health. We eat too much, we eat the wrong mix of foods, and we still get ill from food-borne illnesses. The World Health Organisation estimates that 130 million people in Europe are affected by food-borne diseases each year, with up to 90% of cases being caused by *Salmonella*, and most of the others by *Campylobacter*, *Yersinia*, *Listeria* or *E.coli*. In the USA, the incidence of food-borne illness is greater, perhaps because of the greater industrialisation of agriculture and, in particular, of livestock raising. According to the Centers for Disease Control, 76 million people in the USA fall ill each year from food-borne illness, more than 300,000 are hospitalised and 5000 die.

The costs of food-borne illnesses are massive. In the USA, they are between $3 and $10 billion per year. In the UK, the government's Food Standards Agency estimates that the average cost to the health service and to businesses of each of the 5 million cases of food poisoning per year amounts to about £85, or an annual total of more than £400 million. These data suggest that one in four Americans and one in ten Britons suffer from food poisoning each year.

Some of these food-borne illnesses arise from contaminated shellfish and others are associated with mass catering or originate in the food processing chain. However, the increasing frequency of infections that can be attributed to farming practices, particularly the overuse of antibiotics for growth promotion, is a particular cause for concern. The concentration of livestock into factory feedlots, broiler sheds and colossal pig units favours the spread of infection. The pool of infection at the start of the food chain is now very serious. The USDA has found very high levels of microbial infections in US farm animals. For example, *Clostridium* has been found in 30-40% of broiler chickens and turkeys, *Campylobacter* in nearly 90%, *Salmonella* in 20-30%, and *Staphylococcus* in 65%. The incidence of infection in pigs and cattle is much lower, but still constitutes a significant risk, with over 30% of pigs being contaminated with *Campylobacter* (Table 1). These levels of infection are more than matched in some European countries, with over 90% of pigs and nearly 50% of cattle in the Netherlands and Denmark contaminated with *Campylobacter*. With these levels of infection in animals, it is hardly surprising that the incidence of food-borne illness arising from meat consumption is so high.

Table 1. Incidence of microbial infection in farm animals, USA

	Proportion of individuals with infectious bacteria			
	Broiler chickens	Turkeys	Pigs	Cattle
Clostridium	43%	29%	10%	8%
Campylobacter	88%	90%	32%	1%
Salmonella	29%	19%	8%	3%
Staphylococcus	65%	65%	16%	8%

This extraordinary problem is worsened by antibiotic resistance brought on by the overuse of antibiotics for livestock growth promotion and in veterinary practice. Some 23,000 tonnes of antibiotics are used in the USA each year, with 11,000 tonnes being administered to animals of which 80% is for growth promotion. In the UK, 1200 tonnes of antibiotics are used each year, 40% of which is for humans, 30% for farm animals, and 30% for domestic pets and horses.

Only 20% of the antibiotics and other antimicrobials used in modern agriculture is to treat clinical diseases, with the remaining 80% being used prophylactically and to promote growth. The Centers for Disease Control says, *"antimicrobial resistance is a serious clinical and public health problem in the US"*, and one estimate from the Institute of Medicine suggests that such resistance costs $30 million per year. A UK House of Lords select committee enquiry was even more alarmed, recently stating, *"there is a continuing threat to human health from the imprudent use of antibiotics in animals…we may face the dire prospect of revisiting the pre-antibiotic era"*.

In both Europe and North America, the most common forms of antimicrobial resistance are to strains of antibiotics used in treating animals. Some antibiotics, such as fluoroquinones and avoparcin, used to treat infections and as growth promoters in poultry, are now associated with dramatic increases in resistant diseases in humans. As the World Health Organisation puts it, *"Campylobacter species are now the commonest cause of bacterial gasteroenteritis in developed countries, and cases are predominantly associated with consumption of poultry"*. Given the soaring costs associated with such infections, it is increasingly clear that there is no such thing as a cheap chicken.

Jules Pretty

DIETARY IRON – ABSORPTION, BIOAVAILABILITY AND SUPPLEMENTATION

I ron has evolved to be the major trace metal in the majority of life forms. A 70 kg adult has around 4.5 g of bodily iron, with some 65% associated with the oxygen transport protein haemoglobin that is found in red blood cells. Indeed it is interactions with oxygen that are central to the roles of many iron-containing biomolecules, with a further example being the enzyme cytochrome c oxidase, which converts oxygen to water and underpins energy conversion from dietary carbohydrates. These interactions of iron with oxygen and also other functions adopted by the metal in biological systems are in turn dependent on properties that include its redox chemistry. Iron commonly exists in two oxidation states: ferrous (or Fe^{2+}) and ferric (or Fe^{3+}). These states are interconvertible, but the ease with which this may be achieved is dependent upon what other molecules, known as ligands, are bound to the iron. In haemoglobin, cytochrome c oxidase and many other iron containing proteins and enzymes, one of the ligands to the metal is a porphyrin ring, and the resultant compound (also known as a biocomplex or cofactor) is called haem iron.

The human body has an efficient mechanism for the uptake of haem iron from foodstuffs, with a specific pathway existing for its transport across the epithethial cells that form the lining of the gastrointestinal tract. The haem iron found in red meat is therefore said to be highly bioavailable, in that the iron that is present may be readily extracted by the body to meet the normal daily demand for 2-5 mg. Other foodstuffs such as green vegetables contain iron, but at much decreased levels. Furthermore the iron is in a non-haem form, for which bioavailabilty is low and variable with dependence upon the nature of further dietary components. Concerns surrounding the adverse effects of saturated fats in the diet combined with both the recent CJD epidemic and increasing moral objection to animal farming practices have led to a decline in the consumption of beef and lamb in the UK and a trend for vegetarianism. In turn this has caused an upturn in the incidence amongst the population of iron-deficiency anaemia, a condition that is characterised by impaired resistance to infection and reduced physical capacity and cognitive function.

As iron is an essential nutrient, it must be transported and stored safely in the body, and these tasks are performed by the proteins transferrin and ferritin respectively. Transferrin binds iron that has been delivered into the serum from foodstuffs and carries it to cells involved in for example the biosynthesis of haemoglobin, whilst ferritin and its breakdown product haemosiderin hold reserves of the metal equivalent to 25% of the total in the body. In times of iron depletion, most probably resulting from a insufficient dietary supply or blood loss, a complicated series of regulatory mechanisms are triggered which influence the levels of proteins involved in iron metabolism. For instance, the synthesis of ferritin becomes down-regulated, resulting in a lesser storage capacity for iron. Amongst the proteins for which synthesis is up-regulated is DCT-1, which mediates the active transport of ferrous iron and other dipositively-charged cations (including those of copper and zinc) across the gastrointestinal epithelial cells, and so facilitates the absorption of non-haem forms of the metal from foodstuffs.

However, the majority of non-haem iron in the diet is in the ferric state, and must be reduced to the ferrous state prior to uptake. Reduction of ferric iron is performed by the enzyme Dcytb, the synthesis of which is also up-regulated when bodily iron is at a low level. The bioavailabilty of non-haem iron is determined by the limitations of Dcytb, which interacts quite efficiently with small ferric iron clusters, but will not reduce the ferric iron present in large clusters. It is clearly evident therefore that a quite strictly balanced diet is needed to permit the absorption of non-haem iron at a sufficient level.

Supplementation of the diet with ferrous iron salts is commonly recommended in cases of iron deficiency anaemia. However, side effects of this treatment include intestinal damage resulting from the induction of free-radical formation by ferrous iron. Accidental overdoses, particularly amongst children, may result in death. Around 15 years ago researchers at the University of Essex developed the compound ferric trimaltol as an alternative vehicle to provide iron for dietary supplementation. At present this is still the only ferric compound that has been consistently shown in human studies to deliver iron to the body at an equivalent level to ferrous salts, and its efficacy is derived from the ability of the maltol ligand to retain the ferric iron in a non-polymerised and soluble form that is very easily reduced by Dcytb. When designing the drug, it was taken into account that maltol itself is a natural product of extremely low toxicity that is used in many types of food as a flavour and aroma enhancer. However, and quite surprisingly, ferric trimaltol has failed the Ames test for mutagenicity, and this has halted its progress onto the market. Current work is aimed at developing safer yet still effective alternatives by slight modifications of the maltol structure.

Paul Dobbin

GM CROPS AND HEALTH

Biotechnology involves making molecular changes to living or almost-living things. It has a long history, dating back four thousand years to the development of fermentation, bread-making, brewing and cheese making by Egyptians and Sumerians, and later of grafting techniques by the Greeks. Modern biotechnology (also known as genetic modification or engineering) is, by contrast, the name given to the transfer of DNA (usually chromosomal) from one organism to another, so allowing the recipient to express traits or characteristics normally associated just with the donor. As these transfers or mixes do not occur in nature, the scope for genetic modification is greater than in conventional animal or plant breeding - even though advanced breeding already involves types of genetic manipulation, including clonal propagation, embryo transfer, embryo rescue and mutant selection.

The expansion in the development and commercial cultivation of a few types of genetically-modified (GM) crops has been rapid in recent years. Yet many people are concerned about the potential direct and indirect environmental and health risks. Agricultural genetically-modified organisms (GMOs) pose two risks for human health. The degree to which each of these potential risks is "real" is a combination of both the existence of a hazard and exposure to that hazard; thus not all hazards constitute a risk in practice.

Arguably the most significant risk to human health relates to possible allergic responses to novel compounds, usually proteins, produced by GMOs. Conventional non-GM foods already contain a large number of toxic and potentially-toxic products, and so the key question is whether a specific GMO could constitute a new hazard. Approximately 90% of food allergies occur in response to proteins found in just eight foods (peanuts, tree nuts, milk, egg, soyabean, shellfish, fish and wheat., It could therefore be argued that as GM involves transfer of a single or few genes, it should be easy to predict, or to test for the production of new allergens. For example, one GMO, soya containing a transferred brazil nut gene, has been withdrawn from development because of potential allergenic effects.

The greatest controversy regarding allergenicity has surrounded the case of GM potatoes containing a lectin transgene. Immune response effects have been claimed in experiments on rats, but the research has been widely criticised. Anyway, even if the research had conclusively shown an effect, then this would be a problem only for this particular gene and its product. Equally, though, the absence of an effect in one case does not mean that all GMOs are safe. For example, other potential problems might arise in potatoes with modified biochemical pathways that could inadvertently lead to increased levels of toxic or allergenic glycoalkaloids. It is also important to distinguish between consumption of food products potentially containing GM DNA or proteins, and purified food products that are identical to those from conventional crops, such as refined sugar. The latter are unlikely to represent a risk unless they are contaminated.

The second health risk to humans relates not to the manipulated genes themselves, but to "marker" genes that play an important role in the technique of GMO production. Production of the first generation of GMOs used antibiotic or herbicide marker genes to allow easy selection of successfully transformed cells. In theory, antibiotic-resistant marker genes from a GMO could be incorporated into bacteria in the guts of humans and livestock, so rendering them also resistant to the antibiotic. Although this has not yet been demonstrated empirically, antibiotic resistance is still a major cause for concern.

Antibiotics and other antimicrobials are used in agriculture for therapeutic treatment of clinical diseases (20%), and prophylactic use and growth promotion (80% of total). Concern is growing that overuse of antibiotics may render some human drugs ineffective and/or make some strains of bacteria untreatable. The World Health Organisation has documented direct evidence that antimicrobial use in farm livestock (as well as in hospitals) has resulted in the emergence of antibiotic resistant *Salmonella, Campylobacter,* Enterococci, and *E. coli* types.

Alternatives to antibiotic markers now exist, and many believe that antibiotics should not be used to produce commercial GMOs. The Royal Society has said: `It is no longer acceptable to have antibiotic resistance genes present in a new GM crop'. Nonetheless, it is still not clear whether antibiotic marker genes add significantly to the risk of resistance emerging from exposure to antibiotics used elsewhere in the food chain.

Jules Pretty

WEIGHT LOSS DIETS

Dieting is something of a national obsession and diet books, products and plans are big business, with an annual turnover estimated at £335 million in the UK and over \$40 billion in the USA. Despite this frenetic dieting (or at least, spending) activity, it is predicted that 1 in 4 adults in the UK will be obese by 2010. Clearly reading diet books and buying diet products does not result in effective weight control. The simple truth is that weight can only be lost if "energy out" is greater than "energy in". Exercise is the only bit of the "energy out" side of this equation that we can easily manipulate, so exercising more is an important factor in weight control.

The contribution of exercise to body weight regulation has been discussed elsewhere in this volume. On the other hand "energy in" is the target of weight loss diets and in recent years the "New Diet Revolution" of Dr Robert Atkins has been the bible for celebrity dieters and the other ten million or so that have bought his book. This diet has provoked considerable scepticism amongst dietitians and nutritionists because it contradicts the conventional wisdom that the best way to lose weight is to minimize fat intake. Cutting out fat makes intuitive sense because, weight for weight, fat contains at least twice as many calories as carbohydrate or protein and it is stored fat in your body that makes you overweight. Nevertheless there is convincing evidence from a few reliable scientific studies that this heretical diet really does work; at least in the short term.

The Atkins diet involves minimizing carbohydrate intake and consuming foods that are rich in protein and fat. This has a certain popular appeal because fatty food tends to be tasty and a diet of chocolate and steak seems more attractive than one of pasta, rice and vegetables. The Atkins diet seems to work because "rich" food is high in calories and satisfies the appetite so effectively that, paradoxically, fewer total calories are consumed. Reassuringly, in studies lasting several months the Atkins diet does not seem to produce the high LDL cholesterol levels that are normally associated with high fat consumption and that are linked to an increased risk of heart disease, so at least in that sense it may not be "unhealthy".

However, the diet is also low in certain vitamins (particularly vitamin C) and fibre. A multivitamin and mineral supplement can compensate for the low intake of these nutrients. An inadequate intake of vitamins and minerals can otherwise lead to impaired immune system function, susceptibility to infection, and a variety of "deficiency diseases". The lack of fibre can also have health consequences that are far more serious than the inconvenience and discomfort of constipation. In the long term a low fibre diet is also associated with an increased risk of developing varicose veins (including haemorrhoids), heart disease, type II diabetes and certain cancers.

A diet containing minimal carbohydrate depletes our reserves of glycogen; the stored carbohydrate that we use to produce energy during hard exercise such as running. On a normal mixed diet our bodies contain about a kilogram of glycogen, mainly in the muscles, and, because of its sponge-like structure, it is stored along with about three kilograms of water. As the glycogen, and associated water, largely disappears in the first few days of following the Atkins diet, a rapid weight loss of about three kilograms (6.5 pounds) is to be expected. Unfortunately, without glycogen we feel physically fatigued and it is difficult to exercise. This is counterproductive in terms of the "energy out" side of the weight maintenance equation and incompatible with training for athletes and those seeking the health benefits of an active lifestyle.

Studies that have compared long term weight loss in traditional calorie restricted diets containing normal amounts of carbohydrate with that achieved on the Atkins diet have found that they are equally effective. On the other hand, many find that the Atkins diet is easier to stick with and certainly the early weight loss is good for motivation; it's nice to see quick results. As well as celebrity dieters, some recreational athletes have successfully slimmed down on the Atkins Diet and as a short term strategy there is no evidence that it will do you any harm, so, if you really must diet, why not give it a try? Just be aware that it will compromise any training that you try to do while on the diet, and that you will probably put a few kilograms back on as soon as you revert to a more normal eating pattern. What's the alternative? Well, Atkins is a bit passé nowadays, and if you want to keep up with the fashionistas then the GI (Glycaemic Index) diet might be just what you're looking for.

The GI diet is much less heretical than Atkins, and really just follows traditional nutritional advice that has been around, but largely ignored, for decades. The glycaemic index is a measure of the extent to which a particular food causes a rise in blood sugar (glucose) levels. In essence, food containing glucose or sucrose (table sugar) has a high GI, whereas food rich in complex carbohydrates such as starch and fibre generally has a low GI The blood glucose surge that high GI foods produce stimulates the release of insulin, a hormone that functions to promote storage of energy after a meal. Under the influence of insulin the glucose is rapidly removed from the blood to top up the glycogen (carbohydrate store) in muscles and liver, and any left over is converted into fat.

Although this sequence of events is perfectly normal, it is exaggerated with high GI foods because of the large fluctuations in blood glucose levels and consequent large fluctuations in insulin release. Frequent surges of insulin can make the body resistant to its actions and this is the cause of type II diabetes; a potentially life shortening condition that has reached epidemic proportions in much of the developed world. High GI foods are usually full of calories, tasty, but unsatisfying because they lack bulk. The rapid removal of glucose from the blood stimulates appetite, so we have a junk food double-whammy of over eating and potential insulin insensitivity.

The basic message of the GI diet is simple. Replace high GI foods with low GI, bulky foods and you will eat fewer calories and maintain stable insulin levels. There are added benefits to this strategy. Low GI foods are generally those that we have always known are "healthy"; for example fresh vegetables, fruits and cereals without added sugar. Their bulkiness means that they satisfy hunger and the fibre that provides this bulk is good for intestinal and cardiovascular health. High fibre diets are associated with lower risk of colonic cancer and heart disease, as mentioned above. These foods also provide vitamins and minerals that are sometimes lacking in the sugar-rich, processed foods that tend to dominate the modern "convenience" diet.

So what's stopping you? Part of the practical problem is knowing which food to put in your shopping trolley as you get in a bit of endurance training round the supermarket shelves. The contribution of the author of the best-selling book "The GI diet", Rick Gallop, who will, no doubt, soon be a new entry on the Filthy Rich list, has been to put foods in three categories, green (eat as much as you like) amber (avoid in the weight loss phase, eat sparingly thereafter) and red (you guess).

Finally, a couple of complications. Some low GI foods are low GI because they are high fat, low carbohydrate. Remind you of Atkins? These are OK in moderation, but most of the diet should be high carbohydrate, low GI And finally, high GI foods, though they should generally be avoided, do have their place in the diet of those who exercise hard and long. Endurance athletes and gym junkies can use them to get a quick energy boost during prolonged exercise sessions and to aid recovery before their next exercise fix by replenishing depleted glycogen reserves. In fact, the ability of exercise to subvert the rules of dieting carries an important message. If you burn off the calories you take in you can eat almost anything and still avoid obesity and ill health. Don't just sit there dieting; go for a run.

Martin Sellens

A SAFE ENVIRONMENT AND THE HUMAN RIGHT TO HEALTH

Every human being is entitled to the enjoyment of the highest attainable standard of health conducive to living a life in dignity. The right to health is not to be understood as a right to be healthy – that would be absurd. Rather, the right should be seen to include certain freedoms, such as the right to be free from forced sterilisation and discrimination, and certain entitlements, such as the right to health protection.

The right to health is not confined to health care – it also encompasses adequate sanitation, safe working conditions and a healthy environment. Today, over 100 national constitutions include the right to health, the right to healthcare, or health-related rights, such as the right to a healthy environment. While numerous international treaties recognise the right to health, one specifically recognises the right to a healthy environment.

Quite apart from the right to health and the right to a healthy environment, there are many other linkages between human rights and environmental protection. The right to information includes environmental information. For some years, the United Nations has concerned itself with the dumping of toxic waste which impacts upon the right to life. The right to housing has an environmental dimension. But how does it help to frame an environmental problem as a human rights issue? One advantage is in advocacy and campaigning: if a state dumps toxic waste, it is not only being environmentally irresponsible, it is also violating fundamental human rights.

Another advantage arises from the essence of human rights. At root, human rights are about entitlements from which legal obligations derive and in relation to which monitoring and accountability is required. Human rights subject states to accountability for their acts and omissions. In other words, human rights are a check on the abuse of power. So, if environmental protection is a dimension of a human right, this signals a way of holding states to account for their environmental policies. Of course, it is foolhardy to expect too much from human rights. They certainly do not provide all the answers to complex environmental issues. But they can be one element in a multi-dimensional strategy for enhancing environmental protection.

In 2002, I was appointed the UN Special Rapporteur on the right to health. My job is to try to help states - and others - better promote and protect the right to health. Each year, I report to the UN General Assembly and to the UN Commission on Human Rights. And each year I go on two country missions to consider the right to health in the selected countries. The particular themes I focus on are poverty and the right to health, and discrimination in relation to the right to health. The UN only established the mandate of the Special Rapporteur in 2002. As the first post-holder, I have defined the right to health to include a healthy environment. In my work, I aim to explore this vital environmental dimension of the right to health.

Paul Hunt

NATURE AND HEALTH

How does nature make us feel? Much, of course, will depend on what else is important in our lives. Is it a good day or a bad day? Irrespective of where we come from in the world, it seems that the presence of living things makes us feel good. They help us when we feel stressed, and if there is green vegetation and blue sky, and water in the scene, then we like it even more. This idea that the quality of nature in our home neighbourhood affects our mental health is not a new one, but it has not greatly affected the planning of our urban and rural environments, nor of public health priorities.

Since the advent of the industrial revolution, an increasing number of people have found themselves living in wholly urban settings. Indeed, within the next decade, the number of people in urban areas will exceed those in rural contexts for the first time in human history. In 1960, the world population was some three billion; by 2010 there will be more than three billion people dwelling in urban settlements. Some of this will be by choice – some offer the best opportunities for employment. There are more services concentrated together, with better access to schools, hospitals and sports clubs. But one thing is quite clear: an urban setting by definition has less nature than a rural one. And less green nature means reduced mental well-being – or at least less opportunity to recover from any mental stresses. This is unfortunate. As our green environments have increasingly come under pressure from development, so it seems we ourselves have suffered more. Is this all a simple coincidence, or should we have a rethink?

Today, stress and mental ill-health are becoming more common and the costs are high. The World Health Organisation estimates that depression and depression-related illness will become the greatest sources of ill-health by 2020. This is because many other activities, such as smoking, over-eating and high alcohol consumption, are coping mechanisms for depression, and have their own serious consequences. Stress is now a major problem for people living in modern societies. In the late 1990s, some 24% of men and 29% of women in Britain reported having suffered `a large amount of stress' in the previous 12 months. Such self-reported general health, including stress levels, has been shown to be a strong predictor of mortality, and mental ill-health in Britain costs some £77 billion per year for the provision of care, lost outputs and costs to individuals.

Depression is known to be a risk factor for the outcomes of a range of chronic physical illness, including asthma, arthritis, diabetes, strokes and heart disease. On the other hand, emotional well-being is known to be a strong predictor of physical health. In one study, elderly adults in the USA who scored highest in a survey on emotional health were twice as likely to be alive at the study's end.

In most health care systems, the predominant focus for both treatment and expenditure has come to be on people who have become ill. The same is also true for our environments – we tend only to become concerned when something important is harmed. Yet the best approach, and the cheapest, is to focus efforts upstream and try to create healthy environments in which people can flourish rather than flounder. Thus we should be concerned with not just preventing mental ill-health but with creating positive mental health for all.

It is increasingly well established that the natural and built features of the environment affect behaviour, interpersonal relationships and actual mental states. The environment can, therefore, be therapeutic or harmful. Though there are many reasons for preserving nature, from the value of its economic services to the fundamentals of ethics, relatively little attention has been paid to the potential personal health benefits. What makes people care about nature, and why are so many distressed about its loss? Why does nature still seem to have a positive effect on people, despite the increasing urbanization of modern societies?

We have discerned three levels of engagement with nature, each with incremental benefits as we proceed from one to the next:
- The first is viewing nature, as through a window, or in a book, on television or in a painting.
- The second is being in the presence of usually nearby nature, which is incidental to some other activity, such as walking or cycling to work, reading on a garden seat or talking to friends in a park.
- The third is active participation and involvement with nature, such as gardening or farming, trekking, camping, running, horse-riding, hedge-laying or forestry.

Nature seems to make positive contributions to our health, helps us recover from pre-existing stresses or problems, has an immune effect by protecting us from future stresses, and helps us to concentrate and think more clearly.

Jules Pretty

HEALTH EFFECTS OF AIR POLLUTION

Studies in the USA have shown that those living in less polluted cities live longer than those living in more polluted cities. The human health effects of poor air quality are far reaching, but mainly affect the body's respiratory and cardiovascular systems. Individual reactions to air pollutants depend on the type of pollutant a person is exposed to, the degree of exposure, the individual's health status and genetics. People who exercise outdoors, for example, on hot, smoggy days increase their exposure to pollutants in the air.

The health effects caused by air pollutants may range from subtle biochemical and physiological changes to difficulty breathing, wheezing, coughing and aggravation of existing respiratory and cardiac conditions. There are a variety of effects ranging from increased medication use, through to premature death.

Pollutant	Effect
SO_2	Coughing, tightening of chest, irritation of lung
NO_2	Irritation and inflammation of lungs worsening of symptoms of people with heart and lung conditions, linkage of long-term exposure to coronary heart disease and lung cancer
CO	Prevention of normal transport of oxygen by blood, resulting in the reduction of oxygen supply to the heart
Ozone	Pain on deep breathing, coughing, irritation and inflammation of lungs
Benzene	Cause of cancer

Exposure to chemicals by inhalation can affect our lungs and other organs in the body. The respiratory system is particularly sensitive to air pollutants because much of it is made up of exposed membrane. Lungs are structured to bring large quantities of air (on average, 400 million litres in a lifetime) into intimate contact with the blood system, to facilitate the delivery of oxygen. The inhalation of air pollutants eventually leads to their absorption into the bloodstream and transport to the heart. A wide spectrum of chemical and biological substances may interact directly with the cardiovascular system to cause structural changes, such as degenerative necrosis and inflammatory reactions. Some pollutants may also directly cause functional alterations that affect the rhythmicity and contractility of the heart.

The health effects of air pollution can be seen as a pyramid, with the mildest effects at the bottom, and the least common but most severe at the top. The pyramid demonstrates that as severity decreases the number of people affected increases.

mortality
hospital admissions
visit to A&E
visit doctor
reduced physical performance
medication use
impaired pulmonary function
sub-clinical (subtle) effects

severity of effect

proportion of population affected

Although everyone is at risk from the health effects of air pollution, certain groups are more susceptible. Individual reactions to air contaminants depend on several factors such as the type of pollutant, the degree of exposure and how much of the pollutant is present. The elderly and young people and those with respiratory diseases such as asthma or bronchitis are affected the most.

Particles (those below 10 micron in diameter: PM_{10}) are associated with a range of short-term health effects, including effects on the respiratory and cardiovascular systems, asthma and death. In its 1998 report, COMEAP (an Advisory Committee that provides advice to government departments on all matters concerning the potential toxicity and effects upon health of air pollutants) suggested that in 1996 the early death of 8,100 vulnerable people and 10,500 hospital admissions in the UK were associated with respiratory disease affected by particle air pollution.

In a later report COMEAP suggested that the chronic health effects of particle air pollution were more significant than the acute effects. The report concluded that an estimated 0.2-0.5 million life years across the population might be gained in the UK per 1 $\mu g/m^3$ drop in concentrations of particle air pollution. Monitoring data from across the UK show improvements in air quality. Looking towards 2025, mathematical models predict that most pollutant levels will continue to fall, but targets for NO_2, PM_{10} and ozone may be breached in some areas. Thus, adverse health effects will continue, especially with long term exposure.

Ian Colbeck

ENDOCRINE DISRUPTION BY PESTICIDES: COULD THEY AFFECT HUMAN HEALTH?

The direct effects of pesticides are much easier to establish than indirect effects. If humans or wildlife are harmed or killed, and this can be observed, then it may be possible to establish both an association and causality. Indirect effects tangled up with natural variability are much harder. The effect of DDE (a derivative of DDT) on eggshell thinning was the first recognised case of endocrine disruption in wild populations. This is now a reason to be cautious about some pesticides. The endocrine system is the communication system of glands, hormones and cellular receptors that guide the development, growth, reproduction and behaviour of organisms. Endocrine glands include the pituitary, thyroid, and adrenal glands, the female ovaries and male testes. Thus an endocrine disrupter exerts its effect by mimicking or interfering with the actions of hormones.

Many important hormones, such as oestrogen, progesterone, testosterone and thyroxin, are associated with high-affinity receptor proteins in target cells, and when these hormones come into contact with these receptors, they provoke a series of effects. This high affinity is important, as exogenous chemicals can also bind to these sites, either minimising the effects of the natural hormones or blocking the sites, so preventing proper cell signalling. The chemicals that mimic or block sex steroid hormones are commonly called environmental oestrogens or anti-oestrogens.

Several expert working groups of scientists from Europe and North America now conclude that biologically-active concentrations of endocrine disrupting chemicals are having adverse effects on wildlife reproductive health, and possibly on humans too. Many products have been reported to possess endocrine disrupting capacity, including some natural products (eg coumestrol from clover), pesticides (eg dieldrin, DDT, endosulfan), medical drugs (eg tamoxifen), and commercial and industrial chemicals (eg alkylphenols, phthalates, PCBs, and some metals). Endocrine disrupters can mimic or block natural female sex hormones, mimic or block male sex hormones (androgens or anti-androgens), interfere with sex steroid systems, or disrupt pituitary, thyroid and interregnal hormone systems.

There is stronger causal evidence from laboratory studies, but no more than evidence of associations between the presence of certain chemicals and observed adverse effects in mammals, birds, reptiles, fish and molluscs in the natural environment. Nonetheless, the laboratory studies using realistic exposure levels seem to suggest that such causality will eventually be established. Human health risks that may be associated with exposure are still unknown and therefore controversial. Table 1 contains a list of some products known to have endocrine disrupting effects.

Table 1. Chemicals reported to have reproductive and endocrine disrupting effects

Herbicides	Fungicides	Insecticides	Nematicides	Industrial chemicals
2,4-D	Benomyl	ß-HCH	Aldicarb	Dioxin
2,4,5-T	Hexachlorbenzene	Carbaryl	DBCP	PBBs
Alachlor	Mancozeb	Dieldrin		PCBs
Atrazine	Maneb	DDT,		Pentachlorophenol
Nitrofen	Tributyl tin (TBT)	metabolites		(PCP)
		Endosulfan		Phthalates
		Lindane		Styrenes
		Parathion		

One notorious wildlife case is frogs in the USA. Many amphibian species experienced substantial declines in abundance during the 20th century. Many factors are involved, perhaps most importantly the draining of wetlands and loss of habitats. Lab studies have found a range of subtle effects occurring in amphibians exposed to common herbicides such as atrazine. Male frogs exposed to very low levels of atrazine, the most commonly used herbicide in the USA (27 million kg applied annually), develop symptoms of hermaphroditism and demasculinity. The exposure levels causing these effects were 0.1 to 1.0 µg kg^{-1} (or ppb), whilst the allowable level in drinking water is 3 ppb, and short term exposures of 200 ppb are not considered a risk under current regulations. Concentrations in surface waters in intensively cultivated agricultural regions regularly exceed 200 ppb, and can reach 2300 ppb.

It is now clear that many compounds are endocrine disrupters. There are notable problems from effluents from sewage treatment works and the paper industry, and some agricultural pesticides. There are many confirmed laboratory studies showing causality, though as yet most field studies only show no more than associations.

Jules Pretty

MICROBES ARE ESSENTIAL FOR GOOD HEALTH

Microbes have gained notoriety as agents of food-poisoning, hospital-acquired infections, global epidemics and biological warfare, but it is essential that we temper this perception by acknowledging that our existence in a world devoid of microbes would be very brief. Without microbes we would soon be poisoned and submerged by waste – our own, fallen leaves, paper and so on. Microbes drive the global element cycles, resulting in, for example, fertile soils and oxygen-rich air. A balanced microbiota, in and on our bodies, helps keep pathogens at bay.

Many of our current pharmaceuticals, most notably antibiotics, that cure or ameliorate a wide range of diseases and are the basis of modern medicine, derive from microbes. Microbial enzymes are increasingly being used to make new, more specific and safer drugs; and many polluting and energy-intensive chemical manufacturing processes are being replaced by new environmentally-friendly processes based on microbial enzymes. Similarly, the extraction of metals from metal ores in mining operations is changing from thermal (smelting) to microbially-based processes. Understanding, documenting and sustainable use of microbial diversity is essential for creating a healthier planet.

At the University of Essex, we are investigating the immense diversity and metabolic versatility of microbes with a view to applications in medicine and industry. These studies have taken us to unusual and extreme environments, such as the deep hypersaline anoxic basins (regions more than three km below the sea surface characterized by extreme pressure and salinity and no oxygen), which formed from thousands to millions of years ago, and occur in various areas of the Mediterranean Sea. These 'brine lakes' are so dense that they do not mix with the overlying seawater, and they therefore represent unique, isolated environments, that are expected to yield a rich supply of new diversity, novel activities and products with biotechnological potential. We have already cultivated several hundred microbial strains, many of which belong to new genera or species.

Human health and well-being are affected directly and indirectly by pollution of the environment with, for example, oil, pesticides and heavy metals. Many pollutants are toxic to humans even at low concentrations and many cause cancer. Oil tanker accidents are dramatic examples of pollution incidents that have major impacts on marine life, and fishing and tourism industries. Microbes have evolved an astonishing capacity to degrade, transform and detoxify highly toxic and highly resistant industrial and natural chemicals, and thereby play a pivotal role in the elimination of pollutants from the environment. We are investigating how microbes achieve this; with particular reference to oil-polluted groundwater and marine environments.

Groundwater, which supplies one third of the UK's drinking water, is commonly polluted with the carcinogen, benzene. We have shown that a lack of oxygen, rather than high concentrations of benzene, is primarily responsible for the persistence of benzene in groundwater. Nevertheless, we have evidence that biodegradation takes place under anaerobic conditions, and we are in the process of determining how microbes work together to achieve this.

Figure 1. Survey and sampling devices being lowered more than 3 km below the surface of the Mediterranean Sea into deep anoxic, extremely saline basins. Microbes isolated from these extreme environments are being investigated for their biotechnological potential.

Figure 2. Sampling of groundwater pumped directly from a contaminated aquifer in order to measure concentrations of benzene, characterise the *in-situ* microbial community, and measure rates of benzene degradation.

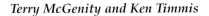

Terry McGenity and Ken Timmis

HUMAN EXPOSURE TO AIR POLLUTION

A irborne pollutants are recognised as a major cause of health problems in Europe. Most adverse health effects come from pollutants in the form of airborne particulate matter or aerosols. However the health risks from these aerosol pollutants are poorly understood. Legislation has been made at various levels to attempt to control the risks but is often based upon available technology i.e. what it is possible to measure conveniently rather than what is most damaging and difficult to implement because of a lack of information on best practice.

Various regulations and guidelines have been published attempting to limit human exposure to potentially harmful particulates (The Air Quality Framework Directive 96/62/EC and World Health Organisation 2000 Air Quality Guidelines for Europe, 2nd edition). These standards are based upon exposure to pollutants measured outdoors. The problem is that in urban environments, most people spend most of their time indoors – at home or at work. This raises two questions:

- How do particulate concentrations from sources outside translate into concentrations inside a building?

- What sources of particulates are there inside a building and what concentrations of these are there in indoor air?

The subsequent questions about exposure, risk and management are being addressed by an EU funded project "URBAN EXPOSURE". The aim of the project is to investigate the toxicological and epidemiological effects of indoor and outdoor pollution in urban environments and to develop and implement integrated modeling tools for calculating exposure through inhalation and through dermal adsorption for compounds relevant to air pollution.

The modeling framework is intended to be modular and very flexible to offer the possibility of evaluating a variety of exposure scenarios. Figure 1 below depicts the environmental framework within which the exposure modeling modules will be built. The final result will be a European exposure database available on a public access website and management decision software tools to enable local authorities to assess the risk presented by measured air pollution levels and act accordingly.

The tools will have a Geographical Information System (GIS) type interface, which is essentially a map from which spatial distributions of pollution sources, monitoring stations, measurement, model results and other geographically linked information can be presented. Two local authorities in urban locations in the EU have volunteered to act as guinea pigs to test the "product" in the last year of the project.

Information concerning concentration and chemical characteristics of particulate matter and gaseous pollutants in urban areas and in indoor air will be used to assess actual human exposure characteristics. The aim is to quantify the correlation between the complex system of human indoor exposure and outdoor monitoring measurements. This will enable governments to quantify risks and hence costs associated with urban air pollution and ultimately to produce abatement strategies.

Ian Colbeck and Guy Coulson

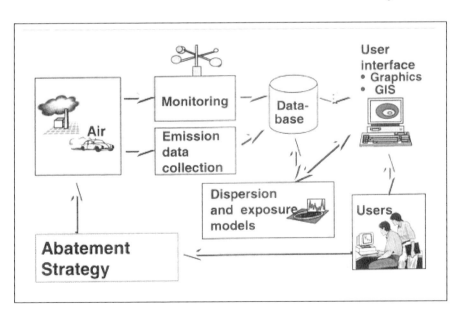

HEALTH AND ILLNESS IN THE BOLIVIAN ANDES

The high Andes of Bolivia are the home of Aymara and Quechua-speaking peasants with a long history of expert knowledge of medicinal plants and herbs. One group, the Kallawayas, travel far beyond the borders of their native country, healing the sick from Colombia to Argentina and many of their medicines have been carefully researched and then patented for sale in pharmacies.

Compounding the injustice of such exploitation, most rural Andean have limited access at best to Western pharmaceuticals and continue to rely on their own knowledge of herbs and plants as well as those of the ritual specialist, the *yatiri*. Although Andean medicines are much sought after by Western pharmaceutical companies who recognise their efficacy, the model of health and illness that generally operates is quite different from the standard Western one.

The model of health and illness in the community of Pocobaya where I have conducted fieldwork since 1989 is based around complementary life forces called the *chuyma* and the *ajayu*. The *chuyma* is the physical 'heart' (although not clearly identified with any particular organ) and its diminution through illness can be corrected through the use of herbs and plant medicines. The *chuyma* is affected when a person has a fever, a broken leg, or an infection. The model of health and illness is a relatively simple one: the medicines restore the strength of the *chuyma* which brings the patient to full health; older people have relatively weak *chuymas* and younger people much stronger ones.

The reverse is the case with the *ajayu*, a more spiritual life force which increases with age even as the *chuyma* diminishes. Illnesses relating to the *ajayu* are much more serious: the permanent loss of the *ajayu* leads to death and prolonged or severe illness relating to the *chuyma* will also lead to the loss of the *ajayu*. Whereas any competent individual can cure illnesses of the *chuyma*, only the shaman can return the *ajayu* back to the human body through the intervention of the ancestral mountain spirits, the *achachilas*. Children are particularly susceptible to *ajayu* loss which is reflected in the high child mortality rate.

The *ajayu* may depart if the child gets a fright and it is for this reason that people never physically punish children as it could lead directly to their death. The *ajayu* is returned to the patient through offerings to the ancestral mountain spirits which vary considerably according to the specific diagnosis made by the shaman. Diagnosis is often made through the casting and subsequent 'reading' of coca leaves although more powerful shamans use a human skull. The required offerings to encourage, entice or placate the ancestral spirits take many forms: it may involve a complex offering of candles, coloured powders and herbs; a llama foetus; a libation of alcohol; some candles; or indeed a combination of all of these.

Rural Andeans continue to rely on their own medicines and cures for many illnesses, partly because they have very limited access to Western medicine but also because they know from their experience that their own medical system continues to be effective; moreover, their understanding of health and illnesses fits in with a broader vision of how humans relate to ancestral spirits and the mountain environment they inhabit.

Andrew Canessa

THE TRAGEDY OF NO LONGER KNOWING: INDIA AS A CASE STUDY

For as long as humans have relied upon natural resources, they have been accumulating an equally valuable wealth of knowledge on those resources, through engaging in activities such as hunting and gathering, fishing and farming. This knowledge has been transferred between generations as a key survival tool through community exchanges such as songs, stories and traditional practices, especially where development is at a slower pace. This knowledge base is termed Local Ecological Knowledge (LEK).

Like gene pools, when these knowledge pools are dissipated due to ineffective transmission, it is impossible to regain such an accumulation of observations since they often go unrecorded. Inefficient transmission, combined with reduced time spent in contact with nature, termed as the 'Extinction of Experience', is contributing to the demise of this knowledge resource. As a result, LEK levels have diminished in communities worldwide.

The huge potential LEK holds as a contributor to the global pharmaceutical industry has only been realized in recent years. Although health benefits are offered worldwide, the potential also exists for exploitation of the knowledge-holders and their resources, hence a multitude of policies and Intellectual Property Rights have emerged targeting this. The vast majority of LEK is held within developing regions, namely in indigenous and tribal groups who have suffered social, political and economic deprivation. Their in-depth knowledge of local species has been key to their survival, as it was to that of their ancestors.

The People of India Project identified 461 tribal communities in India amounting to over 67 million people, the majority of whom lack access to, belief in, or the funding to access modern medicine. They rely on local species and household remedies to cure common ailments (cough, cold, digestive problems, fever, headache and skin infections), and traditional healers and Ayurvedic medicine to cure more serious disorders.

Healers are traditional figureheads in Indian Panchayat villages. Their status is acquired through their knowledge of local wild plants and their healing properties. To protect this status, secrecy of their techniques is very important to them. Often family members may be let into the circle of knowledge to help with gathering and preparation, but many healers insist they will not burden their children with the full depth of their knowledge unless their children wish to follow in their footsteps.

Traditional healers often use over 100 different local species for healing different ailments, although admit this is far less than their predecessors. They can treat a number of local villages including their own, and may be responsible for over 1000 people. They rarely get paid for their work, but instead receive donations in the form of food or wares.

Female medical treatments within the home are commonly known as 'grandmother treatments' and have developed in India for over 40 centuries, although recognition of their value is only recent. As the primary holders of LEK, women are thought to have developed this knowledge as a result of their historical and cultural bonds with nature through their roles as mothers and nurturers. In this role they feed and care for the health of their families, traditionally using only the fruits of the local land. At present using this knowledge, women are believed to be responsible for 80% of the world's medical care without external consultation.

Examples of wild plant species used for home healing in Tamil Nadu, south India:

Sirianangai	Poisonous bites. Tastes bitter normally, but sweet if suffered a poisonous bite.
Karuvelam	Diarrhea, dysentery, gums, cough, throat, discharge, eyes, cystitis, leucorrhoea
Seerukeerai	For pregnant females, urine retention, fits
Vilvam	Diarrhea, dysentery, constipation, jaundice, asthma, bronchitis, seminal weakness, one grown in every Shiva temple
Thulasi	Respiratory problems, piles, stomach, bowel, diarrhea, dysentery, cough, labor pain, diuretic
Adathoda	Diarrhea, constipation, jaundice, TB, cough, asthma, diphtheria, bronchitis, gonorrhea, kidneys, conjunctivitis
Segapu munthari	Salivation, piles, diarrhea, worms, cough, gonorrhea, blood in urine
[name reserved]	Single leaf can be eaten by women each day as a natural contraceptive

Women are also traditionally key to their family's nutritional health as the primary gatherers, cooks, and often-agricultural laborers. They are thought to grow 60-80% of the world's food. The gender imbalance in food production derives from women tending food crops and men cash crops, and is indicative of their knowledge bases; women describe plant health benefits whilst men describe economic income. This female knowledge base of health and subsistence is vital in famine regions, such as the drought-prone plains of southern India, where local wild foods are relied upon when crop yields fail.

A variety of activities can be observed upon entering an Indian Dalit community, cooking over fires, traditional medicine preparation, livestock-rearing, house building and much more. All of these activities have one factor in common; that is their application of wild plant knowledge and its accumulation and transfer through generations. Such knowledge is not just exclusive to developing regions. In the past, now-developed regions held the same value and reliance upon LEK. Horsemen in England for example used to be experts in the treatment of equestrian ailments with local wild plants, including belladonna for colds and apples for flu, but this knowledge was lost alongside the tradition of horsemen and the breeds they worked with, such as the Suffolk Punch. The bark of *Acacia* as a treatment for malaria and ash to cure milk were other traditional health remedies once used in Britain. Sphagnum moss was even used as an antiseptic and for women menstruating or in labour in Stone Age Britain.

LEK decline due to language loss, modernization, urbanization and globalization encompasses a cultural loss and an environmental loss, but possibly of greatest importance is the health loss. This decline in knowledge could be the most important knock back of the pharmaceutical industry as it searches to find treatments that exist in isolated communities after years of knowledge accumulation. It could take our scientists hundreds of years to discover what has been lost in just one tribal generation on the other side of the world. It seems the travesty of no longer knowing threatens human health in both developed and developing regions. Thus a successful integration of ethno-medical preservation and biodiversity conservation could offer an everlasting value to humanity as a whole.

Sarah Pilgrim

AMBIENT INTELLIGENCE, THE IDORM AND SOCIAL CARE

The concept of ambient intelligence refers to a world in which people are surrounded and empowered by networked digital technologies that are sensitive and responsive to their needs. In practical terms this means creating a domestic environment composed of appliances containing `hidden' computers, which connect to other similar appliances. Users are empowered, as they can design the functionality of the environment by managing how these devices coordinate their actions. This new functionality is different to that offered by any separate appliance as it relates to collective social actions that are not possible from individual appliances, and even not envisaged by the original appliance manufacturer. These spaces are called intelligent environments and open up new and creative possibilities for supporting the lives of ordinary people in their homes, particularly those people in need of home care services.

The world's ageing population poses challenges to society in terms of funding the cost of the care that will be needed. For instance, it is predicted that the number of people aged 60 years or older in the world will rise to over 20% by 2050 which will have serious consequences for the future development of human society. In some countries, such as the UK, with a greater proportion of older people, this problem will be even more acute. In addition, there are predictions that an increasing proportion of the population will be living alone. As a consequence of these trends, the task of providing care will fall to a diminishing pool of people, with an increasing financial burden on the people of working age. Fortunately, new technology has the potential to counter this problem, by harnessing advances in ambient intelligence and intelligent environments.

An intelligent environment is a space that people live in (eg a room, a house etc) in which all the services (eg heat, light, communication, entertainment, security etc) are managed intelligently by computers so as to support the occupants in their daily activities. These environments vary in complexity being in their most simple form just a collection of automated systems or in their more complex form "intelligent" systems that can be taught by the user, or even learn for themselves, how best to serve the occupant's needs. The Intelligent Inhabited Environments Group (IIEG) at the University of Essex (http://iieg.essex.ac.uk) is exploring new ways to apply the notion of ambient intelligence to care services. We have built what we term the intelligent dormitory (iDorm - see Figure 1). This is a real pervasive computing testbed comprised of a large number of embedded sensors, actuators, processors and networks in the form of a small self-contained room containing areas for different activities such as sleeping, communicating (writing or video conferencing with remote family and friends) and entertaining (watching TV, listening to music etc).

All the appliances have tiny computers in them, with network connections; even the fridges, chairs, tables and beds have computers and sensors fitted. The aim is not to use these sensors to "spy" on occupants (in fact privacy, security and safety for the individual are the highest priority) but rather to sense and affect their world in a way that would resemble the actions of a caring companion sharing the room with them. Videos of the iDorm in use are available on our web-site http://iieg.essex.ac.uk.

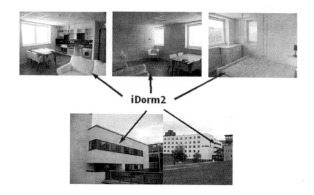

iDorm2

With the success of the iDorm, the University of Essex is constructing a more realistic test-bed for exploring care applications of ambient intelligence in the home. The new facility takes the form of a domestic apartment and has tentatively been called the iFlat. The flat has been built from the ground up to be an experimental ambient intelligence environment with many special structural features such as hollow internal walls to contain sensors and processors etc. All the basic services are electrically controlled (eg heating, water, doors etc). The basic layout of the flat is shown in the figure.

One of our projects involves the use of what we term an intelligent-agent; an entity that can learn about the normal habitual behaviour of a person and later detect deviations from that norm. We aim to characterise the behavioural changes associated with the onset of illness or physical disability such as Alzheimer or dementia where there are changes to the person's habitual behaviours. These vary from changes to sleep/wake rhythms to omitting steps in daily routines.

In our research, we are looking at ways of constructing intelligent agents that can both detect the early signs of the onset of these conditions by finding smaller, more subtle changes in behaviour and trends in behaviour change at an earlier stage, together with providing a means of supporting people so as to extend the time they may live independently in their own home. For example, as the agent learns what a person normally does, it could command the house to do this at the appropriate time (eg lock the doors and windows, switch off unattended appliances etc when the person is in bed), as though the intelligent-agent was a loving companion, caring for the person in the house (another branch of our work is agents that react to emotions!).

Fernando Rivera-Illingworth, Vic Callaghan, Martin Colley and Hani Hagras

WHEN IS WATER HARMFUL?

S ome of us think of ourselves (at least in the material sense) as
consisting of the biological molecules that make up cells and tissues,
along with inert substances like bone mineral and tooth enamel. But it
would be equally valid to look upon ourselves as a solution; we are 60-
80% water, and our cellular membranes, enzymes and proteins, and the
nucleic acids which make up our genes, are all either dissolved in water or
water-covered (hydrated). Even where water is excluded from a molecule,
its behaviour is determined by the surrounding watery environment.

When water is extremely perturbed
Once you think of yourself as a solution, you are no longer surprised to
find that human beings are exceptionally sensitive to changes in the
chemistry and physics of water. There are each year about 25 million
deaths around the globe due to diarrhoeal diseases induced by microbial
infection but fatal due to severe dehydration. But remarkably, drinking too
much water can also cause severe illness or even death; the relationship
between blood, tissue fluid and biological molecules is upset. Too much
salt or alcohol can also have disruptive effects on water-biomolecule
interactions. Secondary effects include swelling of the brain (in the case of
water intoxication) or water imbalance (in the case of salt). Some
compounds (eg urea and alcohol) cause chaos in cells by weakening
bonding between water molecules, fluidising membranes and loosening
protein structure; these compounds are known as chaotropic solutes.

The idea of homeostasis
The body regulates itself to maintain temperature, acid-base balance,
oxygen supply and water content at finely controlled steady levels. This
phenomenon is known as homeostasis. Numerous clinical conditions
perturb homeostasis, such as those involving hormonal imbalances (eg
diabetes and Addison's disease) or kidney failure. Many drugs, from
caffeine and alcohol to the Class A designer drug ecstasy, also affect
homeostasis and interfere with water regulation. Ecstasy can cause death
directly due to dehydration or indirectly when a user rehydrates too
rapidly.

Water in foods
Processed foods constitute a main part of the western diet and are often
supplemented with high levels of sugar (sucrose) and salt (sodium
chloride) to act as preservatives. These substances reduce the availability

of water by effectively dehydrating the food; they thereby prevent microbial growth and food spoilage. Although sugar and salt are not really toxic when eaten, the body must rapidly remove them from the blood stream before the concentrations become dangerously high and cause water stress. This has long-term health implications: ingesting too much sucrose over many years may increase the risk of diabetes, whereas overdosing on salt can eventually lead to hardening of the blood vessels as well as heart disease. Eating a greater proportion of fresh foods (with no added salt or refined sugar) is generally a good idea!

Pollution and drinking water

The main value of water in the body may be to dissolve things, but this is also its main danger. Water acts as a vehicle for dissolved toxic compounds to enter our bodies. Drinking water can contain a multitude of pollutants ranging from agricultural pesticide residues to the chlorine added to prevent microbial growth. Industrially-produced or natural pollutants, such as compounds related to phenol or benzene (some of which come from crude oil), enter aquifers, rivers and lakes, and are extremely toxic.

Like alcohol, a large part of their toxicity may relate to the disruption of water-biomolecule relations, although most pollutants are far more potent and dangerous in their chaotropic activity. The destabilising effect on membranes, proteins and nucleic acids reduces the metabolic activity, growth rate and vitality of cells; this is why they are termed stressful. Here at the University of Essex we have created a new paradigm that cellular water stress is caused by these chaotropic compounds due to disruption of the function of biological molecules. Chaotropes, including the urea that is produced as a waste product by animals but also applied to soils as an agricultural fertilizer, are pervasive major stressors both in the environment and for animal (including human) tissues. We are currently studying the effects of chaotrope-induced stress, and biological responses to it, in various biological systems.

John Hallsworth, Peter Nicholls and Ken Timmis

HEALTH ISSUES RELATED TO THE FAECAL CONTAMINATION OF WATER BODIES

Over one billion people worldwide do not have access to clean and safe water. A child dies every 15 seconds from diseases related to unsafe water, inadequate sanitation and poor hygiene. Faecal pollution is arguably the most important health hazard of all pollution such is the extent of the problem. This article examines some of the problems associated with "fouled water" both in undeveloped and developed nations. Diseases and illnesses caused by "fouled water" can be divided in to two main types; diarrhoeal diseases and diseases caused by worms.

Diseases causing diarrhea

Diarrhoea is not a disease; rather it's a symptom of many different diseases that causes the death of over 2 million people annually whilst severely affecting four billion. Diarrhoea is caused by over 100 different bacteria and

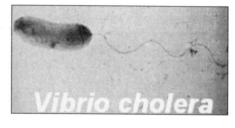

viruses which are primarily spread through polluted water. Diarrhoea usually results in severe dehydration causing salt imbalance and a 10 % loss of body fluids generally results in death. The three mostly deadly diseases that result in diarrhoea are Cholera, Bacillary and Typhoid.

Cholera can cause large scale epidemics. It arises from a bacterial infection and sudden large outbreaks are usually caused by contaminated water supply. A toxin produced by the bacteria prevents the victims from being able to absorb water through the intestine and severe dehydration often results. Dehydration caused by this lack of water absorption and the passing of up to 14 litres of diarrhoea a day, causes decreased blood pressure, kidney failure and death, often within 24 hrs.

Approximately 140 million people are infected with Bacillary dysentery each year resulting in around 300,000 deaths annually. The disease is caused by Shigella bacteria which generally enters the body through contaminated drinking water. The symptoms can include fever, abdominal pain, nausea, cramping and severe, frequent, watery diarrhoea that can contain blood, mucous and pus. Typhoid fever can affect up to 17 million people worldwide annually and results in approximately 600,000 deaths per year. It is contracted when people drink water or eat food infected with a bacterium called *Salmonella typhi* found in human faecal pollution.

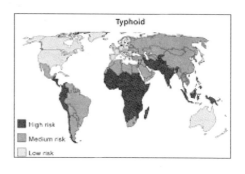

There are several other diseases which cause diarrhoea that are spread in similar ways and hence the eradication of the most important three would also decrease the risk from diseases such as giardiadis, salmonella, camplyobacteriosis and cryptosporidiosis. Prevention of diarrhoeal diseases can be brought about by improving access to clean water and sanitation so that bacteria cannot re-enter water supplies and through education programmes. Many global initiatives are now focused on improving water quality, sanitation and hygiene standards.

Diseases caused by worms
Many thousands of people die each year from diseases caused by worms, the vast majority of these people are from developing countries. The most common diseases include ascaris; whipworm and thread worm, but the most dangerous are bilharzia, hookworm and guinea worm. The treatment and production of safe water coupled with effective sanitation could significantly reduce the number of deaths arising from aquatic worms. As with diarrhoeal diseases these can also be prevented through safe water, effective sanitation and good hygiene.

The larvae of Schistosomiasis

Bilharzia, otherwise known as Schistosomiasis, infects over 200 million people and kills some 20,000 people each year. It is caused by a small flat worm that lives in blood vessels and excretes between 300 and 3000 eggs into the bloodstream. After boring into the intestine, a proportion of the eggs are passed into the environment when people go to the toilet. If this "fouled water" carrying the eggs enters lakes or streams, the eggs hatch into larvae which are then eaten by aquatic snails. The larvae develop within the snail and are passed back into water courses where they can penetrate the skin of its human host. Once in the bloodstream the eggs can cluster and damage blood vessels, the bladder, intestine, liver and kidneys. Programmes developed to eradicate the snail host have also been successful in reducing the incidents of Bilharzia.

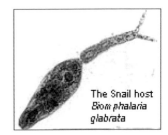

The Snail host
Biomphalaria glabrata

Guinea worm does not generally cause fatalities and the number of reported cases has reduced by some 97 % over the last decade (from 3.5 million to 150,000). The worm, which can be 1m in length, enters the body and lives under the skin. Its presence causes severe pain and the worm eventually emerges through the skin leading to ulcers and fevers. Hookwoorms are common intestinal parasites, the larvae of which generally enter the body by burrowing through the feet of people walking barefoot through fouled water. 900,000 people are thought to be infected each year. Eggs produced by the worms enter the faeces of its host and are therefore readily introduced into water courses. By feeding on the blood of its host, hookworms can cause stunted growth in children, loss of blood and anaemia. In severe cases anaemia can cause heart failure.

The Industrialised World

The developed world also faces significant problems relating to the faecal contamination of water bodies. Generally the proportion of the population that are most at risk from fouled water are those people who have an existing illness that severely impacts on their immune system such as people undergoing chemotherapy, AIDS/HIV sufferers, transplant patients; the very young and old are also at considerable risk.

In the UK, over 300 million gallons of sewage are discharged into the sea each day. Clear links have been made between faecal associated pathogens and incidences of disease. More than 20 separate illnesses have been identified as being associated with `fouled waters' in the UK and illness caused by sewage pollution in the UK stems from direct ingestion most often by water sport enthusiasts and bathers.

It is difficult to gauge the risk of an individual to exposure to pathogens in `fouled water'. The safety of a water body for a bather is covered under the Bathing Water Directive which stipulates mandatory as well as guide-line saftey limits for indicator species. However no single indicator of water quality as it directly relates to the risk to human health has been identified. Despite this, during the 1950s the first systematic study was undertaken to identify the safe-levels of faecal bacteria (faecal coliforms) that could be present within bathing water and not represent a significant threat to bathers.

Values of 200 coliforms per 100 ml water were obtained but despite this the mandatory level for the UK is 2000 per 100 ml, an order of magnitude higher. But it is not just bathers that are at risk from water borne illness resulting from faecal pollution exposure. Food product extracted from aquatic environments can also represent a threat to human health. One such case is the harvesting of shellfisheries, which by means of their feeding strategy can bioconcentrate pollutants in their flesh. The Shellfisheries Directive examines these issues and shellfisheries waters are graded in relation to their indicator loadings.

The current indicators used are under review and research into the use of other, more specific, indicators is underway. The situation is further complicated by the fact that it is not only human contaminants that can result in illness; several livestock species can also contribute to the health problems relating to water use. Traditional techniques are not very good indicators for the potential risk faecal contamination may pose to human health.

Concluding Remarks

In industrialized countries problems with water born illnesses are relatively small when compared to the huge problems facing developing countries. Regular analysis of water samples from areas utilised by bathers and for shellfisheries harvesting does occur. However the uses of the traditional microbial indicators do not allow different types (ie species) of faecal contaminant to be identified. Consequently further research, such as the research currently being undertaken by the Environmental Microbiology group at the University of Essex, is required immediately to address these issues and suggested changes in protocol and perhaps legislation should result.

Andy Ball and Dave Smith

THE SPREAD OF ANTIBIOTIC RESISTANCE

The first antibiotic (origin *anti- against; biotics derived from bios – life*) was discovered in 1928 by a chance observation by Alexander Fleming, working in St Mary's hospital in London when he observed that a fungal contaminant inhibited growth of the bacterium *Staphylococcus* cultured on an agar plate. Fleming realised that this fungus (*Penicillium*) was producing some compound that had antimicrobial activity, and recognised that this could form the basis of a therapeutic treatment to counter infectious disease. Two years later Cecil Paine demonstrated the first successful treatment with penicillin using a crude filtrate from a culture of *Penicillium* to successfully treat two babies suffering from eye infections. The subsequent commercial development of the antibiotic 'Pencillin' followed painstaking research by Howard Florey and Ernst Chain during the late 1930s and early 1940s to purify sufficient quantities of the compound to allow its application for treatment. This research was driven in particular with the aim of developing treatments for bacterial infections in wounds in soldiers during the second world war.

The next twenty years represented the golden age of antibiotics when it was widely hoped that antibiotics would deal a lethal blow to pathogenic diseases. Numerous new antibiotics, including streptomycin and chloramphenicol, were isolated, developed and found widespread clinical use during this period. However, since this time we have been fighting an increasingly intensive battle with bacteria as they have evolved resistances to nearly every antibiotic that we have discovered. Antibiotic resistance in bacteria is arguably one of the classical examples of Darwinian evolution.

At its simplest level it involves selection for bacteria that may have undergone tiny mutations in their DNA that enable them to survive in the presence of an antibiotic. Under such conditions bacteria that are resistant to the antibiotic will be selected for, whilst bacteria lacking the mutation will die. More dramatically a whole series of genes have evolved in bacteria that encode enzymes which inactivate antibiotics rendering them useless. Whilst in themselves these evolutionary processes would make an increasing number of bacteria resistant to different antibiotics it does not explain the dramatic rates by which antibiotic resistance has spread. This spread of antibiotics in bacteria is largely a consequence of bacterial gene transfer in combination with our own misuse of antibiotics.

Bacterial gene transfer is the movement of genes between individual bacteria and occurs by three main mechanisms: transformation (uptake of naked DNA), transduction (DNA transfer mediated by viruses that infect bacteria) and conjugation (plasmid-mediated gene transfer). The most important of these mechanisms in the spread of antibiotics has been plasmid-mediated conjugation. In simple terms, plasmids are circular regions of DNA that can replicate independently of the bacterial chromosome and in many cases be transferred between bacterial cells. These plasmids are typically mosaic elements that carry a whole variety of genes and in many cases will include genes encoding antibiotic resistance. Consequently, if a plasmid carrying an antibiotic resistance gene is transferred to another bacterium the latter will also now be capable of surviving in the presence of that particular antibiotic. Bacteria and their plasmids have now evolved to such an extent that some bacteria will carry genes conferring resistance to ten or more different antibiotics.

The widespread transfer of antibiotic resistance has been accelerated by our own misuse of antibiotics, with as many as one in three antibiotic prescriptions being unnecessary. For many years antibiotics have been prescribed inappropriately for patients suffering from viral infections (eg the common cold), when it has long been known that antibiotics have no inhibitory effects on viruses. Similarly, where patients fail to complete courses of prescribed antibiotics this can provide the ideal selective environment for antibiotic resistance strains. Such misuse of antibiotics and the amazing ability of bacteria to adapt to challenges to their existence means we once again face a return to a time in which bacterial pathogens will pose a significant threat to human health. With almost daily reports in the news of MRSA (methicillin resistant *Staphylococcus aureus*) infections in hospitals and the spectre of bioterrorists using antibiotic resistant anthrax bacteria (*Bacillus anthracis*) we stand at a crossroads in our battle with bacterial pathogens, a mere 76 years after Fleming's original discovery.

f 12

Our current and future battles against antibiotics will rely both on the identification of new antimicrobial agents that are reliant on preserving the ever-dwindling biodiversity present in the natural world, and the specific developments of new antimicrobial agents that will be based on our improved biological understanding of pathogenic bacteria that will result from our interrogation of their genomes.

Mark Osborn

THE HEALTH BENEFITS OF COUNTRYSIDE ACTIVITIES: FISHING IN ESSEX

A s part of research that we have done for the Countryside Recreation Network, we published a report entitled *"A Countryside for Health and Well-Being"*. Here we summarise the findings from analysis of fishing in Essex.

The Colchester Angling Preservation Society (CAPS) manages Layer Pits Fishing Lake, near Colchester in Essex for its members. Layer Pits is a picturesque lake, rich in wildlife and is said to be one of the most popular fishing spots in the county. Anglers fish the various swims around the lake and although fishing can be quite sedentary until fish bite, the fishermen here are usually outside in all weathers for long periods of time, frequently in excess of 10 hours. Most of the anglers know each other and even though they usually fish individually many meet up for a chat over a cup of tea on the lakeside. Fishermen at Layer Pits are predominantly male, with an average age of 43. The average calories (kcal) used per visit was 3528 and at 294 calories per hour this represents gentle physical activity but for long periods of time.

Our questionnaire examined the psychological health of those fishing at Layer Pits, and showed that as a group, their self-esteem improved as a result of the activity (see Figure 1). Self-esteem scores in this group may well be influenced by the degree of success of the fishing trip ie the number or size of fish caught.

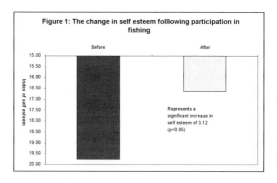

Figure 1: The change in self esteem folllowing participation in fishing

Changes in mood after the conservation activities is shown in Figure 2. Anger, confusion, depression and tension all decreased markedly, suggesting an overall improvement in mood. Levels of fatigue also decreased and vigour levels increased.

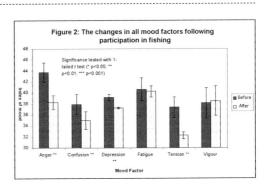

Figure 2: The changes in all mood factors following participation in fishing

It is clear from the comments of the fishermen that it is the combination of the beautiful surroundings, the fishing and the meeting up with others that makes fishing so enjoyable. Many mentioned the value of getting back to nature and away from the stresses of day to day life.

"As we go on we can't help but develop a love of the countryside and the environment we fish in and the things we see when we are out there. We are very lucky to have a hobby that places us in some of the best bits of the country. All anglers can list a series of unforgettable wildlife encounters they've had, or envisage the perfect sunset or sunrise, which is always somehow better when looked upon with water in view."

"The thrill of silently creeping around to see the big fish lurking in the water. The relaxation of sitting amongst nature, watching the world go by, accompanied by the background orchestra of the dawn chorus.

The wonder of watching a kingfisher land on the end of your fishing rod and being able to admire its beauty while too scared to move for fear of making it fly away."

"The tranquility of being on your own, or the comradeship when fishing with your friends."

"Getting up to find the frost has frozen everything or the wonderful dew is covering everything really helps you realize that you are away from it all and that there is no pressure."

Jo Peacock and Rachel Hine

SOCIAL CAPITAL AND HEALTH

S ocial capital is a contentious idea. There is a good deal of agreement as to what is meant by human capital and financial capital, probably because these are relatively easy to conceptualise and measure. Much of the relevant debate surrounds the question of whether a person or a 'community' *has* social capital. In our research we investigated how a person's social capital, measured by indicators such as social participation, contact with friends and attachment to neighbourhood, was associated with their mental and physical health. We analysed data from the first nine years of the British Household Panel Survey – an ongoing annual survey of about 5,500 households carried out by the University of Essex.

We found that most of our measures indicating the presence of social capital reduced the chances of poor mental and physical health. These effects were net of any effects of demographics which persist in being strong determinants of health. Some interesting interactions were found. The one illustrated below is between social participation and working status for working-age women. It suggests that social participation negates the difference in risk of poor mental health that exists between working and non-working women.

We were surprised to find that, overall, our measures of social capital played only a minor role in the processes leading to the start of and recovery from states of poor mental and physical health compared to strong demographic effects. However, we did find some interesting interactions (see below) which shows that men are more affected by their level of 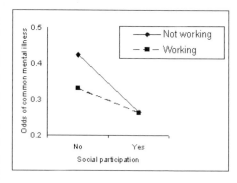 neighbourhood attachment when it comes to recovering from poor mental health whereas women have about the same chances of recovering regardless of their level of attachment.

We also looked at the way that differences in the way that couples feel about their neighbourhood are associated with their own mental and physical health, risks of moving and risks of separation. This type of analysis is only possible with the British Household Panel Survey data as it follows all members of a household over time.

We found that the association between neighbourhood attachment and poor mental health in women was significantly affected by the neighbourhood attachment level of their *spouse*. This suggests that information on a *spouse's* level of attachment would need to be collected to correctly interpret the apparent association for women. When we examined the onset of common mental illness it was for only men that intra-couple differences in attachment significantly raised the likelihood of an onset while such differences did not affect women.

However, when we followed these couples over the next two years we found that intra-couple differences, where the woman had a low level of attachment but the man did not, almost trebled the chances of a separation.

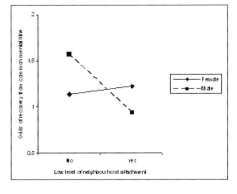

Also, if any one or both of the couple had a low level of attachment then their chances of moving to another neighbourhood within those two years was three to five times more than if both of the couple had high levels of attachment.

David Pevalin and David Rose

AGEING POPULATIONS AND HEALTH

People aged 65 and over currently account for 16% of the UK population. But they absorb over 40% of what we spend as a nation on hospital and community health services and 45% of what we spend on social services provided by local councils. Over the next half century, the proportion of the UK population who are aged 65 and over will rise to more than a quarter, prompting fears that this will place impossible burdens on our health and social services, and on the taxpayers who fund them.

Much of the forecast increases in the numbers of older people is accounted for by increases in life expectancy. A boy born fifty years ago could expect to live until he was 67, and a girl could expect to reach 73. In fifty years' time life expectancy is forecast to have reached 83 for a boy and 87 for a girl. The hotly-debated question is whether these extra years of life will be spent in good or poor health. The more of them that are lived in good health, the better it will be for older people themselves and for the financing of our health and social services. To consider this, people have developed the idea of 'healthy life expectancy' – the remaining number of years which can be expected to be lived in good health. Trends suggest that the forecast increases in life expectancy will be split between extra years in good health and extra years in poor health, implying that the increases in life expectancy will place extra burdens on our health and social services though the picture is not as gloomy as it would be if all we were doing was keeping people alive longer in states of poor health.

Projections for fifty years from now are subject to a great deal of uncertainty. But they are needed if we are to design financially sustainable systems of health and social care which can respond to unforeseen changes in people's health care needs. Nowhere is this more true than in the case of long-term health and social care for older people. Beyond the age of about 85, the proportion of people needing on-going health and social services attention in their own homes or in residential or nursing homes rises fast. The proportion of the population in this age group is expected to rise steeply – from just under 2% now, to 6% in fifty years' time.

At the University of Essex, we have been involved in developing and using computer simulation models designed to see how our system of paying for long-term care would cope in the future under different assumptions about life expectancy, the health and social care needs of older people, the costs of providing health and social services, and the availability of informal care from family members and friends. The models are also able to look at the effect of different ways of financing long-term care. For example, currently, older people in care homes get their nursing care paid for by the state but have to contribute towards their personal care depending on their income and wealth. Scotland has introduced free personal care where the state pays for personal care as well as nursing care. Some people think that the rest of the UK should introduce free personal care. The models can look at the likely effect of free personal care on public spending on long-term care and also see which groups of older people would gain most from different charging schemes. The figure below, produced using the model, shows the so-called 'funnel of doubt' over the future costs of long-term care, that the Chancellor of the Exchequer and the Secretary of State for Health have to contend with in planning long-term care expenditure.

Ruth Hancock

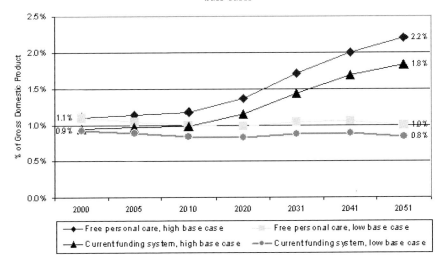

Public expenditure on long-term care as a % of Gross Domestic Product under the current funding system and under free personal care (UK, 2000-2051), low and high base cases

INTELLIGENT ENVIRONMENTS FOR SOCIAL CARE

In January 2004, fourteen residents in a Lanarkshire nursing home suffered pointless deaths due to smoke inhalation from a fire. In the winter of 2004, in England and Wales, 21,800 older people died needlessly as a direct result of the cold; around 180,000 older people every year suffer robbery, injury or death after being targeted by 'bogus caller' criminals. Older people should be feeling supported and cared-for yet instead many are spending the last years of their life living in fear, isolation and distress.

There is already a care crisis in the UK, as society cannot afford to provide the degree of support needed by elderly or disabled people and this problem may soon escalate, spiralling out of control as the ageing population increases. Yet there is a solution: utilise *technology* to supplement and aid the work of carers, to provide better support without the excessive costs of traditional 24-hour care.

There is a growing trend towards the use of simple technology throughout one's home to enhance the environment, providing increased comfort and security. Some gadgets, such as remote-controlled front-door locks or pendant-alarms, have already been used successfully as aids to vulnerable people. Until recently though, such items have only been able to act independently. However, if they are connected together via an electronic network, they have the potential to provide a much greater support system that could go a long way towards enhancing the quality of life of anyone using them.

Such systems already exist to some degree in the form of *Intelligent Environments*: buildings with an infrastructure which allows sophisticated co-ordination of devices such as heating, lighting, blinds and so on, to provide occupants with a comfortable, safe environment. In the Department of Computer Science at the University of Essex, research in the *Intelligent Inhabited Environments Group* is centred upon such systems. One of our aims has been to investigate the use of this technology to provide enhanced safety and quality of life to vulnerable groups.

However, we are not interested in adding intrusive cameras or resorting to "Big Brother"-style monitoring; rather, we are focusing on exploiting the new rise of *embedded technology* - everyday objects like passive sensors and smoke-detectors, door-locks, telephones, or radios, that each contain a tiny computer processor which enables them to be controlled electronically. These devices can communicate with each other across a network to share information and form a fully controllable environment for occupants. Such systems are in fact becoming widespread, since they are already being installed in hotels and offices all over the world. Far from being excessively expensive, in fact they have been shown to be very cost-effective, as they can save considerable amounts of money, for example by switching off devices when not needed or by optimising heating for economy (making savings of up to 40% on energy bills).

For some time our research group has had an experimental system, called an Intelligent Dormitory, or *iDorm* (featured on TV on Tomorrow's World), consisting of a bed-sit room such as one might find in University student accommodation but equipped with many embedded sensors and devices. Now a larger prototype, this time an entire flat - the *iDorm2* - has been developed in the new Network Centre building. The iDorm2 has been designed to provide a cohesive intelligent environment, featuring a sophisticated network of hi-tech equipment and gadgets.

Traditionally, such systems have required significant knowledge or skills on the part of the user to control them effectively. However, our research is primarily based on *Artificial Intelligence* - computers that exhibit elements of "human" thinking and are capable of reasoning, learning, and adapting to new circumstances. So our system incorporates methods that enable it to *learn* from a resident without being "programmed"; thus, it is ideally suited to vulnerable people who may not want or be able to interact with the technology themselves. The system uses the wealth of information available from its sensors and devices to learn about an occupant's lifestyle and preferences.

We call this *Evidential Learning*, since, over time, it builds up patterns (or *evidence*) of actions that are repeated or occur regularly. It is then able to perform some of these actions itself, thus gradually reducing the need for the occupants or carers to do so (unless they wish to). This might include simple tasks like switching on the lights as it gets dark, through to more complex sequences of tasks, for example, as the occupant retires for the evening, locking the doors and windows, turning off lights and heating in the living-room, and switching on an electric blanket to warm up the bed. This will obviously help occupants who physically have difficulty performing these tasks due to limited mobility but it would also help those who are mentally- or memory-impaired and may not always remember, or may not even understand the importance of, certain actions like locking a door or switching an oven off.

This type of system could be implemented either in a residential home, or in sheltered housing, or even in a resident's own existing house, enabling him or her to remain independent for longer without being so reliant on carers. The intention though is that it will supplement, rather than replace, human care, while also relieving care-givers of some of the more mundane tasks and enabling them to spend more quality time with their clients.

The system is designed with certain safety features - such as how to respond to a fire or how to prevent the internal temperature from falling low during cold weather. Unlike other systems though, it does not impose rigid pre-programmed inflexibility on occupants. Since it learns most of its behaviour from the occupants themselves, it appears "tailor-made" to suit any occupant, and it will even adapt if they or their preferences change. An added advantage is the possibility that the system could (with the occupant's permission) also be used to monitor his or her health, either by detecting long-term gradual deterioration, or by alerting a doctor to a more immediate situation such as a fall or a stroke.

In large companies, electronic ID-tags are worn by occupants, used as a means of tracking them and locating them in an emergency. In a residential care-home such devices could be an invaluable aid to health and safety. Worn as a non-intrusive bracelet, pendant or badge, they could act as a personal alarm button (similarly to existing pendant-alarms) to alert a carer that the wearer needs urgent assistance; they could be used to locate occupants in a fire or other emergency situation; and they could even supplement the role of Hearing Dogs or Guide Dogs, by notifying the blind or hard-of-hearing of a doorbell, phone ringing, or smoke-alarm, via a warning light or sound. When communicating with the environmental system too, they could even detect if an intruder (such as a bogus caller's accomplice) was in another room and signal an appropriate alert.

Although this type of research may clearly raise some issues about personal privacy, it has the potential to significantly improve, and even save, many lives. The majority of people we have interviewed about this have said they would welcome such technology and the increased feelings of safety, comfort and independence it would provide. In fact it seems likely to us that only through the use of such technology will we have the power to improve the current abysmal state of the care industry, and to significantly increase the quality of life of those vulnerable people who most need our help.

Sue Sharples, Vic Callaghan and Graham Clarke

SOCIAL CLASS AND HEALTH INEQUALITIES

For more than 150 years the measurement and monitoring of health inequalities has been a central concern of UK government statisticians. Medical and social scientific researchers have also undertaken wide-ranging analyses of health inequalities. The weight of all this scientific and statistical evidence points to a socioeconomic explanation. That is, as in many other areas of life, inequalities in health reflect the differential exposure, from pregnancy, through birth and across the life course to death, to the risks associated with socioeconomic position.

There are many ways of measuring socioeconomic position: income, education, housing tenure and occupation have all been used for this purpose, both separately and together. However, in the UK the traditional way to measure socioeconomic position has been via a socioeconomic classification and specifically by *social class* as a measure of the social structure. This tradition dates back to 1913 with the creation of the Registrar General's Social Classes (RGSC). RGSC brought together into each of its classes, occupations of similar 'social standing'. It was used by researchers in both government and universities to analyse fertility, mortality and morbidity. The point of these analyses was to show that health inequalities are the outcome of causal processes that are inextricably linked with the basic structure of society. For example, researchers showed that there was a health gradient – people in Classes I and II (professionals and managers) had consistently better health and longer lives than people in Classes IV and V (partly skilled and unskilled occupations). Even as the overall health of everyone improved during the twentieth century, the class gradient in health remained and then began to widen after the 1980s.

The RGSC was modified many times between 1913 and 1991. Eventually, it became difficult to maintain because of uncertainties about how best to allocate different occupations to its six classes. Useful as it was empirically, it was unclear what it was actually measuring and, indeed, whether it was still necessary for government to produce this type of classification. So, in 1994 the government commissioned the Economic and Social Research Council (ESRC) to review its social classifications and make recommendations for their revision or replacement. In turn, ESRC appointed University of Essex sociologists David Lockwood and David Rose to undertake this work. The result was the creation of a new government classification to replace RGSC, the National Statistics Socio-economic Classification (NS-SEC). The NS-SEC became the official UK measure of social class from 2001 and is used for the analysis of all government social surveys as well as Population Census data.

Like the RGSC, the NS-SEC is an occupationally based classification but has rules to provide coverage of the whole adult population. The basic information required to create the NS-SEC is occupation, coded to the unit groups (OUG) of the Standard Occupational Classification 2000 (SOC2000), and details of employment status (whether an employer, self-employed or employee; whether a supervisor; number of employees at the workplace).

The version of the classification, which will be used for most analyses (the analytic version), has eight classes, the first of which can be subdivided.

The National Statistics Socio-economic Classification		
1	Higher managerial and professional occupations	
	1.1	Large employers and higher managerial occupations
	1.2	Higher professional occupations
2	Lower managerial and professional occupations	
3	Intermediate occupations	
4	Small employers and own account workers	
5	Lower supervisory and technical occupations	
6	Semi-routine occupations	
7	Routine occupations	
8	Never worked and long-term unemployed	

The NS-SEC was developed from a social class measure designed by the Oxford sociologist John Goldthorpe. The decision to adopt the Goldthorpe classification as the basis for the NS-SEC was made because it was widely used and accepted internationally, had conceptual clarity, and had been reasonably validated both as a measure of class and as a good predictor of health and educational outcomes.

Thus, as with Goldthorpe's class schema, the NS-SEC has been constructed to measure the employment relations and conditions of occupations. Conceptually these are central to delineating the structure of socioeconomic positions in modern societies and helping to explain variations in social behaviour and outcomes, such as health inequalities.

The NS-SEC distinguishes four basic employment positions - employers, the self-employed, employees and those involuntarily excluded from paid employment. Within the category of employers, a further distinction is made between large and small employers according to the number of employees in the organisation. Employees are sub-divided into classes according to the type of contract they have with their employer. Two basic contract types are distinguished - the labour contract and the service relationship.

Labour contracts involve a relatively short-term and specific exchange between employers and employees of money (a wage) for effort. This is the situation which pertains for the whole working class, although its most basic form is found in the case of routine occupations in class 7. The service relationship, however, is typical for managerial, professional and senior administrative positions, and its basic form is found in class 1. This form of contract involves a longer-term and more diffuse exchange in which employees render service in return for both immediate and future compensation (a salary, regular pay reviews, perks of various types, a career, generous pension schemes etc). Other types of employee, for example clerical and technical workers in class 3, are defined as intermediate in terms of employment regulation, having contracts with elements of both the service relationship and the labour contract.

The excluded comprise those who have never worked but would wish to, and the long-term unemployed. However, other non-employed persons, such as those who look after the home, the retired, the short-term unemployed, the sick and disabled, etc., are classified according to their last main occupation. Full-time students can also be treated similarly if required. In this way, it is possible to classify most of the adult population within the NS-SEC.

The NS-SEC has been shown to be a good discriminator in terms of earnings, unemployment experience and duration, smoking behaviour, morbidity, mortality and subjective health. For example, comparing Classes 1 and 7 in terms of the major causes of early death, men in Class 7 are 2.5 times more likely than men in Class 1 to die early from heart disease, 3.5 times more likely to die from a stroke, twice as likely to die from cancer and more then four times likely to commit suicide. Findings such as these are of great concern to the present government and are featured in recent government commissioned reports both on health inequalities and on public health. One of the government's main health targets will be to reduce health inequalities between the NS-SEC classes. History suggests that this will be no easy task. As the health statistics show, the inequalities of class are not easily eroded. Whatever we may think to the contrary, there is a class destiny that shapes our ends – and, for that matter, our beginnings and middles.

David Rose

WALKING ECONOMY: A HIDDEN RESOURCE IN SEVERELY IMPAIRED CHRONIC HEART FAILURE PATIENTS

Walking capacity is an important factor determining quality of life in patients with chronic heart failure (CHF). The ability to walk decreases progressively from New York Heart Association class I to III, and has been shown to be an independent predictor of hospitalization rate and mortality in CHF patients. Additionally a high correlation between psychosocial adjustment to advanced CHF and walking capacity has been demonstrated. The aim of the present study was to analyse the effect of a three-week exercise program on performance and economy of walking in CHF patients.

Sixteen male patients with severe CHF (age: 52 yrs, height: 175 cm, body mass: 75 kg, VO_2Peak: 11.9 ml.kg^{-1}.min^{-1}, ejection fraction: 20.8%) participated in the study. Eight patients were on a heart transplant waiting list. The training program included three treadmill walking sessions 10 min each and five times cycle ergometry for 15 min each with a weekly energy cost of approximately 650 kJ and 270 kJ for cycling and walking, respectively. Before and after the three-week program each patient was submitted to a self-paced 6 min - walking test on a treadmill. Walking power and energy cost of walking were calculated from respiratory gases, changes in blood lactate concentration and walking speed.

The exercise training increased the 6 min maximal self-paced walking speed by 88.5 ± 48.7 %, whereas the corresponding oxygen uptake and metabolic walking power above rest increased only by 15.7% and 33.7% (all significant differences). The blood lactate concentration response was unchanged, and the energy cost of walking decreased (Table 1).

Table 1. Walking performance and economy pre and post three weeks of exercise training

	Pre	Post	P-value
Speed (m·s^{-1})	0.68 ± 0.33	1.16 ± 0.30	0.001
VO_2Peak (ml·kg^{-1}·min^{-1})	10.0 ± 2.2	11.6 ± 2.3	0.01
Blood lactate (mmol·l^{-1})	1.0 ± 0.3	1.1 ± 0.2	n.s.
Power (W·kg^{-1})	2.16 ± 0.89	2.73 ± 0.91	0.01
Energy Cost (J·kg^{-1}·m^{-1})	3.31 ± 0.66	2.33 ± 0.38	0.001

Approximately two thirds of the improvement in walking economy resulted from a better walking technique. The remaining fraction was the consequence of a more adequate self-paced walking speed.

An approximately 89% higher self-paced walking speed offers an essentially augmented potential to sustain physical stress of normal life and an enormous success concerning the quality of life. The present results demonstrate that in CHF patients with severe exercise intolerance walking capacity can be dramatically increased within a three-week rehabilitation program. The benefit for self-paced walking which can be attributed to the increase in metabolic power was smaller, compared to the improvement in walking economy.

Therefore, in severely de-conditioned patients, standard exercise tests for the determination of central hemodynamics and metabolic capacity should be combined with tests for performance of basic activities providing for daily needs, because the latter do not necessarily represent metabolic capacity. The economy of motion may be the dominant factor for improved performance capacity after exercise training programs, especially in patients with severe exercise intolerance. Adequate exercise training programs and their evaluation should contribute to both favourable metabolic changes and positive effects on the economy of motion.

Ralph Beneke, Renate Leithäuser and Katharina Meyer

ETHICAL ISSUES RAISED BY INFERTILITY TREATMENTS

Some argue that there is a human right to reproduce or to found a family. How best to formulate and to construe this right, if there is one, is an important and controversial matter. It may be modestly interpreted as a right to be free to have children without interference from the state or others. Or it may be more robustly construed as including a right to be given assistance to reproduce artificially when one is either unable or unwilling to have children by the normal sexual means. If the latter is the preferred interpretation, then it can be argued that the state should fund infertility treatment more generously that it presently does.

Those who present for treatment at infertility clinics are subjected to a regime of moral scrutiny. Many clinics have ethics committees to which cases can be referred and, even in the absence of such committees, clinicians are obliged by law to consider the interests of any child that may be born as a result of the treatment before agreeing to the treatment. Ordinary parents undergo no such moral investigation and it has been argued by the leading medical ethicist, John Harris, that this discrepancy is both irrational and discriminatory. I believe it to be neither.

There are moral puzzles surrounding the creation of people that we do yet fully understand. As mentioned, clinicians are required to take account of the interests of the prospective child before agreeing to treat the parents, and they will sometimes refuse treatment on the apparently sensible ground that the child will or may incur certain disadvantages when it is born. And yet to deny the child life in this manner seems an odd way to protect its interests.

From the child's point of view it seems almost always better to be born than not to be born, even if it has got some of the disadvantages that sometimes lead clinicians to refuse treatment. There is something of a paradox in the fact that the law by implication takes the view that the interests of the child are likely to be the prime reason, if there is one, for refusing treatment, when on further reflection it seems that the interests of the child almost never tell against treatment.

Will Cartwright

EMPLOYMENT EXPERIENCES OF PEOPLE LIVING WITH NEUROLOGICAL CONDITIONS

E xperiencing an illness or injury of the brain or spinal cord, conditions which often produce variable symptoms over time, can reduce employment opportunities. The British Household Panel Survey (BHPS), managed by the University of Essex, has followed over 10,300 persons living in a random sample of over 5,500 households in England, Wales and Scotland since 1991. The BHPS includes questions recording whether respondents have experienced neurological conditions as well as periodic batteries of questions about physical functioning. The BHPS thus offers the opportunity to compare the experiences of working aged people living with neurological impairments with those of working-aged people with other impairments or no major health concerns.

Slightly more women than men aged 20 to 65 reported a neurological condition in the BHPS main sample. The proportion of the population in this age range reporting such impairments has risen over the last decade, while the proportion of people reporting other forms of disability has remained roughly constant.

When they find paid employment, people with neurological conditions work similar hours to people with no major health problems. People living with a neurological problem, however, are more likely to wish that they could work more hours than other sample members. People with any form of health problem are less likely to work for themselves and also are more likely to travel to work as a passenger in a private vehicle than to drive themselves. Curiously, though, people with neurological conditions are more likely than the rest of the population to walk or cycle to work.

This group does not appear to gravitate to some forms of employment (such as self-employment or working at home) which might offer more flexibility for meeting their health care needs. Even so, people living with neurological impairments were more likely than other Britons throughout the life of the panel to express complete satisfaction with their job, though the level of complete job satisfaction has declined over the last decade for all working people. The process of finding a new job after losing a job takes longer for people with neurological conditions than for people without impairments, though people with other forms of disability face even longer periods of unemployment.

When background factors are held constant, people with neurological conditions and people with other impairments are similarly less likely to work than the rest of the population, though people with neurological conditions of working-age are more likely than people with other impairments to have left the paid labour market. Similar factors affect the likelihood of working or of being outside the paid workforce for all Britons. While having responsibility for a child aged less than 12 serves as an incentive to work, this incentive is particularly strong for people with neurological impairments. Also, in contrast to the rest of the British population, losing a partner (and thus a level of both personal and financial support) also proves a powerful incentive to work for people living with neurological concerns.

Kimberly Fisher

Factors Associated With Paid Work for People Aged 20 to 65 (from Logistic Regression modelling)

	Exponential ß	Significance
All people aged 20 to 65		
Factors that increase the likelihood of working		
Having responsibility for a child aged <12	17.96	0.000
Household has access to a car	1.61	0.000
Household owns or is buying home	1.60	0.000
Holds a university or advanced degree	1.51	0.000
Age (older people more likely to be working)	1.29	0.000
Member of a club or organisation	1.19	0.045
Higher equivalised household income	1.00	0.000
Age squared	1.00	0.000
Factors that decrease the likelihood of working		
Had a stroke/has a chronic neurological condition	0.53	0.006
Women	0.55	0.000
Lives in Wales	0.56	0.005
Increasing numbers of people living in the household	0.57	0.000
Has a disability but reports no neurological condition	0.68	0.000
Lives in the North of England	0.78	0.036
Number of weeks not working in the last 5 years	0.98	0.000
People living with a chronic or acute neurological condition only		
Factors that increase the likelihood of working		
Having responsibility for a child aged <12	93.09	0.000
Has lost a partner in the last 5 years	19.81	0.025
Higher equivalised household income	1.00	0.005
Factors that decrease the likelihood of working		
Increasing numbers of people living in the household	0.42	0.006
Number of weeks not working in the last 5 years	0.97	0.000

Source: British Household Panel Survey 1991-2001

CRIME AS A PUBLIC HEALTH ISSUE

I n one classic in the post-war public health literature, Morris (1955) observed that:

"Epidemiology may be further defined as the study of health and disease of populations in relation to their environment and ways of living. In a society that is changing as rapidly as our own [i.e. in the 1950s], epidemiology has an important duty to observe contemporary social movements for their impact on the health of the population."

Morris then queried what the public health impacts of the dramatic social and economic changes of the 1950s might be – for example, car-usage, persistence of poverty, the end of rationing and changes in diet, and the growth of urbanization. But, importantly, he also added:

"And what can we learn from other indicators of community health: crime, for example – the ups and downs of juvenile delinquency, and the apparent increase of sex crimes and of crimes of violence during a period when so much other crime is decreasing?"

Both the incidence of crime and its' impact on the community have increased enormously in subsequent decades. Around 40 years after Morris, the Acheson Report (1998) on inequalities in health noted that both victimisation *and* fear of crime and violence can have damaging consequences for health. Importantly, Acheson noted the simple but important point that increased risk of ill health and of crime are highest amongst those already most disadvantaged. Furthermore, *"Although the evidence is incomplete, the link between income inequality, social cohesion and crime has important policy implications"* (Acheson, 1998: 54).

Following from this and a variety of sources in the health and criminology literatures, we can propose a broad idea of public health that includes crime-related matters. Some of the connections that follow are represented in the Typology below in boxes 1, 2 and 3, while more sceptical and critical positions are summarised in box 4.

Toward a Public Health Approach to Harm Reduction and to Crime Prevention

Moore (1995) observes that *"the criminal justice approach sees violence primarily as a threat to community order; the public health approach sees it as a threat to community health."* Public health approaches stress primary prevention but also work toward prevention at other levels - secondary (identifying cases as early as possible to try to prevent more serious problems) and tertiary (minimising long term consequences of disease or injury). Medicine and criminal justice on the other hand, work mainly at tertiary levels hence the public health approach is an obvious route to develop in relation to crime prevention and community safety planning. Public health is increasingly a social and holistic field and there is considerable scope for future imaginative thinking about its wider relevance for communities today.

Nigel South

1 Crime and Victimization from a Health Service perspective	2 Health Impacts of Crime on Individuals and the Community
Hidden victimization revealed by studies of A&E attenders > possible contribution to community crime survey data; violence against health service staff; impact of staff exposure to crime and violence as post-traumatic stress etc; crime / violence producing financial costs to the health service [eg Shepherd, 1990]	Impacts of crime on physical health Impacts of crime on psychological health Fear of crime and social consequences Costs and impacts of crime on health services [eg Robinson et al, 1998; McCabe and Raine, 1997]
3 Public Health Approaches to Harm Reduction and to Crime Prevention	4 Sceptical and Critical positions
The need for 'joined-up' thinking, multi-agency approaches, redefining some 'crime' matters as public health matters (Moore, 1995; Maher and Dixon, 1999). Public health law and regulation enforcement (eg environmental health officers, health and safety inspectorate) as forms of 'community policing'.	The idea of introducing a Public Health perspective into crime control may be over-optimistic and unrealistic in practice; it may also represent unwelcome extension of surveillance and regulation; such proposals have possible strengths and possible weaknesses (Keithley and Robinson, 2000). For others (Rose, 2000) health perspectives in criminology can be seen as a manifestation of disturbing popular acceptance of eugenicist ideas and biological racism.

g8

HATE CRIME

S ome notorious 'hate crimes' have made the national and international news, pricking the public conscience and sometimes having major public policy repercussions. Take the racist murder of Stephen Lawrence by a gang of white youths in south London in 1993. The Macpherson Inquiry into the flawed police investigation of the crime alleged that 'institutional racism' characterised the investigation: that conclusion led to fundamental changes in the organisation of policing and police training. Clearly, the phenomena of 'hate crimes' have serious consequences for the health and wellbeing of individuals and their communities.

In the United States the callousness of the homophobic attack on the young gay man Matthew Shepard in Wyoming in 1998, who was pistol-whipped and left lashed to a fence in freezing conditions to die later in hospital, generated considerable public debate about homophobic bigotry. The incident was portrayed in the play and the film *The Laramie Project*.

Behind such infamous incidents there are thousands of hate crimes that don't make the news. Estimates from the annual British Crime Survey for 2002/03 suggest that there were 200,000 racially motivated incidents committed in the twelve month period covered by the survey. That number does not include incidents motivated by other forms of bigotry, such as homophobia and antisemitism for which there is little official data.

The United States Federal Bureau of Investigation (FBI) defines 'hate crime' as offences that are 'motivated in part or singularly by personal prejudice against others because of a diversity—race, sexual orientation, religion, ethnicity/national origin, or disability.' Whilst the term 'hate crime' is institutionalised in law in the United States—as in the Hate Crime Statistics Act (1990)—it has no legislative status in Britain. However, the term has been adopted by the Metropolitan Police Services and other police services, and the media, and has become established in popular discourse.

A significant public policy response to hate crime in the United States has been the enactment of laws providing extra punishment for crimes motivated by certain forms of bigotry compared with punishment for the same underlying offences without the bigoted motivation. Similar provisions were enacted in Britain in the case of racially aggravated crimes by the 1988 Crime and Disorder Act and they were extended in 2001 to cover religiously aggravated crimes.

In the United States hate crime laws have been subject to a fiercely contested debate about whether they are desirable and constitutional. Controversy has centred on the alleged restriction by laws of fundamental human rights to freedom of expression and thought. Critics argue that the additional punishment of an offender for the bigoted thoughts in their head when they carry out their crime amounts to the punishment of the expression of ideas and values that government deems abhorrent. Opponents of legislation raise the prospect of the 'slippery-slope' whereby hate crime laws open the door to the punishment of other thoughts that governments consider undesirable. Against the critics, advocates of the laws argue that expression, the thought behind the crimes, or the motivation, are not being punished. Instead, they argue that the laws impose greater punishment for the greater harms they believe are inflicted by hate crimes. The challenging arguments levelled by both sides are explored in in my book *The Hate Debate: Should Hate be Punished as a Crime?*

For many people the term 'hate crime' arguably conjures-up an image of a violent crime committed by extremists or other committed bigots: in other words, hate-fuelled individuals who subscribe to racist, antisemitic, homophobic, and other bigoted ideologies. It's not surprising why many people think this way about hate crimes, because the media focuses on the most extreme incidents as is the case with crime reporting in general.

However, the research suggests that extremists are only likely to be responsible for a small proportion of incidents. Data on the characteristics of offenders supports this assertion. An analysis of the relationship between victim and suspect in homophobic incidents in January 2001, published by the Metropolitan Police Service, London, showed that:
- in just over one-fifth of incidents the recorded suspect was a neighbour,
- in 25% of incidents the suspects were other local people (eg youths).

A similar analysis of racist incidents involving a snapshot of forty-nine incidents recorded by the Metropolitan Police in January 2001, showed very similar proportions of neighbours and other locals as suspects. Nearly one in five incidents were committed by schoolchildren. Such research, limited though it is, barely paints a picture of pre-meditated extremism at work behind incidents. Instead the data suggest that many incidents occur as part and parcel of the victim's and the perpetrator's everyday lives and the volume of incidents clearly shows that hate crime is a serious social problem with implications for health, social work and education issues.

Paul Iganski

^g10

GROWING OLD: THE SCIENCE OF GERONTOLOGY

"*The years of life are threescore and ten, or even by reason of strength fourscore; yet their span is but toil and trouble; they are soon gone and we fly away*," wrote the psalmist, reflecting realities of life in pastoral Palestine nearly three thousand years ago. Despite advances in medical science and changes in social conditions, diet, sanitation, pollution, stress and so on, 70 is still considered a respectable age, 80 is considered elderly, 90 very old and centenarians are exceptional. Certainly improvements in the quality of life and in medical care mean that fewer people die prematurely, but ageing still continues in the same way and at the same time as it did centuries ago. We have not solved the problems of ageing (and its associated diseases such as rheumatoid arthritis, Alzheimer's senile dementia and Parkinson's disease) and dying.

Understanding ageing with a view to ameliorating its effects and perhaps to reverse it has long been a human preoccupation. Marlowe's Dr. Faustus sold his soul to the Devil to regain his youth. The alchemists, when trying to transmute lead to gold, sought an Elixir of Youth. Today much of the cosmetics industry is concerned with creaming over the ravages of age. More profitable than satanic transactions or spending a fortune on 'age-smoothing crème', hair toners or dubious cosmetic surgery might be a study of gerontology, the science of the biology of ageing. Gerontology seeks to understand `senescence', the decline with age in a person's 'vitality', his or her ability to withstand changes in homeostasis and insults from the environment, with a resultant increase in the chances of dying.

We do not know why we senesce. We see the signs of ageing: cateracts, atherosclerotic plaques, loss of muscle tone, skeletal degeneration, and a myriad other manifestations, but we do not know how these relate to the whole picture. The overall sum of ageing is more than its component parts. Numerous theories of ageing have been proposed, each with its passionate supporters and its detractors. For every scientific paper setting forth observations or experiments in favour of a given theory there is another to refute it. Much of the evidence is anecdotal and incomplete. Every answered question seems to pose several new, unanswered questions.

Nature *versus* nurture figures large in gerontological debate. Humans live to ninety, but dogs are old at twenty – our genes make us humans and dogs dogs. Within the species the evidence is less clear-cut. There does seem to be some evidence that human longevity (and slow senescence) is inherited: if you want to live to ninety, choose parents who will become nonagenarians! However the evidence is controversial. Identical twins have more similar lifespans than do non-identical twins, but identical twins are often subject to very similar environmental influences in their early lives. There are a number of conditions such as Hutchinson-Gilford's progeria where patients senesce prematurely – a child of ten has facial, skin and other features of a person of eight times their age. This and some similar conditions are inherited through an autosomal recessive gene, but the details of the "ageing" changes in these children show some major differences to those in natural ageing. Genetically associated susceptibility to certain environmental stresses (e.g. ultra-violet light in people with xeroderma pigmentosum) is linked to hastened senescence.

Environmental factors can promote senescence. Culprits suspected include ionising radiation, toxic chemicals, deficient diets, drug-abuse including alcohol and smoking, obesity and prolonged stress. The evidence is, as always in gerontology, inconclusive. It is hard to sort out cause and effect. Does a disease, the result of environmental damage, cause senescence, or is it the result of senescent changes that make the body less able to cope with environmental insults and so prone to further damage? Random changes at atomic and molecular level also seem to be implicated.

Theories to account for ageing include damage to biological molecules, especially in cell and organelle membranes, by free radicals, often from the diet. Free radical scavengers such as vitamin E are known to prolong the lives of cultures of lung fibroblast cells *in vitro*. Error-prone nucleic acid polymerases and helicases result in a catastrophic positive feedback process in cells whereby further errors upon errors are generated in the synthetic machinery of those cells. Mutant DNA helicases are known to be implicated in Werner's syndrome, another progeria. Cross-linking of molecules ranging from DNA to collagen is known to occur in ageing; somatic mutation of the genome of cells can impair cellular function. At the organism level, breakdown and imbalances of complex homeostatic regulatory mechanisms can compromise the physiological functioning of the body. One of the most exciting modern theories for ageing involves telomeres, the subject of a separate article in this book.

g10

In the vertebrates there is an increasing inefficiency and imbalance in the immune system as we grow old. Involution of the thymus in our teens is followed by a decline in T-lymphocyte function, such cells being all-important in the control of the immune response. The body is less able to cope with infection, and the self-censoring mechanisms of the immune system break down, with an increase in autoimmunity (immune reaction to self), a characteristic feature of many diseases of old age such as rheumatoid arthritis and autoimmune thyroiditis. This anarchic immunological "decadence" could lead to the body's self-destruction.

Gerontologists are far from understanding their subject – we feel we are playing with a huge jigsaw puzzle, trying to see the whole picture from a few pieces, only some of which are joined together. We can say that in the foreseeable suture it is unlikely that human lifespans will be increased significantly (perhaps as well, for socio-economic reasons). But gerontologists are trying to understand ageing to help people live happier, healthier, but not excessively prolonged old age, and to alleviate some of the distressing diseases and disabilities of growing older.

Richard Jurd

THE ART OF THE HEART

W hat has human organ transplantation got to do with art or social harmony? In conjunction with Paris-based artist Jorge Orta, the Departments of Art History and Biological Sciences at the University of Essex collaborated on an art-science project to consider the human heart and to raise public awareness of issues relating to immunology and the transplantation of human organs. Orta's art explores the human heart as a biological entity, as a synecdoche for the whole person, as a metaphor for the centre or powerhouse of a place, community or family, and, more generally, in relation to human expression, social harmony and communication.

The project aimed to investigate these ideas and to encourage an understanding of the science involved in organ transplantation. A series of workshops brought together people from different backgrounds including artists, scientists, nurses, teachers and transplantees. Everyone was actively involved in what has been termed *arte co-creativo*, a process similar to that used in scientific projects whereby a 'sensitised' person, a research team or community responds to input signals or messages from, in this case, the artist. The results of these interactive workshops were works of art and performance that addressed the issues of organ transplantation and immunological tolerance at the bio-medical level as well as acceptance, rejection and social harmony at a metaphoric and poetic level.

It is often hard for scientists to communicate with the wider public. Subjects such as *in vitro* cloning, *in vitro* fertilisation, transgenic or genetically-modified organisms and the mapping of the human genome raise bioethical questions that have major implications for society as a whole. This art-science initiative highlighted how artistic language and symbolic expression can help people to understand scientific issues. One of the findings of the project was that through symbolic language the problem of organ transplantation becomes intelligible to a wider audience and the non-connoisseur. Another finding was the way in which a metaphoric analogy can be drawn between the human immune system and the displacement and migration of human populations around the planet. The central paradigm of immunology as defined by the British immunologist Peter Medawar is that it is "...*a system that has evolved to recognise self from non-self*..." In the case of transplants the recipient's immune system recognises the transplanted organ as non-self and thus mounts an immune response. These are often termed 'rejection episodes', like an encounter between two clashing cultures. The rejection can be ameliorated by donor-recipient biological matching and by suppression of the immune system with drugs. In society, laws and human predisposition to tolerance can ease the blending of cultures.

The best outcome and only way forward for a transplanted organ without a full biological match is to undergo a process of donor-recipient adaptation and immunological tolerance. A parallel can be drawn with society where the patient development of mutual tolerance is essential if displaced communities are to settle and contribute to their recipient countries. The implication of the biological metaphor is that the continued health of a country depends upon the successful incorporation of new elements. This would ensure *'hybrid vigour'* leading to diversity; a precondition for evolution and survivability of the species.

In the past – and the paradigm case would be Leonardo da Vinci –art and science were part of a single body of enquiry. Today art can be used as a strategy to teach and practice science, and to communicate scientific ideas to society at large.

Nelson Fernandez, Gabriela Salgado and Valerie Fraser

209

THE ETHICAL AND METHODOLOGICAL ISSUES OF ASSESSING THE REPRODUCTIVE HEALTH NEEDS OF YOUNG ASYLUM SEEKERS

People who have fled their homelands to seek asylum in other countries may have suffered sexual exploitation or abuse. Where healthcare has not been easily accessible, the reproductive health needs of asylum seekers may go unmet. Even when healthcare is available, it is not always sought. War related sexual violence has been widely reported across Sub-Saharan Africa and Eastern Europe. But because of the cultural stigma attached to rape, many of its victims are unwilling to speak about their rape.

Young asylum seekers are subject to the same sexual health risks as older female asylum seekers. However, their predicament is compounded by their limited knowledge of physiological changes in adolescence and sexual health matters. In refugee camps in Angola, young people suffering from STDs or HIV often self-diagnose and use unsafe traditional treatments. In some parts of the world, maturity of age does not always mean a greater understanding of sexual health. The majority of Iranian women refugees in Turkey have never heard of HIV/AIDS.

Moreover, the reproductive health needs of young asylum seekers and their sexual behaviour are largely determined by their cultural and economic backgrounds. Adolescent refugees in Bangkok who have been separated from their families tend to engage in high STD/HIV risk behaviour. The internal conflicts in Columbia and the resulting poverty force many adolescents into prostitution to provide for their families. Against this background, international studies have found that the reproductive health needs of young refugees and asylum seekers are unmet. The World Health Organisation and United Nations High Commissioner for Refugees (UNHCR) have highlighted the provision of reproductive health services as an important element of health care for refugees and asylum seekers.

Parts of Essex have a large population of asylum seekers who come from sub-Saharan Africa and Eastern Europe. Local health and social care providers are keen to ensure that their needs are accurately identified so that limited resources are appropriately targeted to meet these needs. To this end, they commissioned us to undertake a healthcare needs assessment on the local asylum seeker population, focusing on the reproductive health of young asylum seekers.

Healthcare needs assessments can be performed on individual patients as and when they present themselves for treatment. However, this approach risks ignoring those individuals with healthcare needs who do not seek treatment. On the other hand, assessing the reproductive healthcare needs of young asylum seekers at a population level raises a number of ethical and methodological issues.

The project sought to explore issues that are culturally sensitive. Some of the participants were therefore concerned that their involvement and the information they disclosed might compromise their relationships with family, friends and partners. The assessment process was therefore designed to ensure confidentiality and sensitivity. Since most of the assessments involved translators, selection and training was carefully managed to safeguard the interests of participants.

The assessment required participants to recount the events that led them to seek asylum, which inevitably evoked painful memories. "Debriefing" or counselling support was provided in order to minimise distress. The Government is keen to promote needs-led and evidence-based health care. However, the current dispersal policy hinders the gathering of evidence from which to plan health care services for the local asylum seeker population and in general for asylum seekers across the UK. Over the course of the study, a number of participants were relocated to other parts of the country, resulting in a decrease in the original sample size. In addition, a number of participants who had agreed to take part did not keep their appointments.

Assessing the reproductive health needs of young asylum seekers poses a number of challenges. We found that with careful planning, we were able to overcome the ethical and methodological issues. However, the dispersal policy, which was introduced to relieve pressure on London and the South, continues to disrupt health service planning, thus increasing ill health amongst an already vulnerable population.

Kimmy Eldridge and Robin Mutter

ASYLUM SEEKERS: THE PROBLEMS OF HEALTH AND SOCIAL CARE PROVISION

Contrary to British media images, the majority of refugees in the world seek asylum in neighbouring countries and their intent is to return home as soon as it is safe to do so. This is born out by recent figures.

. . in 2000 almost 800,000 refugees throughout the world returned to their home country.

Applications to the UK are controlled through a number of Asylum Acts dictating and restricting lengths of stay and rights of citizenship. However, refugees have the right to seek asylum in the UK under the directives of the 1951 Geneva Convention and this right is reinforced by the Human Rights Act 1998, which means the UK has to adopt some national, European and global responsibilities for displaced peoples.

Those asylum seekers who make it to the UK are entitled to access primary health and social care while their applications are being considered. In spite of the fact that the majority of asylum seekers arrive in good health, there are some who require medical and social care whose needs will depend on the country of origin and living conditions both at home and in temporary accommodation within the UK. It is not just the availability of health and social care services that is important but also their accessibility.

Planning service provision

Any service provision needs planning, a factor which is more complicated when dealing with unknown or highly mobile populations. This does not just apply to asylum seekers but also to other groups like travellers, the homeless and migrant workers and most health and social care provision can be absorbed within mainstream services, given appropriate strategic planning and resources.

There are however a number of particular challenges to planning services for asylum seekers and refugees.
- The most important challenge is ensuring the cultural competency of staff by offering cultural awareness training and an understanding of the potential health and social care problems faced by asylum seekers. However, the resourcing of such projects, especially in terms of cover supply, can represent difficulties for professionals working in the field.

- The second challenge concerns the preparation of the local community. *Planning needs to be particularly sensitive towards the host communities ensuring that existing services can, and are seen to, meet the needs of the local population.*

Some local government agencies have enlisted the support of the media in presenting positive images of asylum seekers and refugees in an attempt to curb racism. But there are other approaches that could be considered, as this community worker suggests:

'Myths needs busting. When Bolton asylum team place asylum seekers in houses, they visit the neighbours on either side and explain who the people are, where they have come from and why they have come to the UK. They find this reduces the tension.'

- The provision of health and social care services is enhanced by multi-agency collaboration but while working together is well-documented as good practice, it can be difficult to convert well-intentioned, multi-agency meetings into action on the ground. Often no-one wants to take responsibility and no-one wants to budget for multi-agency work. Taking a holistic and multi-disciplinary approach when working with asylum seekers is important. It not only enables an exchange of expert knowledge and highlights areas where good practice exists but it also accommodates a pro-active, rather than reactive, response to service provision.
- Probably the least recognised but most vital component to health and social care provision is the involvement of voluntary and community groups, especially asylum seekers and refugees themselves, in planning services. Most voluntary and community organisations have considerable experience in working with minority groups and displaced peoples and may be better placed to provide emergency front line services than statutory organizations.

Accessing service provision

Dealing with the problems of provision for asylum seekers and refugees is just one side of the coin, we also need to consider just some of the difficulties these groups have in accessing services.

- Lack of communication is the key difficulty for non-English speaking groups. Until recently the interpretation and translation services within health and social care have been in disarray. And while the supply and quality of interpretation is improving there is still some way to go. Interpreters should be offered to all non-English speakers who access the health services. However, there are several issues to be taken into account, such as the appropriateness of a male interpreter for a female client. For some cultures and in some circumstances this situation would be unacceptable. Furthermore problems of confidentiality can occur if community interpreters, family or friends are used, particularly in cases involving sexual health, domestic violence or child abuse.

- For some asylum seekers and refugees it is the nature of the health condition that acts as a barrier to service provision. Mental and psychological distress, for instance, is stigmatised in many cultures and given that it is estimated that 5-30% of asylum seekers have witnessed or experienced torture, cultural disparities need to be taken into account. This requires a two pronged approach in order to disclose the cultures of difference about mental health and expected responses and to develop more holistic and less westernised models of therapy.

- Accessing services can be even more complicated for unaccompanied children who are seeking asylum and who face particular health and social care needs. It is estimated there are over 8,000 of such unaccompanied children in the UK. All of these have suffered separation and loss and many have witnessed war and torture. This group of young people face a high rate of mental and psychological distress and illness which is exacerbated for some by bullying, racism and low self-esteem.

Conclusion

The adequate provision of health and social care services for asylum seekers and refugees involves thoughtful strategic planning within multi-agency management teams. But it does not stop there. The professional workers in the field need more than additional financial and staffing resources, they require cultural competency, information and in some cases specialist training to be able to offer appropriate services.

Asylum seekers represent one of the most stigmatised and excluded groups in society. Taking steps to ensure access to public sector services is empowering and creates better opportunities for successful integration.

Jackie Turton

CHANGE AND CONTINUITY IN THE NATIONAL HEALTH SERVICE

Contemporary debate about the National Health Service (NHS) such as the development of Foundation Hospitals and the Private Finance Initiative (PFI) demonstrates how continuity intersects with change. In particular it illustrates the search for the answer to the problems of how to recognise and cater for local diversity within a system whose aim is to provide universal health cover.

Prior to the inception of the NHS, provision of hospital care was divided between the voluntary hospitals and the ex-Poor Law municipal hospitals. The voluntary hospitals were founded as charitable institutions and maintained by voluntary subscription. They ranged from large teaching hospitals, concentrated in London and the larger provincial cites to small cottage hospitals. Consultants gave their services free and wages of nurses and junior medical staff were kept at a lower level than in the public sector. By the 1930s less of the teaching hospital funding was coming from charitable donations and shortfalls had to be made up from paying patients in purpose built private wings. Although equipment could be bought with the proceeds of funding raising drives, there was often a shortage of staff trained to use it.

The municipal hospitals, run by local authorities, had developed gradually from destinations of last resort to significant health care providers. They dealt with people suffering from chronic and infectious conditions and, increasingly, for acute care that the voluntary hospitals (overwhelmed by demand) could not see. In London the authority with responsibility for the municipal hospitals was the London County Council (LCC), from 1934/40 under the leadership of Herbert Morrison. With 75,000 beds (including 35,000 mental) the LCC was arguably the largest hospital authority in the world, rivalling in size the entire voluntary sector of England and Wales.

However, many smaller and less resourced authorities perpetuated the low image of the municipal services in public and professional consciousness. New management could not altogether remove the stigma of the Poor Law from the municipal hospitals. Geographical disparity and their Poor Law legacy affected the perception of municipal hospitals.

This may have been one explanation for the antagonism of the medical profession towards them but another related to the management arrangements of municipal health services. Unlike their colleagues in the voluntary sector, doctors working for local authority health services were salaried employees. For the majority of the medical professional this was regarded as anathema and a threat to their professional authority. In the municipal hospitals the senior doctor was the medical superintendent whose role had more management than clinical elements. The medical superintendent was considered by colleagues to be less of a specialist and working under them was considered to be a threat to clinical expertise.

During the inter-war years there was a growing realisation that a solution had to be found to the problems of health provision nationally. During World War II hospital services were co-ordinated nationally by means of an Emergency Medical Service (EMS). The success of the EMS during wartime was powerful evidence that a National Health Service was possible in peace too. Because of the financial problems of the voluntary hospitals and the achievements of authorities such as the LCC, there was strong support in the Ministry of Health for a municipal model of health service. The support of the medical profession was crucial to any plans; this meant that the 1944 White Paper based on local authority management of the proposed service would not be acceptable.

Aneurin Bevan, the Minister of Health in the 1945/51 Labour government, implemented the bold solution of incorporating both hospital sectors and making them accountable to the Minister of Health, thus nationalising the hospital service. He also negotiated favourable contractual terms with the doctors, memorably declaring that he had silenced their protests by stuffing their mouths with gold. The terms of the settlement also meant that the LCC hospital service was dispersed to four metropolitan health regions which met at a central point, allowing no region and no one entity to run London's health care. Countering the disappointment of Morrison at the LCC's loss, Bevan pointed out that local authority control of health services would always be a varied experience which would be prevented by the universal principle embodied in his solution. It was to be fifty years before London again had a unified health authority. It may be accurate to describe the creation of the NHS as a monument carved by the art of the possible, the best of the feasible options at the time. While this short account has demonstrated the truth of the evaluation by Powell, it must also be remembered that in selecting the most feasible options for the operation of the NHS at any given time, account has to be taken of the multifactoral socio-political variations on continuing themes.

Stephanie Kirby

RATIONING HEALTH CARE RESOURCES

I n the modern world, health is viewed as a right. In economically developed societies (the USA being the great exception), this has come to mean that all citizens secure access to health care in terms of need rather than the ability to pay. The exact institutional means by which this happens varies from country to country. Some societies fund health care directly out of taxation; others use publicly regulated health insurance funds. But the principle of access as a right is established.

The right is not just a right to basic care, but to high quality care that covers a range of services. Hence, access is not simply to life-saving care (resuscitation from a heart attack or an operation for cancer), but also to medical interventions aimed at improving the quality of life, including dental care, joint replacements and mental health services. The modern health care state is based on the principle that citizens should enjoy comprehensive, high quality care without financial and other social barriers to access.

Yet public policies of this sort pose a problem. How is it possible to finance the economic demand that the right to health care involves? Over the last fifty years, since systems of public health care provision have been in place, expenditure on health care has risen in all societies faster than general income. The effect has been that health care spending has taken up an increasing proportion of national income, so that across OECD countries health care spending takes up around ten per cent of national income on average. The problem of health care rationing is how to balance the right to health with economic feasibility.

There are no easy solutions. In the early days of public provision, in the 1950s and 1960s, some economists argued that the problem was publicly provided care itself. Because consumers of health care in public systems faced no price constraint on the use of services, it was argued that they 'over-consumed' resources as a consequence.

The trouble with this line of argument is that in the US, where health care is predominantly a private matter, health care expenditure has risen to higher levels than anywhere else in the world, so that Americans spend some 15 per cent of their average income on health care. Privatising health care provision would both deny the right to health and increase spending.

An alternative approach is to ration by trying to cut down on demand. If people could be encouraged to lead healthier lives, and if risks to health from the environment could be reduced, then it is argued that demand on medical care could be reduced. Yet, life-style measures can only deal with part of the problem. There are many causes of the most prevalent diseases.

Even if everyone exercised regularly and ate well, heart attacks, strokes, diabetes and other diseases would still occur. Also, many people do not want the state to possess the power to police what ordinary citizens eat, drink and do in their spare time. And as people live into old age, so the diseases of old age – dementia, prostate cancer and joint failure among others – await to cause further demands on health care.

In the UK at present, the main body making recommendations on the sort of treatments that the NHS should fund is the National Institute for Clinical Excellence (NICE). It looks at specific medical conditions or technologies (for example what should be done to reduce blood pressure) and makes recommendations as to the most cost-effective strategies. It strives to ensure that treatments are good value for money, but observers agree that the effect of its recommendations has been to increase demand for medical services, particularly in connection with drug treatments.

From one point of view, the demand for medical care is endless, for human beings will always want to live longer and happier lives. What health care citizenship means in a democratic society is that, though we all cannot live for ever, we should all have an equal chance of a long and healthy life. How to achieve that, however, is a large problem.

Albert Weale

NEW TYPES OF LEADERSHIP FOR A NEW NHS?

The NHS is currently experiencing the most ambitious modernisation programme since its creation over 50 years ago. There are a number of key drivers that have brought about this significant change agenda.

The NHS has always been a secondary and tertiary led service because traditionally the power base for health care has been with hospital consultants. However, most people's experience of healthcare is in primary care, for example with general Practitioners, health visitors and school nurses. There is a strong belief that the NHS should be led by Primary Care, particularly because of the increasing importance of the public health agenda in relation to issues such as obesity and sexual health. The creation of Primary Care Groups, and then Trusts, by the 1997 White Paper 'The New NHS; Modern, Dependable' sets out the government's vision for a primary care NHS that can truly reflect the health needs of its local population.

The increasing specialisation of medicine along with technological advances and patients living for decades with chronic illness has led to a shift in thinking about how healthcare should be delivered. There is a continuing debate about the fast disappearing role of the 'generalist' doctor both in primary and in secondary care as it is clear from the evidence that patients managed by a specialist practitioner in a specialist centre have much better health outcomes. But what if your local specialist is 100 miles away? The need to create 'hub and spoke' models of healthcare, such as in cancer care as well as specialist networks, spells out new ways of working collaboratively across geographical and professional boundaries.

The public demand for and expectation of healthcare is very different to what can actually be delivered. Bevan's vision in 1946 was that once the newly created NHS had 'mopped up' all the ill health backlog in the population the demand for healthcare would actually decrease. This could not be further from reality. Despite year on year real increases in health spending for the last five years the public have yet to be convinced that the health service can deliver. It has been difficult for any government to admit that demand for health care will always outstrip supply. How to provide an efficient and effective health service free at the point of delivery, as the NHS is, remains an intractable problem for all of Europe and beyond. This government's current strategy of forming partnerships with the private sector to increase capacity is fraught with difficulties and many would argue that the bigger questions of whether it is realistic for the NHS to meet all health needs or even if that is a desirable state must be asked.

The NHS plan, which set out the modernisation agenda in 2000 spells out huge increases in key professional staff such as doctors and nurses. However this coincided with a significant downturn in 18-25 year olds choosing a career in public services (although there is evidence that this has recently changed) as well as legislation around Working Time Directives which have significantly impacted on the way junior doctors in particular have worked. This has led many organisations to question the way healthcare professionals traditionally work (which is usually that the patient fits in around the working practices of different professional groups) and instead to consider that other healthcare professionals other than a doctor may be in a better position to develop services around patients' needs, especially in areas such as chronic illness and rehabilitation.

The changing face of nursing
The impact of all of these drivers has affected all professional groups in the Health Service but nursing in particular has been well placed to respond to them by developing a range of nurse led services; often in the initial assessment and treatment of patients presenting in hospital and in health centres as well as taking the lead in chronic illness management such as asthma and diabetes care. The introduction of the Nurse Consultant in 2000 was, for many in the profession, the final acknowledgement that nursing had come of age. Nurse consultants, experts in their field, educated to Masters level, would develop more opportunities for nurse led services, provide expert clinical support and demonstrate much needed leadership and role modeling. Many of the Nurse Consultants in this region are enrolled on the Clinical Doctorate programme in the Department of Health and Human Sciences at the University of Essex. It has become clear how hard many of these pioneers have found the process of establishing their role in organisations often inadequately prepared for their arrival.

Nursing education has for over a decade been preparing nurses to take on flexible roles that question existing practice, advocate for their patients and challenge traditional boundaries. However it has not always been possible for nurses to actually practice in this way, not only because of the challenges it has presented to the medical profession but often because of constraints within nursing itself - a profession often practising within a rule-bound, autocratic culture that could be defensive and suspicious of nurses who wanted to try out new ideas and challenge existing practice.

The modernisation agenda has opened up unprecedented opportunities for nursing to grow and develop professionally, so why have some service developments been so much more successful than others?

One major factor in successful reform has been leadership. Nursing leadership in the past has mirrored the hospitals that it ran; autocratic command and control ensuring that all decisions were made by Matron, then the Ward sister, which junior nurses were expected to follow without question. It has been clear for many years that this model of leadership is not only problematic but undesirable; many of the decisions made by the ward sister were in fact simply unquestioning of medical decisions made by the consultant and demanded a compliant patient. It is probably the changing expectations of patients more than anything else that has challenged this model of leadership, brought sharply into the foreground by the Kennedy report of the Bristol Inquiry.

The inquiry investigated why so many children failed to survive cardiac surgery at the Bristol Royal Infirmary in the mid-1990s and found an organisational culture where it was impossible for staff to raise their concerns or question the appropriateness of surgery. The NHS has since invested heavily in leadership development for senior health care professionals and managers but it is a leadership model very different to one the NHS has been used to. Modern NHS leaders, particularly nurses as they are the largest workforce, are expected to lead in a collaborative, team orientated style, to be questioning of decisions and to be prepared to take risks to ensure patients get what they need. While this is to be applauded, this 'bottom up' approach to leadership does not always sit comfortably in organisations which still covertly have an autocratic culture and/or are struggling with risk management issues.

This paradox is perhaps most apparent with the hapless NHS General Manager, often a nurse by background, who truly believes in leading collaboratively but recognises their job is on the line if they do not meet the specific targets set by the government for their service, often forcing them into a command and control model of leadership with their staff. The government cannot have it both ways; it cannot expect its leading lights to develop new innovative services that truly meet the needs of the patient group while at the same time insist that often incompatible performance targets must take priority. The government intends to relax its targets in 2006 as its view is most of the health service modernisation will be complete. While few believe this will be the case, perhaps in 2006 the health service can truly embrace new models of leadership to develop the services patients really want.

Linda Crofts

221

HEALTHCARE IN ESSEX

T he statutory health, social and community care providers in Essex are the Essex Strategic Health Authority, Essex County Council, Southend and Thurrock Unitary Authorities and the Local Authorities*.

Essex Strategic Health Authority

In April 2002, the North Essex and South Essex health authorities merged and became Essex Strategic Health Authority (Essex SHA), covering the needs of all of Essex. The Essex SHA sets the healthcare strategy for the county, helps NHS Trusts and Primary Care Trusts (PCTs) put national policies into practice, supports modernisation across the county and monitors performance for the Department of Health. Primary Care Trusts receive annual funding from the government and provide healthcare services in the community including GP practices, dentists, opticians and pharmacists. The PCTs also manage community services such as district nursing, community hospitals and clinics. The number of GP practices by PCT can be seen in Figure 1.

Figure 1. Number of GP Surgeries by PCT in Essex 2004

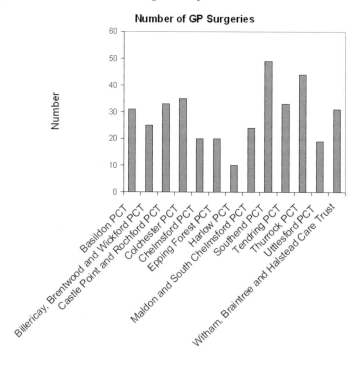

The PCTs and Hospital Trusts in Essex also cover services such as collaborative care, health promotion, health visitors, chiropody, diabetes, occupational therapy, midwifery, dietetic services, community nursing and physiotherapy. Currently in Essex there are 13 Primary Care Trusts:

Basildon PCT	Maldon and South Chelmsford PCT
Billericay, Brentwood and Wickford PCT	Southend PCT
Castle Point and Rochford PCT	Tendring PCT
Chelmsford PCT	Thurrock PCT
Colchester PCT	Uttlesford PCT
Epping Forest PCT	Witham, Braintree and Halstead Care Trust
Harlow PCT	

Essex also has one of the few Care Trusts in the country. Care Trusts are relatively new organisations which have the responsibilities of PCTs but also provide social care in addition to healthcare. Witham, Halstead and Braintree Care Trust operates in an integrated way in a partnership with Essex County Council and Braintree District Council to provide health and social care services. Changing to a Care Trust stemmed from the recognition of the confusing divisions between health and social care for patients by healthcare workers such as GPs and their realisation of the need to unite the two services for better patient care.

Primary Care Trusts buy hospital and other secondary care services from five NHS Trusts across the county: Basildon and Thurrock University Hospitals NHS Trust; Essex Rivers Healthcare NHS Trust; Mid Essex Hospital Services NHS Trust; Southend Hospital NHS Trust and The Princess Alexandra Hospital Trust. In addition Essex SHA oversees ambulance services in Essex provided by Essex Ambulance Services NHS Trust and mental health services provided by North Essex Mental Health Partnership NHS Trust and South Essex Partnership NHS Trust.

In order to reach healthcare service provision targets set by the government, SHAs are implementing Local Delivery Plans (LDP). These LDPs look at tackling issues and improving services such as - waiting times in Accident and Emergency departments; waiting times to see a GP and in Hospital outpatients departments; cancer care provision; coronary heart disease; mental health; older peoples' services; services for people with learning disabilities; and children's services.

Essex County Council, Southend and Thurrock Unitary Authorities
Essex County Council is one of the largest authorities in the country and serves a population of 1.3m people. Southend UA serves a population of

159,000 and Thurrock a population of 143,000. These populations are set to grow as development of the Thames Gateway, north Essex and Stansted Airport area gets underway.

In Essex, social care services (including: community care, children and family services, fostering and adoption, services for people with physical, sensory or learning disabilities, mental health and substance misuse services and older people's services) are the responsibility of Essex County Council and the two Unitary Authorities of Southend and Thurrock, often in partnership with local authorities, PCTs and the voluntary sector.

Community Care in the administrative county of Essex is part of the Learning and Social Care services of Essex County Council, and is overseen by the Head of Community Care. The Community Care Service identifies its top priorities in the coming years as:
- The improvement of care-at-home services, to encourage more people to stay living in their communities
- Deliverance of quicker and better assessments of social care needs
- Help for people with disabilities and for those with mental health or substance abuse problems to lead an independent life.

Social carers focus on helping children to reach full potential at all stages in their development and, as part of the Children and Young People's Strategic Partnership in Essex, work together with the SHA and the education and voluntary sector. Local Authority social services have responsibility for Residential Services and Fostering and Children's assessment and Care management.

Essex County Council Social Services, Southend Social Services and Thurrock Social Services all work in partnership with PCTs, district councils and voluntary sector providers in the care of older people. Through the Age Matters Strategy there is a strong emphasis on enabling and supporting older people living independently at home in the local community.

Mental Health Services in Essex also exist as a partnership between the Essex Mental Health NHS Trusts, Essex County Council, Southend UA, Thurrock UA and the voluntary sector. Most Social Services carers operate as part of multi-disciplinary Community Mental Health teams although Mental Health Services also include Adult Mental Health teams and Adolescent, Substance Misuse and Criminal Justice specialist areas.

Voluntary and Community Sector (VCS)

Under the general umbrella of organisations such as Councils for Voluntary Services and the NCVO, there are many voluntary and community groups in Essex. In addition to smaller locally based groups and charities there are also the local branches of large national organisations and charities such as Age Concern and InterAct for example.

There are fourteen Councils for Voluntary Services (CVS) in Essex which cover similar areas to the district and borough councils within the county. Although these vary from area to area in terms of size, charitable status and member composition they all have similar core functions and are essentially there to provide a supporting and enabling environment for voluntary and community groups to develop in their area.

In Essex there are 15 Local Strategic Partnerships, all of which were started at different times, so community strategies and Compacts across the region are in different stages of development. As well as the District LSPs there is also an Essex Strategic Partnership which was set up in 2001 and aims to pull the county-wide voluntary and business organisations, statutory agencies, district councils and unitary authorities together to consider the county-wide picture. Unsurprisingly but of key importance, one of the major threads of the partnership looks at 'being healthy' in Essex and covers all health issues in the county.

Rachel Hine and Jules Pretty

* This was the case at the time of writing. In 2006, further mergers of SHAs and PCTs will be formalised.

HEALTH TRENDS AND SUPPORT IN ESSEX

There are several areas of priority for health within Essex. These concern hospital and GP waiting times; cancer care, coronary heart disease, mental health services, older people's services, services for people with learning disabilities and children's services. Essex County Council has also set priorities both for social services and for community care as a whole. Nationally, concerns for the government and health promotion information campaigns include the rise in obesity, diabetes and "binge drinking", all health concerns with the potential of putting great strain on healthcare services in the future.

Mortality rates
As illustrated by the government strategy "Our Healthier Nation", four major causes of premature death and illness are cancer, circulatory diseases, accidental injury and suicide. Health indicators show that the biggest killers in Essex are heart disease and strokes and this is also the case for England as a whole. However mortality rates from both heart disease and strokes are slightly lower in Essex than they are nationally and records show that these rates have fallen over the last five years.

Mortality rates from cancer are generally lower both for men and for women in Essex than nationally. Fewer deaths from lung cancer occur in Essex compared to the national picture but mortality rates from breast cancer are close to those in England as a whole. Deaths from accidental injury in Essex are below the England rate, and deaths by suicide show a similar pattern.

Limiting long-term illness
16% of Essex residents described themselves as having a limiting long-term illness in 2001. This was an increase from 11% in 1991. Essex had a similar rate to the region, and was slightly below the national level. Within Essex, Tendring district had a very high rate with nearly a quarter (24%) of residents saying they had a long-term illness.

Within Essex as a whole, 12% of working age residents described themselves as having a limiting long-term illness. For Tendring district the level was 17%, which is still considerably higher than in other districts in

Essex or than nationally (14%). The results also show that illness is not just high amongst the elderly population. The 2001 census also found that 31% of all Essex households contained one or more people with a limiting long-term illness in 2001; regionally this ranged from 27% in Uttlesford to 41% in Tendring.

General Health

A question on general health was included for the first time in the 2001 Census. In Essex, 71% felt they were in good health, 22% in fairly good health and 8% not in good health. This was more positive than nationally and similar to figures for the East region. Tendring residents again felt markedly less healthy.

Disability

People with disabilities can feel isolated in the community in the same way as other minority groups. Access to all services including those of healthcare can be problematic with a physical disability and issues of communication (lack of signers and Braille) may also cause problems.

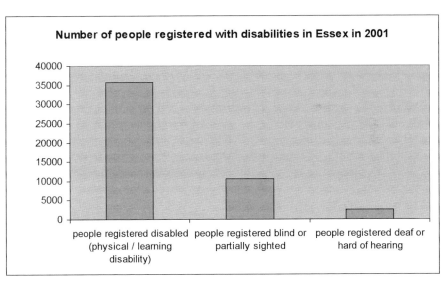

Number of people registered with disabilities in Essex in 2001

There is no single source of information about numbers of people in Essex with disabilities but estimates can be obtained from various indicators, for example i) Labour Force Survey (number of disabled working age adults) ii) disability benefit claimants and iii) those registered disabled with Essex County Council Social Services. In 2002 there were an estimated 121,000 disabled working age adults in Essex which represents approximately

15.6% of the working population in Essex which is slightly lower than the national figure of 18.7%. The number of people in Essex claiming disability benefit in May 1999 was 60,155 which represents 4.6% of the population. This varies across Essex with the highest numbers of disability claimants in Tendring (7%), Harlow (5%) and Basildon (5%) and the lowest numbers in Uttlesford (3%). Tendring District has a high number of people under 65 on Disability Living Allowance.

Social Services supported 1,068 adults with disabilities in residential and nursing care in 2003, of whom 205 had a physical disability and 863 had a learning disability.

Voluntary and community groups are varied over the county of Essex but include:
• Essex Coalition of Disabled People (which also provides disability training for statutory and voluntary organisations and businesses)
• Essex Disabled People's Association
• Disablement Income Group
• Community Care Access website (provides information for all those who work in community care).

Mental Health
Mental health problems are common and widely misunderstood and can vary from conditions such as anxiety to psychotic disorders such as schizophrenia. According to the Office for National Statistics, at any one time, one adult in six suffers from mental health problems of varying severity. Mental health conditions can also vary widely from person to person and may also appear, disappear and reappear at any time throughout an individual's life creating special challenges for healthcare. As with other potentially socially excluded groups, people with mental health problems are often linked with other health problems and socioeconomic factors such as poverty, homelessness, substance misuse, learning disability, poor physical health, and old age.

Nationally, every year, more than 250,000 people are admitted to psychiatric hospitals and over 4000 people take their own lives. In the UK, 628,000 adults of working age regard mental health problems as their main disability and government departments are looking at improving access to healthcare services for people suffering from mental health problems. The National Service Framework for Mental Health (Department of Health) aims to raise standards in health and social care for those with mental

h 5

health problems and in line with this Framework, Essex Mental Health teams have developed 24 hour services and outreach teams.

Mental health service providers in Essex have concluded that given the nature of mental health being intertwined with other health and social issues the most effective way to plan and deliver what people need and want is through both formal and informal collaborative partnerships. These partnerships include those:

- Between service users and service providers
- Between carers (most often close relatives and family) and service providers
- Between statutory and voluntary organisations that provide mental health services
- Between those that commission services and those who provide services

Both Essex Mental Health Partnership NHS Trusts are formal partnerships as integrated health *and* social care providers and link with Essex County Council and also Southend and Thurrock unitary authorities. There is also a partnership with Essex County Council and PCTs in North Essex including Uttlesford, Harlow, Epping Forest, Maldon and South Chelmsford, Witham, Braintree and Halstead, Colchester and Tendring.

Essex Child and Adolescent Mental Health Services (CAMHS) deal with the youth offending teams in North Essex and are responsible for services in four key areas: i) assessment of a young persons mental health state in court ii) advice to the criminal justice system beyond the courts regarding the young persons problems iii) liaison with other services regarding on-going therapeutic care and iv) limited on-going treatment in the community. The youth offending teams in North Essex include those in Chelmsford, Colchester, Harlow, Basildon, Southend and Thurrock. The CAMHS also provides young people and their carers with information and support with issues such as abuse, bullying, child protection, depression, eating problems, phobias, relationships and self esteem.

Recently North Essex Stronger Together (NEST) has been established. This is a Mental Health service user network which is managed and run entirely by current and previous mental health service users. This network works across the whole of Essex and represents users on a range of different committees and groups. NEST aims to be the single point of entry to user involvement in Essex and enables as many people as possible to get involved.

Rachel Hine and Jules Pretty

CONTROLLING THE USE OF PHARMACEUTICALS

In many advanced industrial societies the quantity of prescribed medicines taken by individuals has reached enormous proportions. For instance, in England the number of prescriptions issued in community settings (that is excluding those dispensed in hospital) had reached an average of 12.5 per person by 2002. This is one for every person for every month of their life, and is an increase of 56% in 13 years.

It might be argued that this level of use of prescribed medicines is necessary and beneficial; however, there is evidence that medicines are prescribed and used too readily. Certainly, where illness is severe, drugs can be very valuable, the benefits outweighing the side effects. Yet in more marginal cases the side effects and dangers often outweigh the benefits. It is now well recognised that antibiotics have been overused both in relation to humans and animals.

There is also clear evidence that minor tranquillisers, which are quite frequently addictive, have been prescribed too freely and for too long a period of time. There is recent evidence that hormone-replacement therapies have far more adverse side effects than previously recognised. Medicines are also frequently prescribed in too high dosages. Moreover it is clear that the interaction effects of multiple drug use, particularly common amongst the elderly, have been poorly studied.

The cost of this indiscriminate prescribing is high both in terms of the direct financial costs of the drugs and medical time, and in terms of the high levels of side effects and adverse drug reactions (ADRs). A recent study found that 6.5% of all admissions were the result of ADRs; it also found that the majority resulted from inappropriate prescribing.

The reasons for the high levels of pharmaceutical use are diverse. There is evidence that as people become more affluent and their health and longevity improves, they actually report more ill-health, seek more frequent medical help, and so end up taking more medicines. Affluence allows individuals to attach greater weight to their health and also facilitates the development of more extensive health services. And the highly commercial, multinational pharmaceutical companies encourage people to believe that medicines are the solution to a wide range of problems, and are generally supported in this, for a number of reasons, by the medical profession.

Yet, the evidence suggests that it is the social and cultural circumstances of people's lives – the way the economy and society are organised, the levels of sanitation and standards of living – and the implications of these for people's lives, including diet and exercise, that largely determine health, not the extensive use of pharmaceuticals.

Medicines can be invaluable. Yet nowadays they are often used far too freely and readily with too little regard for their adverse consequences. What is needed is a greater awareness of the risks associated with the taking of medicines, especially when they are taken over long periods of time, and far greater caution over when they should be prescribed and used.

Joan Busfield

PATIENT AUTONOMY AND ITS LIMITS
AT THE END OF LIFE

In the context of medical practice, many problems that need legal answers can arise. Usually, a physician faced with a patient seeking medical advice and treatment will suggest a form of treatment he/she regards as the best possible way of redressing the patient's medical problems. However, many patients have their own views of what they regard as best, so that situations might arise in which patients reject the physician's recommendation of the course of treatment to take. For example, a patient might not like the idea of taking medication, believing that it is better for his/her health to resort to alternative forms of medicine; a patient might disagree with a certain type of medical treatment for religious reasons; or a patient might decide that on the balance, he/she is better off without medical treatment.

What should the physician do in such a situation, if he/she sincerely believes that treatment is necessary in order to cure the patient? Does the physician have the right and maybe even the obligation to do whatever he/she regards as best for the patient, or should the patient's choices be respected? In this scenario, the law needs to decide the conflict between the principle of beneficence, that is that the physician is under an obligation to do good and improve the patient's health, and the principle of patient autonomy, that is that adult patients without mental impairments can determine themselves which course of treatment is best for them, aided by the physician's expertise.

It is now widely accepted that in principle, the adult patient's wishes are determinative. However, in some situations, this might be difficult to accept. Jehovah's Witnesses, for example, refuse blood transfusions, even if these transfusions are necessary to save their lives. Therefore, if a Jehovah's Witness is brought to a hospital, for example after an accident, and needs a blood transfusion in order to survive, the patient's life could very easily be saved by the administration of treatment that normally does not have any adverse consequences. While this causes a difficult dilemma for the physician who, contrary to the values of his/her profession, needs to stand by and see a patient die whose life he/she could save, and while the religious beliefs of Jehovah's Witnesses are not widely shared, the law has nevertheless decided the conflict in favour of patient autonomy. It is submitted, rightly so, because it is primarily the patient who is affected by the consequences of treatment, and to force the values of the medical profession, or the majority in society, upon the individual would mean an important invasion of personal freedom.

Other cases in which patients might reject life-saving treatment are cases of patients who are suffering from terminal illnesses. These cases differ from those of Jehovah's Witnesses mainly in two respects: the decisions are usually not religiously motivated; and death itself might be a desired outcome, as it might provide relief from suffering. Where a patient who is suffering from a terminal illness needs medical treatment, the decision to refuse such treatment needs to be respected as long as the patient is still competent to make such a decision, based on the principle of patient autonomy. However, while the legal principles are straightforward, patients might nevertheless sometimes find it difficult to have their rights respected in the clinical setting.

A recent case demonstrates some of the problems that can arise in this context. Ms B, a woman in her forties, developed medical problems and ended up paralysed from the neck down. She was conscious and able to speak with the assistance of a speaking valve, could move her head and use some of her neck muscles, but not her torso, arms or legs, and was totally dependent on her carers, who fed, clothed and washed her and assisted with her bodily functions. Her life needed to be supported by artificial ventilation through a tracheostomy, a tube in her windpipe, as she was not able to breathe independently. She stayed in an intensive care unit in an NHS hospital and at some point decided that she wanted the ventilation to be withdrawn. Given that she was competent, and given that artificial ventilation is regarded as medical treatment, the legal principles applicable in this case are straightforward – the physicians would have to respect her wishes and switch off the ventilator.

This, however, was not what happened, as the treating physicians felt unable to do so, based on their convictions that it would be beneficial for her at least to try rehabilitation therapy, a therapy which would not improve her physical condition, but they felt might help her live with her debilitated state, before taking such a drastic decision as having life-support terminated. The patient disagreed. The conflict was eventually resolved when Ms B went to court demanding that the court declare the continued ventilation against her wishes to be unlawful, which was granted. This demonstrates that even the existence of clear legal principles, giving patient autonomy precedence over all other interests potentially involved in such cases, do not necessarily guarantee that the patient's wishes are respected in day-to-day medical practice, as paternalistic views of 'doctor knows best' can still be found.

Courts thus have an important role to play in giving patient autonomy the protection it deserves as a matter of law. However, rather surprisingly, in the case of Ms B the court found that even though her treatment had clearly been unlawful, and even though the treating physicians had openly disregarded her autonomous decision, the court stressed that the carers had looked after her 'to the highest standards of medical competence and with devotion. They deserve the highest praise.' This gives a conflicting message, given that treatment against the patient's wishes constitutes a criminal offence as well as a tort, and can therefore hardly be praiseworthy. It can be seen that the courts, while upholding patient autonomy as the predominant principle, are uncomfortable with attaching blame to physicians who act according to their clinical judgment and their conscience, even if they do so in an open disregard of the law.

It would seem that, in the light of this tolerance towards the medical profession and the lack of clear and serious consequences in the case of a violation of patient autonomy (the court, following its own logic, decided that the physicians were not liable for damages, but awarded damages of £100(!) against the hospital), a lot of work still needs to be done to give patient autonomy in practice, and not just in theory, the protection it deserves. This is necessary to ensure that patients who find themselves in such tragic circumstances as Ms B will not be treated against their wishes and kept alive by medical treatment they do not want, as it prolongs their painful condition and causes them anguish, pain and suffering.

More difficult still are cases in which the patient is suffering from a condition that causes tremendous physical and/or mental suffering and faces the prospect of a very long and painful death but does not need medical treatment in order to stay alive. In such cases, the patient therefore does not have the possibility to accelerate the dying process by refusing life-saving treatment. Patients who still have the physical ability to do so, could choose to commit suicide in such a situation. However, in some cases this is not a possibility. In the case of patients suffering from motor neurone disease, for example, in the advanced stages of the illness the patient is fully conscious, but loses all control over his/her muscles, can at some point only communicate with an eyelid, and will eventually even lose this last form of communication.

Thus, in the final stages of the disease, when the patient might decide that he/she is better off dying quickly than having to face the anguish of a drawn out dying process without any possibility to move or to communicate, the patient no longer has the physical ability to end his/her life without assistance. Some patients faced with such a diagnosis express that their quality of life would be enhanced if at least they knew that when they reach a stage of total dependency someone would be willing to give them the assistance they need in order to end their lives and avoid the agony of a slow and painful death. However, in English law assisted suicide is a criminal offence, and actively ending the life of a patient, even if the patient begs the physician to do so, would be murder, to which the patient's consent provides no defence.

In the highly publicised case of Diane Pretty, a woman suffering from motor neurone disease, she wanted the assurance that her husband would not be prosecuted if he helped her with her suicide at a moment chosen by her. She argued that to apply the general prohibition of assisted suicide to her particular case constituted a violation of her right to end her life, her right to be free from inhuman and degrading treatment, and her right to private life. Furthermore, the law was discriminatory, in that it unduly affected disabled persons, as able-bodied people could end their lives without needing assistance. Her claim was rejected by English courts, including the House of Lords, and also by the European Court of Human Rights in Strasburg. From a legal point of view, this outcome was to be expected and even seemed unavoidable but, given the ethical issues involved, the case raises questions of the appropriateness of the law as it stands.

While the state argued that it needs to protect vulnerable patients from potential abuse and therefore defends the need to criminalise assisted suicide and active euthanasia without exception, from the point of view of patients in very painful conditions and who, as in the case of Mrs Pretty, do not feel vulnerable, this seems a harsh approach that does not do justice to the individual case. Taking into account that many physicians admit that at some point in their career they have helped a patient to die, it seems as if the law does not necessarily achieve its' aim nor that euthanasia or assisted suicide are not happening, but rather that these practices are happening in secrecy, without any possibility of state control. It then seems justified to ask whether a system such as that adopted by the Netherlands, where euthanasia can lawfully be practised under certain conditions and with control mechanisms in place, might be a desirable alternative.

Sabine Michalowski

HEALTH POLICY ISSUES IN CENTRAL
AND EASTERN EUROPE

A ll countries, without exception, face problems in relation to the health of their citizens. The post-communist states of Central and Eastern Europe share many of these with their advanced Western counterparts but they must also deal with distinctive problems arising from the 'transition' from communism to democracy. Transition proved a complex process because of the simultaneous introduction of so many profound changes. States in the region changed their political systems with new democratic constitutions, new institutions, free elections and multi-party competition. They moved from an economic system based on central planning of production and distribution to a system based on capitalism, private property, and the market. Economic changes also led to changes in the social structure and new social problems such as increased crime. Those responsible for social policies needed to rethink the ways in which the state provided for its citizens as well as address unemployment, homelessness, and drug abuse which had not featured under the old system.

Indeed, transition proved generally bad for the populations' health. The processes of socio-economic transformation exacerbated certain traditional problems associated with the communist period: these included poor working conditions and lax standards of industrial safety, poor housing, inadequate diet, and too much smoking and drinking. Growing insecurity increased levels of stress, resulting in pervasive mental health problems. Basic indicators such as life expectancy and infant mortality fell in most countries, leading some to speak of a looming 'demographic disaster'. Rates of cardiovascular disease and neoplasms rose, while infectious diseases such as tuberculosis re-emerged at alarming rates and new conditions such as HIV/AIDS began to spread, especially in Russia and the Ukraine.

Existing health care systems were ill equipped to deal with these problems, as well as with the 'normal' demands of the population. For a time, communist systems functioned well. They provided state-funded, comprehensive preventive, curative and rehabilitative care, free at the point of delivery. Quantitative indices were high, especially for the number of doctors and hospital beds, as well as for vaccination programmes and health checks for industrial workers. However, concerns grew in the 1980s over low levels of funding and a failure to respond to new technologies. Aside from the lack of modern equipment, in many countries shortages emerged of basic essentials, such as disposable needles, drugs, bandages and the like. There was wasteful duplication of provision, including health care facilities in large factories as well as in neighbourhoods, along with an underdeveloped primary care sector and over-reliance on specialist clinicians. All health care workers, including doctors, were badly paid. Problems of poor quality and difficulties of access were met with the growing use of 'informal charges' (bribes or 'tips') and the practice of using personal connections for access to the 'best' doctors and hospitals.

When the communist systems fell (1989-92) the ailing health care systems were in dire need of treatment. The conceptual debates underlying discussions of what medicine was needed sound much like those in virtually every other industrialised society: what should the state provide, who should pay for health care, how should provision be structured, and what incentive structure should be adopted to influence physicians' and patients' behaviour. The difference was that in post-communist countries these debates - and early reforms - took place in the context of deep economic recession, general institutional upheaval, and widespread public insecurity.

Reforming health care systems
Health funding was the first major issue to be tackled, and most countries moved to new insurance-based and/or contract-based systems financed from employers' and employees' contributions and modelled on the perceived successes of the Bismarckian model common in Western Europe. It was widely believed that this would increase health funding and protect it from annual battles over the state budget. At the same time, contracts between purchasers and providers would generate greater efficiency in resource allocation and stimulate evidence-based clinical practice. Patients would gain from choice and responsiveness.

In some cases it was assumed that privatization of existing facilities would accompany reform, with (for example) groups of doctors buying up primary care clinics. New private facilities were also permitted. By 1997 health insurance systems had been introduced in the Czech Republic, Russia, Romania, Estonia, Slovenia, and Hungary, and they were later introduced elsewhere. The state continued to make an (often considerable) contribution to health, including public health provision, funding teaching hospitals, and paying contributions for certain groups. In many cases patients were also now expected to pay something for their care. These co-payments were seen as increasing people's responsibility for their own health and thus predicted to have major 'life-style' effects.

The Consequences of Change

It is not surprising that changing the basis of health funding did not prove the magic bullet that many had anticipated. Citizens remained deeply unhappy with access to and the quality of health care provision. Health workers often expressed their discontent over pay and working conditions with strikes and demonstrations. For a variety of reasons overall funding remained low for many countries. High levels of unemployment reduced the numbers contributing to the new funds. Many firms failed to make their scheduled contributions, and even governments did not transfer funds for contributions on behalf of the unemployed, pensioners, children etc. Levels of corruption also remained high, with health-procurement scandals in many countries - Poland and Russia are just two examples. At the same time inflation was high in the health sector, with dramatic price increases for pharmaceuticals and medical equipment. There were *ad hoc* responses, the most common of which was the accumulation of indebtedness to suppliers: clinics and hospitals simply failed to pay their bills. Poland bailed out its hospitals three times in the 1990s, but in 2004 the problem remained acute.

Moreover, the difficulties of measuring costs, including the absence of developed information systems, coupled with inexperience with technical processes of drafting contracts and the lack of competition among providers meant that the new systems did not operate as expected, particularly in regards to efficiency gains. Sometimes reform elements proved contradictory. Although Croatia attempted to strengthen primary care, its use of a capitation system for primary doctors (payment per patient) alongside fee-for-service payments for specialists led to more referrals up the specialist ladder: primary care doctors could get rid of their patients and specialists could earn more fees for more services.

Since citizens retained expectations of comprehensive provision that could not be realised in practice, many countries tried to define what was covered by their new health insurance schemes. This attempt to define the 'basket of services' proved generally unsuccessful, for both political and technical reasons. In Poland, however, it became urgent in 2004: the Constitutional Tribunal declared the amended (2003) health insurance law unconstitutional on the grounds that it did not define what people could expect to receive for their money. Certainly it is the case that without such a basket, it is purchasers who effectively decide - and this itself can undermine equity of access. Indeed, with the partial exception of the Czech Republic, patients everywhere continued to make significant informal payments to secure access to health services. Those who can afford it are also increasingly able to take advantage of private practitioners and (still few) private hospitals.

h
8

Some categories of patients, particularly in areas of disability or mental health, remained badly provided for and for them choice was illusory. Tens of thousands of people continue to be locked away from society in overcrowded and often degrading conditions. In 2003 the international Mental Disability Advocacy Center released a report documenting the use of cage beds in social care homes and psychiatric hospitals in the Czech Republic, Hungary, Slovakia, and Slovenia. These beds are surrounded by metal bars or a strong net and fixed on a tubular metal structure that is closed with a padlock.

In general, patients' rights still remain very undeveloped - not just for socially excluded categories of the population - though the concept made quite an early appearance and some countries tried to formalise Charters of Patients' Rights. But clinical dominance is still strong, and humility and good communications' skills are not notable characteristics of physicians in the region.

Some signs of enlightened practice are emerging. Strong primary care is recognised as essential, and more family doctors are being trained in general practice. Hospital visiting is now far easier, and family and friends are no longer regarded merely as unwelcome intruders. International organisations have provided funding and advice. There are signs that certain groups, especially the more educated strata, are taking healthy living seriously. It should be said, however, that health workers are not always ideal role models. Russia, Bulgaria and the Czech Republic provide just three examples of populations with very high rates of tobacco consumption; in these countries many doctors smoke (some 52% in Bulgaria, where smoking is still permitted in hospitals). However, health care provision remains a serious concern for governments, health professionals, and citizens alike.

Conclusion
Although regional disparities remain considerable, both among and within countries, health issues in post-communist Europe are very similar. The general failure of health care reform shows the need to take into account historical legacies and cultural specificities in promoting change and ensuring its successful implementation. At the same time, the capacity of the state to generate a coherent policy, to communicate effectively with its citizens, and to monitor change are also important factors. Although economic growth would go some way to increasing resources for health care, there can be no quick fix for the multi-faceted problems of the region.

Frances Millard

MRS BEDFORD FENWICK AND THE DEVELOPMENT OF THE NURSING PROFESSION

W hen asked to name a nurse the most frequently mentioned name would probably be that of Florence Nightingale. Florence Nightingale (1820-1910) deserves her reputation as a famous nurse, famous woman and an eminent Victorian. She achieved celebrity status in her own lifetime. Her experience of the Crimean War, which is responsible for much of her fame, took just two years of a long, busy life. The legacy she left to nursing was to make it secular and a career opportunity for women of all classes. However, her reputation has been such that other contributors to the development of the nursing profession have been over-looked.

In 1855, while Miss Nightingale was still in the Crimea, Sidney Herbert of the War Office, set up a committee to collect money from a grateful nation; £45,000 was collected in the form of a fund to enable Miss Nightingale to train nurses. Surprisingly this was not her first priority, her energies being with the needs of the army. The School opened at St Thomas' Hospital in 1860. Monica Baly has shown that the first years of the school were hardly spectacular but publicity for the school was good and by the 1880s hospitals in London, the provinces (and later across the British Empire) had nurse training schools along Nightingale lines. Unlike earlier training institutions, notably St John's House founded in 1848, the new schools were secular with no religious affiliation.

By the 1880s, the leaders of this new reformed nursing movement were beginning to ask whether nursing should be tested by public examination and only those passing an examination be entered on a register and entitled to call themselves 'nurse'. Miss Nightingale was opposed to state registration on the grounds that it would impose a lower uniform standard. She also was of the opinion that examinations could only test technical not personal qualities of the nurse.

The main protagonist for state registration was Ethel Gordon Manson (1857-1947). In many ways she was a product of the reformed training schools. She trained as a lady probationer at Nottingham and Manchester and after a position as ward sister at the London Hospital was appointed Matron of St Bartholomew's Hospital in 1881 at the age of 24.

This experience convinced her of the necessity of a uniform training to raise standards, protect the public and guarantee a professional status for nursing. An active suffragist she also believed that improving the status of nursing would enhance the position of women. As a result of her connections with other activists she founded the International Congress of Nurses. On her marriage to Dr Bedford Fenwick in 1887 she had to resign her clinical post. With his support she then harnessed all her energies to the politics of nursing, predominantly the registration campaign.

One of the main vehicles for the campaign was journalism. In 1893 the Fenwicks acquired the *Nursing Record and Hospital World*, changing its name in 1903 to the *British Journal of Nursing*. As editor, a post she occupied for nearly fifty years, Mrs Bedford Fenwick put her arguments across to her readership. The 1902 Midwives Act gave fresh impetus to her efforts. Nursing was divided on the registration question. From the turn of the twentieth century until 1914, Registration Bills were introduced into Parliament and blocked. It was the impact of changes during World War I (1914-18) which hastened the state registration of nurses. The threat of dilution of nursing by the basically trained Voluntary Aid Detachment (VAD) nurses united nurses in favour of registration.

The 1919 Nurses' Registration Act laid the legislative framework. The General Nursing Council (GNC) became the statutory body for nursing in England and Wales. Mrs Bedford Fenwick is recorded on the original GCNC register as State Registered Nurse no 1. The present regulatory body for nursing - the Nursing and Midwifery Council (NMC) - continues to protect the public by setting and maintaining professional standards in nursing. The preparation of nurses continues to be an issue that generates heated debate.

Stephanie Kirby

STATISTICAL ASPECTS OF CLINICAL TRIALS: DOUBLE-BLIND TESTING AND THE PLAY-THE-WINNER RULE

There are probably more statisticians engaged in drug trials than in any other area of activity. When a new medicine has passed all the initial testing, it will be released on a monitored basis for use with patients. One form of evaluating the success of a new drug is the so-called *double-blind* trial. The patient is given a drug (or tablet) by the doctor. However, the drug given is identified only by a code number. Neither the patient, nor the doctor, knows what treatment is being given.

The outcome of the treatment is reported to the trial organiser (and, in the back room, the statisticians start to compute!). This type of trial generally involves just two treatments: the new treatment and either the existing treatment, or a *placebo* (a treatment, without genuine medical content, which, to both patient and doctor, looks like the real thing). One well-known finding is that many patients given the placebo recover quickly (probably because they feel better for knowing that they have been "treated", even though the treatment may have involved no more than drinking a glass of water).

We consider next a rather special type of situation, involving two treatments (A and B), and a rare, potentially fatal, disease. Suppose that, by the time that a new patient arrives, the outcome (survival or death) for the last patient is known. A double-blind trial is not suitable for a potentially fatal disease. Instead the consultant must decide to treat the patient with one of treatment A or treatment B. How should the consultant make the decision? Statisticians have spent a good deal of time trying to answer this question! Here are two of their ideas:

Alternate allocation of the treatments (ABABAB…). Stop when one treatment has resulted in r (a pre-determined constant) ie more successes than the other. The less successful treatment is then abandoned.

This is the "Vector-at-a-time" method. It is easy to administer but ethical difficulties arise if one treatment is "clearly" superior to the other, since half the patients will continue to be given the inferior treatment until the stopping rule is satisfied. This puts pressure on the statistician to choose too small a value for r, (thereby increasing the chance that the test results in the selection of the "wrong" treatment as a consequence of "bad luck").

Allocate treatments according to the success of the previous treatment. Suppose A is given to the first patient. If the patient recovers, then A is again given to the next patient. However, if the patient dies, then B is given to the next patient. The stopping rule is as before.

This is the "Play-the-winner" method. It appeals to those with ethical concerns, since it virtually ensures that the superior treatment is the one used more often. Indeed, the greater its superiority, the greater the proportion of patients that receive that treatment.

Graham Upton

MULTIDISCIPLINARY INTERPROFESSIONAL HIGHER EDUCATION FOR THE NEW NHS: INNOVATIONS FROM A UNIVERSITY DEPARTMENT

The NHS was established in 1948 with ambitious aims to provide the health care needs of the entire population for the whole of life. Today, although NHS hospitals provide intensive and technologically complex care, the overwhelming bulk of health services are provided in the community through Primary Care Trusts (PCTs). The PCTs deliver services through a network of nurses and allied health professionals directly employed by PCTs, and through doctors, dentists, pharmacists, and opticians working under contract in the community. PCTs also commission (or purchase) a vast range of services from hospitals, mental health trusts, voluntary organisations, and, increasingly, private sector organisations.

The consistency of the public branding of the NHS over the past 50 years or so, has masked the fractured structure of this national icon. This contradiction between 'image' and 'reality' may in part explain why so many NHS service users, and a good deal of its own employees, are bewildered by the complexity of the organisation and frustrated by the constantly shifting lines of responsibility and accountability. Although the seemingly endless restructuring of the NHS throughout its history has most often occurred as a result of direct political intervention, the onerous responsibility for turning political vision into service provision will inevitably pass to health service managers and senior practitioners.

Newspaper headlines declaring *"GPs disappearing under a mountain of red tape"* and *"More frontline staff and fewer managers"* are based on a superficial analysis of the challenges facing the NHS. The proposition that health service managers are remote from frontline service provision, or are a burden on health care resources, suggests that the contribution of health service managers to patient services is poorly understood. A far better understanding of the relationships between health professionals and health service managers can be found by examining the experiences of students engaged in higher education programmes at the University of Essex.

The Department of Health and Human Sciences provides vocational, undergraduate, and postgraduate programmes for clinicians and health service managers working in all aspects of health care. The professional diversity of the students, the variety of courses offered, and the approaches to learning reflect the interprofessional and multidisciplinary model of health care provision that is gradually becoming the norm in the NHS. In today's classroom, clipboards and stethoscopes lose their heraldic symbolism, as managers, clinicians, and a new generation of clinical managers experience new approaches to learning.

The concept of evidence-based practice is now embedded in all aspects of clinical decision making and management practice. In order to support evidence-based practice, educational approaches now focus on equipping clinicians and managers with the ability to analyse information rather than store knowledge. These approaches promote the development of a portfolio of skills and experiences, encourage professional development through reflective practice, and engage students in problem-based learning. These approaches also emphasise the role of lecturers as facilitators to self-directed enquiry rather than conveyors of information.

The multi-dimensional characteristics of the Department's learning and teaching strategies are being further enhanced by the introduction of interprofessional pre-registration MSc schemes. Traditionally, clinicians qualify for professional registration by completing *specialised* clinical programmes of study, with the option of pursuing further postgraduate education in specialised clinical fields. The 'Inter-professional learning' approach allows graduates from a wide range of backgrounds to *simultaneously* participate in a *shared* postgraduate programme of study that, upon completion of relevant practice placements, will result in the award of an MSc. It is hoped that this innovative approach to professional education will lead to more integrated approaches to clinical practice.

The NHS has experienced an unprecedented level of reorganisation since publication of the NHS Plan in 1999. The modernisation agenda requires health professionals and health service managers to adopt new ways of working in order to deliver the standard of health care that the public expects. These new ways of working must be supported by new ways of learning and a fresh approach to holistic health care. The aim of the Department of Health and Human Sciences is to work in partnership with the NHS to ensure that we continue to lead in the development of new ways of learning for the health professionals of the future.

Allan Hildon

FURTHER READING

a3. Nicholls and Wilson

Taylor, RW, & Turnbull DM, 2005. Mitochondrial DNA mutations in human disease. Nat Rev Genet. 6(5): 389-402.

Duchen MR, 2004. Mitochondria in health and disease: perspectives on a new mitochondrial biology. Mol Aspects Med. 2004; 25(4): 365-451.

Land JM, Morgan-Hughes JA, Hargreaves I, Heales SJ, 2004. Mitochondrial disease: a historical, biochemical, and London perspective. Neurochem Res 29(3): 483-91.

Salvatore DiMauro. The many faces of mitochondrial diseases Mitochondrion 2004; 4(5-6): 799-807.

United Mitochondrial Disease Foundation at http://www.umdf.org/mitodisease/

The Children's Mitochondrial Disease Network at http://www.emdn-mitonet.co.uk/

a6. Reader

Reeder BJ, Svistunenko DA, Cooper CE and Wilson MT, 2004. The radical and redox chemistry of myoglobin and hemoglobin: from in vitro studies to human pathology. *Antioxidants and Redox Signalling. In press*

Reeder BJ, Sharpe MA, Kay AD, Kerr M, Moore K and Wilson MT, 2002. Toxicity of myoglobin and haemoglobin: oxidative stress in patients with rhabdomyolysis and subarachnoid haemorrhage. *Biochem. Soc. Trans.*, 30: 745-748

Reeder BJ, Svistunenko DA, Sharpe MA and Wilson MT, 2002. Characteristics and Mechanism of Formation of Peroxide-Induced Heme to Protein Cross-Linking in Myoglobin. *Biochemistry* 41: 367-375

Holt S, Reeder BJ, Wilson M, Harvey S, Morrow JD, Roberts LJ and Moore K, 1999. Increased lipid peroxidation in patients with rhabdomyolysis. *Lancet* 353: 1241

a7. Nicholls

Haldane, JBS, (1949) "Life at high Pressures" *in* What is Life? (Lindsay Drummond).

Haldane, JBS, (1946) "The commonest poison gas" *in* A Banned Broadcast (Chatto & co.).

Alvarez, A, (1971) "The Savage God: a study of suicide" (Weidenfeld and Nicolson).

Haldane, JBS, (1925) "Callinicus: a defence of chemical warfare" (Kegan Paul & co.).

Nicholls, P, (1983). The Biology of Oxygen. Carolina Biology Reader #100.

Keilin, D, (1966) The History of Cell Respiration and Cytochrome. Cambridge Univ. Press.

Warburg, O, (1949) Heavy metal prosthetic groups and enzyme action. Oxford Univ. Press.

a8.Svistunenko

Reichard P and A Ehrenberg, 1983. Ribonucleotide reductase - a radical enzyme. *Science* 221:514-519

a9. Thornalley

Thornalley,PJ *et al.* Quantitative screening of advanced glycation endproducts in cellular and extracellular proteins by tandem mass spectrometry. *Biochem. J.* **375**, 581-592 (2003).

Agalou,S., Ahmed,N, Dawnay, A & Thornalley, PJ Removal of advanced glycation end products in clinical renal failure by peritoneal dialysis and haemodialysis. *Biochem. Soc. Trans.* **31**, 1394-1396 (2003).

a11. Cherry
Hope-Simpson, RE 1992. *The transmission of epidemic influenza*. Plenum Press.
Krug, RM 1989. *The influenza viruses*. Plenum Press.

b2. Thornalley
Expert Group on Vitamins and Minerals (UK). Safe upper levels for vitamins and minerals. Food Standards Agency, 1- 360 (2003)
Babaei-Jadidi, R, Karachalias, N, Ahmed, N, Battah, S & Thornalley, PJ Prevention of incipient diabetic nephropathy by high dose thiamine and Benfotiamine. *Diabetes* **52**, 2110-2120 (2003).

b3. Jones
Hall SS, 2003. The Quest for a Smart Pill. *Scientific American*, September 2003, p 36-45
Cognitive enhancement raises ethical concerns. *The Lancet* 2003 Vol 362 , No. 9378

b5. Wilson
Blood substitules: see www.eurobloodsubstitutes.com

b6. Weale
Nuffield Council on Bioethics, *Animal-to-Human Transplants: The Ethics of Xenotransplantation* (London: Nuffield Council on Bioethics, 1996). A copy can be downloaded from www.nuffieldbioethics.org.
The Advisory Group on the Ethics of Xenotransplantation, *Animal Tissue into Humans* (London: Department of Health, 1997).
See also the reports of the UK Xenotransplantation Interim Regulatory Authority at: www.doh.gov.uk/ukxira/index.htm.

b8. Bailey
Bailey, GS, (ed) 1998. Enzymes from Snake Venoms. Alaken Inc., Fort Collins, 736pp
Lewis, RJ, and Garcia, ML, 2003. Therapeutic Potential of Venom Peptides. Nature Drug Discovery 2 (10) 790-802

b9. Gladwell, Head and Beneke
Maniadakas, N and Gray, A, (2000). The economic burden of back pain in the UK. *Pain*. **84** 95-103.
Rainville, J, Hartigan, C, Martinez, E, Limke, J, Jouve, C, and Finno, M, (2004). Exercise as a treatment for chronic lower back pain. *The Spine Journal*. **4** 106-115.
Hodges, PW and Richardson, CA, (1996). Inefficient Muscular stabilisation of the lumbar spine associated with low back pain. A motor control evaluation of the transverses abdominis. *Spine*. **21** (22) 2640-2650.
Muscolino, JE and Cipriani, S, (2004). Pilates and the "powerhouse"-1. *Journal of Bodywork and Movement Therapies*. **8** 15-24

b10. Ahmed
Zimmet, P, Alberti, KGMM & Shaw, J, Global and societal implications of the diabetes epidemic. *Nature* **414**, 782-787 (2002).
Babaei-Jadidi, R, Karachalias, N, Ahmed, N, Battah, S & Thornalley, PJ, Prevention of incipient diabetic nephropathy by high dose thiamine and Benfotiamine. *Diabetes* **52**, 2110-2120 (2003).

b11. Beneke, Leithauser and Hutler

Arcasoy SM, Kotloff RM (1999) Lung transplantation. N Engl J Med 340:1081-91

Broyer M, Otte JB, Kachaner J, Goulet O (1989) Organ transplantation in children. Intensive Care Med 15:S76-79

Hütler M, Beneke R (2002) Herz- und Lungentransplantation. In: Hebestreit H et al. (eds). Kinder- und Jugendsportmedizin. Georg Thieme Verlag, Stuttgart New York, pp 129-132

Kjaer M, Beyer N, Secher NH (1999) Exercise and organ transplantation. Scand J Med Sci Sports 9:1-14

Maeder JP (1993) Rehabilitation nach einer Herztransplantation. In: Saner H (ed). Kardiale Rehabilitation. Georg Thieme Verlag, Stuttgart New York, pp 171-178

Nixon PA, Fricker J, Noyes BE, Webber SA, Orenstein DM, Armitage JM (1995) Exercise testing in pediatric heart, heart-lung, and lung transplant recipients. Chest 107:1328-135

Skinner J (1989) Rezepte für Sport und Bewegungstherapie. Deutscher Ärzte Verlag, Köln

b12. Psaroudakis and Reynolds

Large-scale virtual screening for discovering leads in the postgenomic era by B Waszkowycz, TDJ Perkins, RA Sykes, and J Li, IBM systems Journal, Volume 40, Number 2, 2001,Deep computing for the life sciences

c3. Sellens

A number of relevant articles can be found in the electronic journal "Sports Science Exchange" on the Gatorade Sports Science Institute (GSSI) web site.http://www.gssiweb.com/

Try *Nieman, D.C. (1998) Sports Science Exchange* **69** *(2)*
http://www.gssiweb.com/reflib/refs/42/d000000020000021e.cfm?pid=38

c4. Wilson

Lane MA Ingram DK and Roth GS, 2004. The serious search for an anti-aging pill. Sci. Am,14, 36-42

Trifunovik, *et al*, 2004. Causal link now established between damage to mitochondrial DNA and ageing. Nature 429, 417

Schriner SE, et al, 2005. Extension of murine life span by overexpression of catalase targeted to mitochondria. Science 308: 1909-11.

Vina J, et al, 2003. Mitochondrial theory of aging: importance to explain why females live longer than males. Antioxid Redox Signal 5, 549-56.

c5. Shearman

Rothenbacher, Hoffmeister, & Hermann, (2003) Physical Activity, Coronary Heart Disease, and Inflammatory Response. Arch Intern Med. 163 (10), 1200-1205.

Stampfer, Hu, Manson, Rimm, and Willett, Primary Prevention of Coronary Heart Disease in Women through Diet and Lifestyle. (2000) N Engl J Med 343:16-22.

c6. Sellens and Voutselas

Borsheim E, Bahr R, (2003) Effect of exercise intensity, duration and mode on post-exercise oxygen consumption. SPORTS MEDICINE 33 (14): 1037-1060 2003

c7. Fisher

Fisher K 2002, Chewing the fat: the story time diaries tell about physical activity in the United Kingdom Working papers of the Institute for Social and Economic Research paper 2002-13 University of Essex Colchester

Gershuny JI 2000, Changing times: work and leisure in post-industrial societies Oxford
University Press Oxford
Gershuny JI & Fisher K 2000, Leisure in Halsey AH & Webb J eds Twentieth-century British
social trends 3rd edition Macmillan Publishers Ltd London

c8. Angus, Leithauser and Beneke
Beneke R, Schwarz V, Leithäuser R, Hütler M, von Duvillard SP, (1996) Maximal lactate steady
state in children. Ped Exerc Sci 8(4):328-336
Beneke R, Heck H, Schwarz V, Leithäuser R, (1996) Maximal lactate steady state during the
second decade of age. Med Sci Sports Exerc 28(12):1474-1478
Beneke R, (2003) Methodological aspects of maximal lactate steady state – implications for
performance testing. Eur J Appl Physiol 89: 95-99

c9. Sellens
Hoffman, Jay, (2002) Physiological aspects of sport training and performance. Champaign,
Illinois: Human Kinetics.

c10. Wittekind
Bishop D, (2003) Warm Up II: Performance changes following active warm up and how to
structure the warm up. *Sports Med* 33(7): 483 – 498
Jones A M, Wilkerson DP, Burnley M, Koppo K, (2003) Prior heavy exercise enhances
performance during subsequent perimaximal exercise. *Med Sci Sports Exerc*
35(12):2085-2092
Marino FE, (2002) Methods, advantages and limitations of body cooling for exercise
performance *Br J Sports Med* 36: 89-94
Stewart IB, Sleivert GG (1998) The effect of warm-up intensity on range of motion and
anaerobic performance. *J Orthopaedic Sports Physical Therapy* 27(2): 154 - 161

c14. Pevalin and Robson
UNICEF Innocenti Research Centre, *A league table of teenage births in rich nations* (2003).
Ermisch, JF and Pevalin, DJ, 'Does a 'Teen-birth' have longer-term impacts on the mother?
Evidence from the 1970 British Cohort Study', *Working Paper of the Institute for Social
and Economic Research*, Paper 2003-28 (2003).
Robson, KL and Berthoud, R, 'Early Motherhood and Disadvantage: a comparison between
ethnic groups', *Working Paper of the Institute for Social and Economic Research*, Paper
2003-29 (2003).

d5. Samson
Nancy K, Hanna et al, (2003), 'Diet and Mental Health in the Arctic: Is Diet an Important Risk
Factor for Mental Health in Circumpolar Peoples? – A Review,' *International Journal of
Circumpolar Health*, 62: 3, 228-241
Colin Samson 2003, *A Way of Life That Does Not Exist: Canada and the Extinguishment of the
Innu*, St. John's: ISER Books, and London: Verso Press, 2003.

d7. Micklewright
Hemmings, B, Smith, M, Graydon, J, & Dixon, R, (2002). Effects of massage on physiological
restoration, perceived recovery, and repeated sports performance. *British Journal of
Sports Medicine*, 34, 109-115.

Morgan, W, (1980, August). Exercise as a relaxation technique. *Primary Cardiology,* 25-30.

Tyurin, AM, (1986). The influence of different forms of massage on the psycho-emotional state of athletes. *Soviet Sports Review,* 21, 126-127.

Weinberg, R, Jackson, A, & Kolodny, K, (1988). The relationship of massage and exercise to mood enhancement. *The Sport Psychologist,* 2, 202-211.

d9. Pretty, Griffin, Sellens and Peacock

Pretty J, Griffin M and Sellens M, 2004. Is nature good for you? *Ecos* 24 (3-4), p2-9

Pretty J, Peacock J, Sellens M and Griffin M, 2005. The mental and physical health outcomes of green exercise. *International Journal of Environmental Health Research* 15 (5), 319 - 337

e1. Reid, Hammersley and Rance

Berg, FM, (1992) Harmful weight loss practices are widespread among adolescents. *Obesity & Health,* (July/Aug): 69-72

Casper, RC, Offer, D, (1990) Weight and dieting concerns in adolescents: Fashion or symptom? *Pediatrics,* 86, 384-90.

Nichter, M, Ritenbaugh, C, Nichter, M, Vuckovic, N et al, (1995) Dieting and "watching" behaviors among adolescent females: Report of a multimethod study. *Journal of Adolescent Health,* 17, 153-162.

Polivy, J & Herman, CP, (1995) Dieting and its relation to eating disorders. In Brownell KD, Fairburn CG eds. *Eating disorders and obesity. A comprehensive handbook.* New York Guilford Press, 83-86.

Stein, DM & Reichert, P, (1990) Extreme dieting behaviours in early adolescence. *Journal of Early Adolescence,* 10, 108-21.

e3. Nicholas

American College of Sports Medicine (1996). Position stand on exercise and fluid replacement. Med. Sci. Sports Exerc. 28: i-vii.

Brouns, F, (1993). Nutritional needs of athletes. John Wiley and Sons, Chichester.

Burke L M, B Kiens and JLIvy, (2004). Carbohydrates and fat for training and recovery. Journal of Sports Sciences 22: 15-30.

Coyle E F, (1994) Fluid and carbohydrate replacement during exercise: how much and why? Sports Science Exchange Volume 7 (3).

Grandjean, AC and JSRuud, (1996). Energy intake of athletes. Oxford Textbook of Sports Medicine. M Harries, C Williams, WD Stanish, LJ Micheli (eds), Oxford Univ Press, New York , pp 53-65.

Maughan, RJ, (2000). Water and electrolyte loss and replacement in exercise. In: RJ Maughan (ed) Nutrition in Sport. Blackwell Science Ltd, London. Chapter 17. Maughan, RJ, DSKing, TLea (2004). Dietary Supplements. Journal of Sports Sciences 22: 95-113.

e7. Fryer

Nelson HK, Shi Q, Van Deal P, Schiffrin EJ, Blum S, Barclay D, Levander OA, Beck MA. (2001) Host nutritional status as a driving force for influenza virus mutations. *FASEB J* **15:** 1846-48.

e9. Fernandez

MHC Volume 1, (1997) Edited by N. Fernández and G. Butcher. Oxford University Press.

e13. Sellens
Find the "Tackling Obesity" report from the National Audit Office on
http://www.nao.org.uk/publications/nao_reports/00-01/0001220.pdf
http://women.timesonline.co.uk/article/0,,18030-1440410_2,00.html..
The GI diet can be found at http://www.gidiet.com/
with further information at http://women.timesonline.co.uk/article/0,,18030-
1440410_2,00.html.

f3. Colbeck
http://www.advisorybodies.doh.gov.uk/comeap/
http://www.airquality.co.uk/archive/what_causes.php
http://www.defra.gov.uk/environment/airquality/
http://www.essexair.org/

f4. Pretty
Pretty J (ed). 2005. *The Pesticide Detox: Towards a More Sustainable Agriculture*. Earthscan,
London

f5. McGenity and Timmis
http://www.geo.unimib.it/BioDeep/Project.html (EU project BIODEEP)
http://www.ist.me.cnr.it/project.php (EU project COMMODE)
http://www.clarrc.ed.ac.uk/link/index_flash.htm (UK Programme Bioremediation Link)

f6. Colbeck
http://www.epa.gov/iaq/ia-intro.html
http://www.who.int/indoorair/publications/health_effects/en/
http://www.nilu.no/urban_exposure/

f10. Hallsworth, Nicholls and Timmis
Hallsworth, JE, (1998). Ethanol-induced water stress in yeast. *Journal of Fermentation and
Bioengineering*. **85** 125-137.
Hallsworth, JE, Heim, S & KN Timmis, (2003). Chaotropic solutes cause water stress in
Psuedomonas putida. *Environmental Microbiology* **5** 1270-1280.
Kropman, MF & HJ Bakker, (2001). Dynamics of water molecules in aqueous solvation shells.
Science **291** 2118-2120.

g1. Pevalin and Rose
Cooper, H, Arber, S, Fee, L and Ginn, J, (1999) *The Influence of Social Support and Social
Capital on Health: A Review and Analysis of British Data*. London: Health Development
Agency.
Pevalin, DJ and Rose, D, (2003) *Social Capital for Health: Investigating the Links between Social
Capital and Health using the British Household Panel Survey*. London: Health
Development Agency.
Pevalin, DJ, (2004) 'Intra-household differences in neighbourhood attachment and their
associations with health' in A. Morgan and C. Swann (eds) *Social Capital for Health:
Insights from Quantitative Research*, pp. 69-82. London: Health Development Agency.
Portes, A, (2000) "The Two Meanings of Social Capital." *Sociological Forum* 15: 1-12

g2. Hancock
Hancock, R, Comas-Herrera, A, Wittenberg, R and Pickard, L, 2003. Who will pay for long-term
care in the UK? Projections linking macro- and micro-simulation models. *Fiscal Studies*
24 (4)

g5. Beneke, Leithauser and Meyer

Beneke R, Meyer K, (1997) Walking performance and economy in chronic heart failure patients pre and post exercise training. Eur J Appl Physiol 75:246-251

Meyer K, Schwaibold M, Westbrook S, Beneke R, Hajric R, Lehmann M, Roskamm H, (1997) Effects of exercise training and activity restriction on 6-minute walking test performance in patients with chronic heart failure. Am Heart J 133: 447-453

g7. Fisher

Berthoud, R, (1998) Counting the costs of disability. *The New Statesman*, 16 January, 14-15.

Burkhauser R and M Daly. (1993) The importance of labor earnings for working age males with disabilities. Cross-National Studies in Aging, Program Paper Number 11, New York: Syracuse University.

Thornton, P, R Sainsbury, and H Barnes, (1997) *Helping disabled people to work: A cross-national study of social security and employment provisions: a report for the social security advisory committee.* London: The Stationery Office.

g8. South

The Acheson Report, 1998. *Independent Inquiry into Inequalities in Health Report*, London: HMSO

Keithley J and Robinson F, 2000. Violence as a public health issue. *Policy and Politics* 28(1), 67-77

Maher L and Dixon D, 1999. Policing and public health: Law enforcement and harm minimization in a street-level drug market. *British Journal of Criminology* 39(4), 488-512

McCabe A and Raine J, 1997. *Framing the debate: crime and public health* (a project sponsored by the Public Health Trust) Birmingham: Public Health Alliance

Moore M, 1995. 'Public health and criminal justice approaches to prevention' in M. Tonry and D. Farrington (Eds), *Strategic approaches to crime prevention,* 237-62, Chicago: University of Chicago Press

Morris J, 1955. Uses of Epidemiology. *British Medical Journal*, 13th August, 305-401

Robinson F, Keithley J, Robinson S and Childs S. 1998. *Exploring the impacts of crime on health and health services: a Feasibility study*, University of Durham: Department of Sociology and Social Policy.

Rose N, 2000. The biology of culpability: pathological identity and crime control in a biological culture. *Theoretical Criminology* 4(1), 5-34

Shepherd J, 1990. Violent crime in Bristol: an accident and emergency department perspective. *British Journal of Criminology* 30(3), 289-305

g11. Fernandez, Salgado and Fraser

Medawar, Peter. The uniqueness of the individual (1957) Methuen & Co Ltd.

Brent, Lesley. A history of transplantation Immunology (1997) Academic Press

Medawar, Peter. The limits of science. (1986) Oxford University Press

http://www.essex.ac.uk/ueclaa/english/exhibitions/jorgeorta/workshops/index.htm

g12. Eldridge and Mutter

Beatty M, Jones R K and McGinn T, 2001. *Assessment of Reproductive Health for IDPs, Angola, February 15-28, 2001.* Reproductive Health for Refugees Consortium.
http://www.rhrc.org/resources/general_reports/angola/angola00.html

Carballo, M and Mansfield C, 2000. The complex impact of conflict on women's health. In RHRC (2000) *Findings On Reproductive Health Of Refugees and Displaced Populations. Conference Proceedings, Washington DC, December 5-6, 2000*
http://www.rhrc.org/resources/general_reports/con00/con00.htm

Fain, LK, (2000) Unsafe Haven: Report on the findings of a baseline sexual violence survey among Burundian refugees. In RHRC (2000) *Findings On Reproductive Health Of Refugees and Displaced Populations. Conference Proceedings, Washington DC, December 5-6, 2000* http://www.rhrc.org/resources/general_reports/con00.con00.htm

Human Rights Watch (2000). *Kosovo: Rape as a Weapon of "Ethnic Cleansing".* New York: Human Rights Watch. www.hrw.org/reports/2000/fry

Human Rights Watch (2002). *The War within the War: Sexual Violence against Women and girls in Eastern Congo.* June 2002. New York: Human Rights Watch. http://hrw.org/reports/2002/drc/

g13. Turton

Burnett & Fassil, 2002, Meeting the health needs of refugees and asylum seekers in the UK: an information and resource pack for health workers, Directorate of Health and Social Care

Gardee, 2002, Good practice in integration, NHS Health Scotland

Turton, Chaplin, Ramsay & Skambalis, 2004, Health & social care issues for asylum seekers & refugees: an East of England view, Go-East Public Health Group

Turton, 2002, Ask where it hurts: a qualitative study of interpretation in the National Health Service, London, DoH

Kings Fund, 1999. The health of refugee children: guidelines for paediatricians, London

h1 Kirby

Powell, M, *Evaluating the Health Service.* Open University Press, Buckingham. 1997

Webster C, The Health Services since the War. **3 vols. HMSO, London. 1988**

h2 Weale

Klein, R, Day, P and Redmayne, S, (1996) *Managing Scarcity* (Buckingham: Open University Press).

Oliver, A, (ed.) (2003) *Health Care Priority Setting: Implications for Health Inequalities* (London: The Nuffield Trust).

White, J, (1995) *Competing Solutions: American Health Care Proposals and International Experience* (Washington DC: The Brookings Institution).

For the reports of the National Institute of Clinical Excellence, see the NICE web-site at www.nice.org.uk.

h6 Busfield

Beral V, (2003) 'Breast cancer and hormone-replacement therapy in the Million Women Study' *The Lancet,* Aug 9; 362: 419-27

Cohen, J, (2001) *Over Dose,* New York: Putnam

Colgrove H, (2002) 'The McKeown thesis' *American Journal of Public Health* 92: 725-9.

Department of Health (2000/2003) *Prescriptions Dispensed in the Community,* London.

Pirohamed M et al, (2004) 'Adverse drug reaction as cause of admission to hospital' *BMJ* 329: 30 July: 15-19.

Sen A, (2002) 'Health: perception versus observation' *BMJ* 324, 13 April: 860-1.

h9 Kirby

Baly, M, *Florence Nightingale and the Nursing Legacy.* London, Croom Helm. 1987

Hector, W, *Mrs. Bedford Fenwick.* London, RCN. 1973

Kirby, SA, The Development of the Nursing Profession in: Kenworthy, N; Gilling C and Snowley G *Foundation Studies in Nursing* (2nd). Edinburgh, Churchill Livingstone. 1996

McGann, S & O'Brien F A, 1999. Champion of Nursing. *Nursing Standard* 13, 40, 17

Mrs Bedford Fenwick's *British Journal of Nursing* can be accessed on line at www.rcn.org.uk/historicalnursingjournals